The 1929 Bunion Derby

Sports and Entertainment
Steven A. Riess, *Series Editor*

Editor's Choice

Our Editor's Choice program is an opportunity to highlight a book from our list that deserves special attention. This remarkable account of human endurance unfolds against the backdrop of America's swift decline from the heady Roaring Twenties to the devastating Great Crash, and is precisely the kind of underdog story that university presses continue to bring to light.

Suzanne E. Guiod
Editor-in-Chief, Syracuse University Press

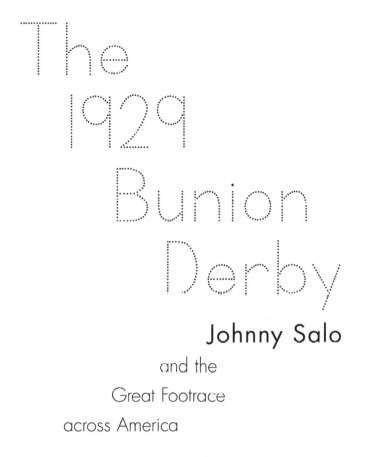

The 1929 Bunion Derby

Johnny Salo
and the
Great Footrace
across America

Charles B. Kastner

SYRACUSE UNIVERSITY PRESS

For a listing of books published and distributed by Syracuse University Press,
visit our website at www.SyracuseUniversityPress.syr.edu.

ISBN: 978-0-8156-1036-6 (cloth)   978-0-8156-5281-6 (e-book)

Library of Congress Cataloging-in-Publication Data

Kastner, Charles B., 1955–

   The 1929 Bunion Derby : Johnny Salo and the great footrace across America / Charles B. Kastner. —
First Edition.

      pagescm. — (Sports and entertainment)

   Includes bibliographical references and index.

   ISBN 978-0-8156-1036-6 (cloth : alk. paper) — ISBN 978-0-8156-5281-6 (ebook) 1. Running races—
United States—History. 2. Salo, Johnny, 1893–1931. I. Title.

   GV1061.2.K369 2014

   796.424097309042—dc23   2014001413

Manufactured in the United States of America

To Eddie "the Sheik" Gardner (1897–1966),
bunioneer and unsung hero in the battle
for racial equality in America.

Charles B. Kastner is a Seattle-based writer and financial manager. In 2007, the University of New Mexico Press published his history of the first footrace across America. He has also contributed chapters to two books dealing with his experience as a Peace Corps volunteer as well as writing about the Bunion Derbies for *blackpast.org* as well as *Marathon and Beyond* and *Northwest Runner* magazines. He holds advanced degrees in business, history, and environmental biology. Kastner is an avid distance runner. He has run more than twenty marathons and one ultramarathon.

Contents

List of Illustrations • *ix*

Acknowledgments • *xi*

Introduction • *xiii*

1. Race Day
   New York City to Elizabeth, New Jersey, March 31, 1929 • 1

2. Down the Eastern Seaboard
   Elizabeth, New Jersey, to Baltimore, Maryland,
   April 1–April 5, 1929 • 12

3. Six Days of Hell—Crossing the Appalachian Plateau
   Baltimore, Maryland, to Wheeling, West Virginia,
   April 6–April 11, 1929 • 36

4. Fast Times in the Old Northwest
   Wheeling, West Virginia, to Collinsville, Illinois,
   April 12–April 23, 1929 • 53

5. On Familiar Ground
   Collinsville, Illinois, to Chelsea, Oklahoma,
   April 24–May 3, 1929 • 75

6. Heading to the Promised Land
   Chelsea, Oklahoma, to Dallas, Texas, May 4–May 10, 1929 • 95

7. Under Western Skies
   Dallas to Pecos, Texas, May 11–May 22, 1929 • 107

8. West of the Pecos
   Pecos to El Paso, Texas, May 23–May 27, 1929 • *121*

9. Across a Rough and Unforgiving Land
   El Paso, Texas, to Yuma, Arizona, May 28–June 10, 1929 • *130*

10. "Overcoming the Killing Distances"—
    The Last Five Days to Los Angeles
    Yuma, Arizona, to Los Angeles, June 11–June 15, 1929 • *150*

11. The End of the Rainbow
    Los Angeles, June 16, 1929 • *161*

12. Searching for the Pot of Gold • *175*

    Appendixes • *191*
    Notes • *255*
    Glossary • *289*
    Bibliography • *291*
    Index • *297*

Illustrations

Photos

1. Cover from *Official 1929 Program* • 3

2. Johnny Salo commissioned as a Passaic city police officer • 6

3. Johnny Salo being sworn in as a Passaic city police officer • 7

4. Andy Payne, from *Official 1929 Program* • 9

5. Pete Gavuzzi wearing his Bunion Derby race number • 15

6. Arthur Newton, England • 16

7. Arthur Newton and Pete Gavuzzi racing together in Canada • 17

8. Unidentified man and Leonard Lewis #39 • 20

9. Official race bib, Leonard Lewis • 21

10. C. C. Pyle's Cross Country Follies • 25

11. Frank "Black Dan" Hart • 27

12. Charley Pyle, 1926 • 30

13. Charley Pyle, 1929 • 31

14. John Stone • 37

15. Eddie "the Sheik" Gardner • 45

16. Eddie Gardner crossing the Free Bridge into Missouri • 76

17. Jim Thorpe • 82

18. Eddie Gardner on Route 66, Oklahoma, 1928 race • 92

19. Runners finishing in Breckenridge, Texas, Photo 1 • 112

20. Runners finishing in Breckenridge, Texas, Photo 2 • 113

21. Muddy road in Texas • 117

22. Johnny and Amelia Salo, Superior, Arizona, 1929 • 140

23. Johnny Salo's legs   •   *141*

24. Arthur Newton, final competitive run, England   •   *181*

25. Director General Charley Pyle   •   *183*

Maps

1. 1929 route, New York City to Los Angeles   •   *10*

2. 1929 route, Elizabeth to Baltimore   •   *13*

3. US Route 40   •   *38*

4. 1929 route, Baltimore to Wheeling   •   *39*

5. 1929 route, Wheeling to Collinsville   •   *54*

6. 1929 route, Collinsville to Chelsea   •   *79*

7. 1929 route, Chelsea to Dallas   •   *96*

8. 1929 route, Dallas to Pecos   •   *108*

9. 1929 route, Pecos to El Paso   •   *122*

10. 1929 route, El Paso to Yuma   •   *131*

11. 1929 route, Yuma to Los Angeles   •   *151*

Tables

Table 1. Finishers, 1929: 3,553.6 Miles in 78 Days   •   *173*

Table 2. Top Ten Finishers, 1928: 3,422.3 Miles in 84 Days   •   *174*

Table 3. List of Runners Who Completed Both   •   *174*

Acknowledgments

TO TELL THE STORY of the 1929 Bunion Derby, I reviewed articles from eighty period newspapers from cities and towns along the 3,554-mile course, memoirs from the runners, Works Progress Administration (WPA) State Guides, and many secondary works. I could have never gathered the primary materials without the help of an army of newspaper editors, archivists, and librarians from cities and towns along the course. I want to express my sincere thanks to John "Charley" Stone for letting me use his treasure trove of photos and primary documents. Charley was born while his father, John Stone, ran the 1928 race and was one of two Bunion Derby babies born during the first derby. I am also indebted to Pete Gavuzzi's grandson, Guy Gavuzzi, for the use of his photos and to author Mark Whitaker for introducing me to Guy. I owe a special thank you to author and runner Rob Hadgraft for the use of his photos and for his help and support while I was writing this book. I also wish to thank Nicki Leone and Dick Lipsey for their editorial expertise. And, finally, I want to express my heartfelt gratitude to my wife, Mary. She never wavered in her support for me during the thirteen years I spent learning and writing about the 1928 and 1929 Bunion Derby races.

Introduction

June 6, 1929, Sonora Desert, Arizona

On a gravel road that had once been the stagecoach route from El Paso to San Diego, an extremely muscular, leather-brown man was flying through a fifty-four-mile course in rough desert country—running at seven minutes and forty-four seconds per mile with the sun beating down and only the howling desert wind to compete with the rhythmic plodding of his feet. His trainer, Bill Wicklund, followed behind him in the well-worn 1921 Ford that had seen them through more than three thousand miles and sixty-eight days of almost nonstop running, averaging almost forty-six miles a day in daily stage-to-stage racing.[1] Just days away were Los Angeles and the twenty-five-thousand-dollar first prize going to the winner of the race—the Second Annual Transcontinental Foot Race across America, or simply the Bunion Derby, as the press had nicknamed the race in 1928. This was a fortune to a workingman when a yearly salary of $2,500 represented a decent standard of living for an American family.[2]

By now, the two men were a well-oiled machine, with Wicklund giving the runner food and fluids every two miles or so. The runner was Johnny Salo, the "flying cop" from Passaic, New Jersey. At about five feet, five inches, and 145 pounds, Salo's muscularity was fit for a statue in ancient Greece. His physique was barely covered under a loose singlet and shorts, with his police-badge emblem embroidered on the shorts.[3] Johnny's style was mechanical and stiff, like a bulldozer that plows its way through mud, rough terrain, lighting storms, and desert sun. He was expressionless, blank in his concentration. He gave off a scent of controlled aggression that he directed fully at the task at hand.

Keeping him in balance at the start and end of each stage of the race was Amelia, his wife. She was a trained massage therapist, cook, counselor, and soul mate. The first woman trainer in this new sport of trans-America racing, Amelia was the glue that kept Johnny going.[4]

Chasing him relentlessly was his old rival, Pete Gavuzzi of England, the trilingual star who had led the first Bunion Derby run from Los Angeles to New York the year before. Gavuzzi had been forced out of the race in Ohio because of an infected tooth, giving the derby to Andy Payne of Oklahoma, with Johnny taking second.[5] Gavuzzi, at 118 pounds, barely five feet, two inches, and just twenty-three years of age, was the Fred Astaire of the derby—flowing, effortless, and beautiful to watch—and he excelled on flat, open terrain.[6] He, too, had an efficient racing team. His mentor and partner was Arthur Newton, the stern, middle-aged Englishman who looked more like a tanned bank executive than someone who had held every world long-distance record from thirty to one hundred miles. Shepherding them both across the country was George Barren, their valet, cook, and driver, who followed in their specially built motor home.[7]

When Gavuzzi and Salo had raced in 1928, they were making up the rules of running a trans-America road race as they went along. In 1929, they had perfected them, turning the contest from a test of survival to a true competition of skill that pushed the limits of human endurance to the breaking point.

Directing the Bunion Derby was Charley Pyle, teetering on bankruptcy after having lost much of the fortune he had earned in a wild four-year ride that took him from obscurity to shining star in the development of professional sports in America. In 1925, he had signed the greatest football player of the 1920s, Red Grange, and together they made a fortune, established the short-lived American Football League, owned a National Football League franchise, established professional tennis in America, and directed the first Bunion Derby in 1928.[8] Pyle proved to be a man of almost evangelical vision, but he was woefully short on managerial skills and bled away most of his fortune as his schemes came unraveled.[9]

In 1929, Charley hoped to rebuild his fortune with one wild grab at glory, staging the second Bunion Derby at the zenith of the Roaring

Twenties, just months before the Wall Street crash. In New York City, Charley cobbled together his Cross Country Follies, complete with dancing debutantes, an all-girl band wearing pilots' outfits, a husband-and-wife acrobatic team, and blackface comedians, all housed under the massive show tent that Charley hoped would pack in audiences and cover the sixty-thousand dollars in prize money that he put up to the top fifteen bunioneers to finish the race in Los Angeles.[10]

On March 31, 1929, Charley Pyle, seventy-seven runners, and his Cross Country Follies left Columbus Circle in New York City for a seventy-eight-day footrace across America. This is the story of that forgotten race that took place just months before the nation began its long plunge into the grim reality of the Great Depression.

The 1929 Bunion Derby

1

Race Day

New York City to Elizabeth New Jersey,
March 31, 1929

Day 1, 77 Men

March 31, 1929. After a decade of peace and unprecedented economic expansion, Americans could look back on the 1920s with an understandable sense of pride. The United States had helped stop the carnage of the First World War and emerged as an industrial marvel. As the decade of the twenties dawned, constitutional amendments gave women the right to vote and outlawed the sale and distribution of alcohol, making Prohibition the law of the land.[1] The country was richer and more prosperous than it had ever been, with annual incomes rising by 30 percent from 1921 to 1929.[2] Key technologies—electricity, motion pictures, autos, and radios—had spread rapidly and profoundly and reshaped the country. Twenty-seven million cars clogged roads that were quiet at the start of the decade, which set off a boom in road construction and oil production.[3]

By race day, the stock market had reached stratospheric levels as money poured into Wall Street to purchase stocks, fueled by broker loans where an investor could put down from 10 to 20 percent of the stock purchase price and use the inflated value of his or her stocks as collateral.[4] The cowboy humorist Will Rogers wrote that "it was a great game. All you had to do was to buy and wait till the next morning and just pick up the paper and see how much you made, in print."[5] President Herbert Hoover had been in office for less than a month. As a self-made millionaire, he symbolized bedrock American values of rugged individualism and unyielding faith in the future. In just seven months, this optimism would turn to despair as the infamous stock market crash started America on its spiral into the Great Depression.

In New York City, thousands of people were unaware of their dark future as they strolled in their Sunday best in and around Central Park on a sunny Easter Sunday afternoon. Spring was in the air. Baseball season would soon begin, and the great Babe Ruth would once again step up to the plate for the New York Yankees.

Many of these strollers were attracted to Columbus Circle on the southwest corner of Central Park, where a seventy-seven-foot granite column supported a marble statue of Christopher Columbus and, wrote syndicated columnist Westbrook Pegler, "A large number of males attired in underwear of various hues" was assembled.[6] The runners, like the famous explorer, were seeking fame and fortune on their own westward journey as part of the Bunion Derby, the nickname for "C. C. Pyle's Second Annual International-Trans-Continental Foot Race" across America.

The wail of sirens from police motorcycles escorting the runners through the city and the large waving flags at the start attracted thousands of New Yorkers to the circle, bringing traffic to a standstill and engulfing Pyle's seventy-seven runners in the crowd.[7] A film taken of the start shows Charley Pyle in an open-air car, shouting instructions to his runners through a megaphone as they snake by in a thin line, an artery of runners moving through a mass of humanity.[8] The curious crowd pushed and shoved its way to the starting line, and the police were powerless to control it.[9] In this chaos, Charley's opening ceremonies came unraveled, and he simply screamed instructions to begin the race. Will Rogers, a friend of the previous year's winner, Andy Payne, had apparently been scheduled to begin the race with a gunshot, but that did not happen.[10]

With the race under way, the seventy-seven men began to weave through the crowd, with their police escorts blaring their sirens as they attempted to clear a path to the Hudson River ferries that would take the men to New Jersey. Two unidentified runners broke out of the crowd and crashed into a parked taxi. The rest weaved their way through dense crowds on onlookers.[11] At several points along the course, patrons of

1. Cover from *Official 1929 Program*. Source: John Stone, private collection.

speakeasies rushed to the doors, holding their steins aloft in a Prohibition-era salute.[12]

Harry Abramowitz, a tiny New Yorker and 1928 derby finisher, reached the 23rd Street ferry first, covering the one and a half miles in thirteen minutes, "a time," wrote the New York Times, "that would have been good for a taxi trip from the circle to the ferry."[13] The men had to wait until all the runners had checked in before boarding the vessel, forcing them to stand sweating in the chilly winds that blew off the Hudson River.[14] The men were delayed again on the New Jersey side when a head count revealed that derby officials had left Polish runner George Jusnick on the New York side. The head referee, Steve Owen, held the men back until Jusnick arrived on the next boat.[15]

Just as in New York, massive crowds, which New York Times estimated at around a half-million souls, jammed the roads to the finish in Elizabeth, New Jersey.[16] Two race veterans, Eddie Gardner and Sammy Richman, burned up the short-by-derby-standards 21.1-mile course, covering the miles at a pace of five minutes and forty seconds per mile, seemingly an impossibly fast pace for trans-America racing since Payne had won the previous year by "stepping along" at the ten-minute-per-mile pace.[17] The veterans drew in rookies Pietro Marini of Italy and the two Cools brothers from Belgium, who tried to match their furious pace.[18] Most of the fans, however, had come to see Johnny Salo, their home-state hero, win the opening stage of the Bunion Derby wearing his trademark number 107 on his racing bib and his blue American Legion cap. One fan shouted, "Come on, Salo. You are going to finish first today, aren't you?" Johnny only grinned and maintained the slow, steady pace he had perfected while logging the brutal miles of the previous year.[19]

The crowd was kind to Sammy Richman, a veteran of the first derby, a New Yorker, and a fellow legionnaire, but it vented its anger at fellow derby veteran Eddie Gardner, an Alabama-born African American from Seattle. The crowd yelled racial slurs at him, but the words did not bother Eddie after his trials in the South in the previous year's Bunion Derby, where he faced a daily dose of death threats and intimidation.[20]

Johnny Salo had become a household in name in New Jersey, the rags-to-riches, against-all-odds story of a common man who had triumphed by sheer guts and an iron will to finish second in the 1928 derby and who earned a ten-thousand-dollar prize. He had arrived in the United States as a Finnish immigrant in his midteens, served in World War I, and risen through the ranks to become a naval officer after making ten trips on convoys across the submarine-infested Atlantic. In 1928, he left his hometown of Passaic, New Jersey, for Los Angeles to enter the first Bunion Derby as an unknown, thirty-four-year-old father of two and an often-unemployed shipyard worker with just eleven dollars in his pocket and a dream.[21] He had survived the first terrible five hundred miles of desert and mountain running. Gradually, he adapted to the rigors of trans-America running, and with the financial support of local American Legion posts along the course, he hired a trainer and was able to avoid Pyle's horrible food and drafty tents that passed for free room and board. By the time Johnny reached Ohio, he was one of the lead runners, racing in the seven-to-eight-minute-per-mile range day after day as he chased front-runner Andy Payne of Oklahoma for first place.[22]

On the second to the last day of the 1928 derby, Johnny led the race into Passaic on his thirty-fifth birthday. Passaic's citizens had decorated the town in red, white, and blue bunting. Newspaper stories about his race across America had become daily reading in every Passaic household. As he neared the finish line, sirens from the town's firehouses blew and a mass of people ten deep parted to let him finish. He declared, "This is the greatest and happiest day of my life. It almost makes me cry to see what the citizens of Passaic are doing for me."[23]

The night before, the town council had appointed him a city police officer as a gesture of thanks for all the positive publicity he had brought the city. His days of unemployment were behind him. He used the second place ten-thousand-dollar prize money to buy a cozy house for his wife and two children on Spring Street and settled down to walk a beat. For Johnny, dreams did come true. He had become the "flying cop from Passaic," a local hero, and the odds-on favorite to win the second Bunion Derby.[24]

As the first day of the 1929 race neared its end in Elizabeth, New Jersey, masses of exhaust-belching cars jammed the roads and forced the runners to weave through them.[25] The bus Pyle used to transport his

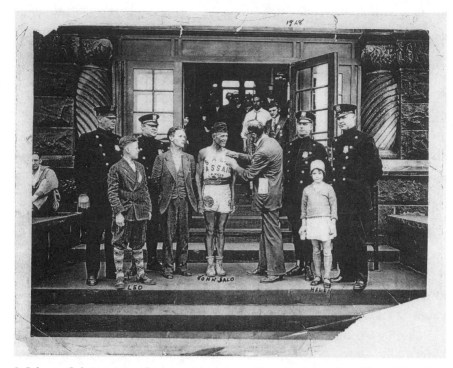

2. Johnny Salo receiving his commission as a Passaic city police officer, May 25, 1928. Courtesy of northjersey.com.

follies cast added to the confusion by trying to get around the jam by weaving in and out of oncoming traffic.[26] This forced many of the oncoming cars to pull off to the shoulder of the road. In the chaos, the derby suffered its first accident when a car brushed Charley Hart, the race's senior runner at sixty-four years of age, and injured his knee, but not severely enough to put this veteran competitor out of the contest.[27] Hart had been one of the race favorites in 1928. He had held the world one-hundred-mile running record before Arthur Newton and had survived the opening weeks of the 1928 race before dropping out from exhaustion in the Arizona high country.[28]

As the men passed through Newark near the end of the race, the townspeople welcomed them, and hundreds watched from their porches while firehouse whistles blew in salute. The reception at the finish in nearby Elizabeth, however, was less than cordial.

2nd Prize Winner   John Salo
(receiving appointment as police officer of
City of Passaic from Comm.Benj. F. Turner)

Of..
Leg..
Van

Harry ..
Donohue

3. Johnny Salo being sworn in as a Passaic city police officer, May 25, 1928.
Courtesy of northjersey.com.

On Saturday morning, March 30, 1929, the residents of this sedate, hardworking community had been awakened by the rumble of Pyle's fleet of heavy trucks heading to Sportsmen's Park, where his work gang planned to erect the massive tent that would house his traveling vaudeville show, "C. C. Pyle's Cross Country Follies," which would accompany the derby across America. Charley planned an exciting finish. For twenty-five cents, fans could watch the bunioneers run the final four miles around an indoor track under the big top followed by a performance of Pyle's show.[29]

The editors of the town newspaper, the *Elizabeth Daily Journal*, were not impressed by the event, claiming that only deranged citizens would come down to Sportsmen's Park to see the bunioneers.[30] The city fathers were even less receptive when Pyle's representative requested a permit to set up his show. Police Chief Michael J. Mulcahy, citing the city's blue laws, which prohibited such activities on Sunday, flatly refused to issue Pyle a permit to stage the follies in town.[31] Charley, who never seemed to bother with such details, began setting up his tent Sunday morning until officers from the Elizabeth City Police Department arrived and ordered his men to pull it down and stop selling programs.[32] This left Pyle's perpetual critic, sportswriter Westbrook Pegler, to quip, "Mr. Pyle's gross receipts for the first day of the tour were, in round numbers, approximately nothing at all, and his net receipts a little less than that."[33]

The postponement of the stage show was a blessing for twenty-two-year-old Andy Payne, the 1928 derby winner turned performer. He had sprained an ankle practicing a rope trick and was, in Pegler's words, "now listing sharply to starboard."[34] Andy had two jobs in the 1929 race: first, to entertain the crowds with rope tricks and jokes while the other performers changed costumes, and second, to serve on the race patrol, which involved driving the course in one of Pyles's six bright-red patrol cars to ensure that none of the runners accepted rides from sympathetic motorists.[35]

Most of the fans who milled around at Sportsmen's Park were wildly pro-Salo, with a huge contingent from Passaic on hand. Johnny would not indulge them and finished a distant eleventh.[36] Gardner finished first with a fast pace of five minutes and forty seconds per mile, with Sammy Richman fifteen seconds behind him. For his trouble, Eddie finished to a hail of catcalls and racial slurs.[37] When Johnny finally arrived, a huge roar went up from the crowd, but Salo was in a foul mood, complaining of stomach trouble and stating that he felt terrible. His ailment was brought on by the heat and left him considering whether to drop out of the contest. Fast work that night by his wife, Amelia, and his trainer, Bill Wicklund, got him back in shape by morning.[38]

The unluckiest man in the race was Louis Perrella of Albany, New York. He tripped at the finish, injuring himself, and was unable to start the next day. Perrella had finished seventh in the 1928 race and had endured painful shin splints as he raced over the rolling hills of New York in the last days of that year's derby.[39] The second unluckiest man was novice Merle A. Trapp of Atchison, Kansas, who was hit by a car and had to drop out the next day.[40]

The surviving men had entered a new world ruled by a simple repetitive pattern that would go on for the next two and a half months. Each

4. Andy Payne, from *Official 1929 Program*. Source: John Stone, private collection.

morning, the contestants would assemble at the prior day's finish line, where the head referee would call the roll. Once completed, he would give the starting command and an official timer would record the start time. The men would then race to the next finish line that Pyle had set up in some town down the road. In the terminology of the Bunion Derby, the finish line was the "control point" and the daily race, the "stage race." As each man crossed the finish line, a timer would record his time in the official log and add it to his cumulative time from the prior stage races. The man with the lowest cumulative time in Los Angeles would win the twenty-five-thousand-dollar cash prize, the second lowest, ten-thousand

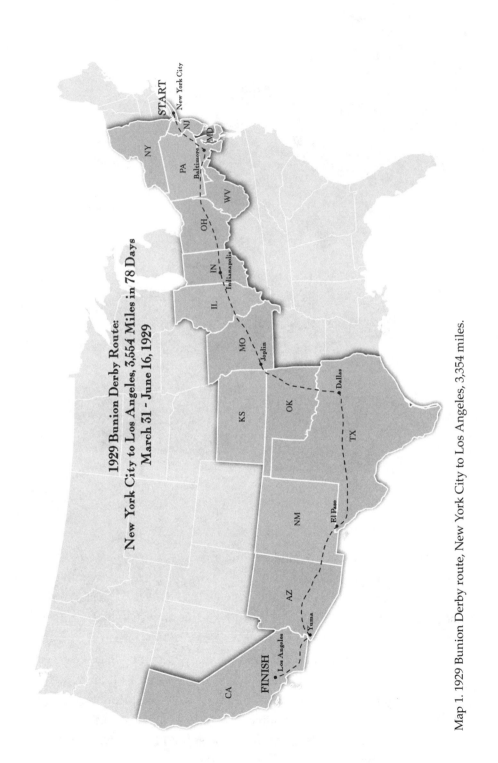

1929 Bunion Derby Route:
New York City to Los Angeles, 3,554 Miles in 78 Days
March 31 - June 16, 1929

START

New York City

NJ

MD

Baltimore

NY

PA

WV

OH

IN

Indianapolis

IL

MO

Joplin

KS

OK

Dallas

TX

NM

El Paso

AZ

Yuma

CA

FINISH

Los Angeles

Map 1. 1929 Bunion Derby route, New York City to Los Angeles, 3,354 miles.

dollars and so on, with the fifteen lowest finishers winning a share of the sixty-thousand dollars in prize money. The "Director General," as Pyle had grandly dubbed himself, set two simple rules for his competitors: run on your own two feet and finish by midnight. Any man who violated either rule would be disqualified from the derby.[41]

The first day of the Bunion Derby had gotten off to a very rough start. If Pyle wanted to make enough money to pay out sixty-thousand dollars in prize money, he needed to get the follies up and running quickly. The bunioneers had had their first taste of transcontinental running—less than half of what they would run on a daily basis for the next seventy-seven days. Already, one man had dropped out, another would soon follow, and a third, Charley Hart, had injured his knee. Johnny Salo, the derby's star runner, seemed on the verge of making a quick exit from the race. Charley Pyle hoped for better results on the second day of the Bunion Derby.

2

Down the Eastern Seaboard

Elizabeth, New Jersey, to Baltimore, Maryland,
April 1–April 5, 1929

Trouble in Trenton

Day 2, 76 Men

The bunioneers had five more days until the serious running began after racing down the Eastern Seaboard to Baltimore. Then they would turn west to tackle the Appalachian Mountains, the traditional barrier to the hinterland that had challenged pioneers ever since the first European colonists arrived in America more than three hundred years before.

Both the veterans and the rookies needed to work out the kinks in their routines with their trainers, both on the course and before and after the daily runs. A myriad of decisions about pacing, diet, hydration, clothing, and footwear and about dealing with blisters, sunburn, chafing, muscle pulls, and a range of other ailments needed to be made, any one of which could spell success or failure as the runners ascended the mountains.

On the morning of the second day, Pete Gavuzzi and Arthur Newton's valet, George Barren, had cooked scrambled eggs and delivered them to Sportsmen's Park for the 6:30 start.[1] Newton was two decades older and a foot taller than Gavuzzi, but both were equally blessed with talent and skill. "His style attracts attention at once," wrote a reporter who watched Gavuzzi run. "He bounds over the ground with a grace and agility that is almost astonishing; only a man who was born to be a great runner could develop such a natural and perfectly effortless gait."[2] Born in England to

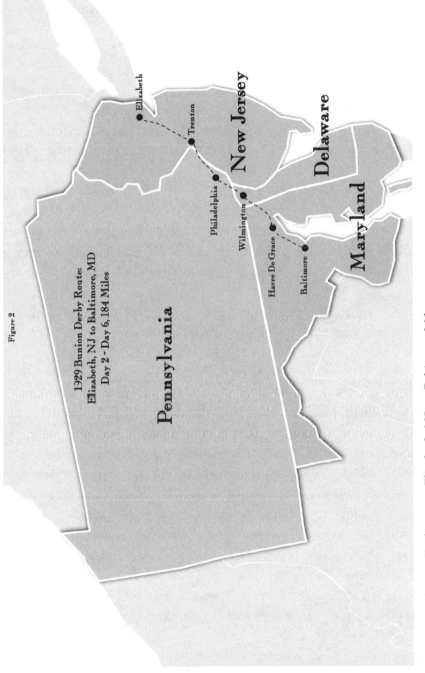

Figure 2

1929 Bunion Derby Route:
Elizabeth, NJ to Baltimore, MD
Day 2 – Day 6, 184 Miles

Pennsylvania

New Jersey

Delaware

Maryland

Elizabeth

Trenton

Philadelphia

Wilmington

Havre De Grace

Baltimore

Map 2. 1929 Bunion Derby route, Elizabeth, N.J., tc Baltimore, Md.

a French parlor maid and an Italian chef, he grew up trilingual and spoke English with a working-class cockney accent.[3] In his teen years, he went to sea on an ocean liner where he worked as a ship's steward and won every cup offered for shipboard racing.[4]

In the 1928 race, Pete started out slowly, mixing race walking with running, which gave his body time to adjust to the rigors of racing across America.[5] In Arizona, he gained a trainer when Charley Hart, a sixty-three-year-old London boot maker, dropped out of the derby from exhaustion. In a donated car with a Union Jack tied across the trunk, Hart shepherded Pete across the country.[6]

By the time the derby reached Oklahoma, Gavuzzi was battling the eventual winner, Andy Payne, for the lead. On the flat roads of Illinois and Indiana, Pete showed himself to be an exceptional runner, gifted with both endurance and speed. He had built a sizable lead over Payne until disaster struck in Ohio; an infected tooth forced him to abandon eating solid food and switch to drinking soup and sucking on hard candy, a diet that could not provide him the with the massive calories needed to sustain transcontinental running. Pete literally ran out of fuel with the twenty-five-thousand-dollar first prize in his grasp.[7]

When Arthur Newton entered the 1928 Bunion Derby, he needed no introduction. He was heavily favored to win the race.[8] Tall, nearsighted, and in his midforties, he looked more like a senior schoolmaster than the world's greatest ultramarathoner.[9] Born in England, Newton had spent most of his adult life in South Africa, where he broke all established training rules for long-distance running—often running more than two hundred miles a week while his competitors would run only thirty, since it was common wisdom that running longer distances would strain their hearts.[10]

With his tougher training regimen, Newton smashed the course record for South Africa's brutal fifty-six-mile Comrades Marathon, winning it six times in the 1920s as well as setting every world distance-running record between thirty and one hundred miles.[11] He led the first Bunion Derby until a leg injury forced him out of the contest in the mountains of Arizona.[12]

Back in England, Newton and Gavuzzi trained hard for the next derby, which Pyle had tentatively set for March 1929. Pete ran the length of

5. Pete Gavuzzi wearing his Bunion Derby race number. Source: Guy Gavuzzi, private collection.

Great Britain in September 1928, covering its north-south length in thirty days, and setting what he claimed to be a new record for the distance. Both men raced in the fifty-mile Glasgow to Edinburgh, Scotland, run on New Year's Day in the middle of a snowstorm. Sometime after the race, Newton had a proposition for Gavuzzi for the upcoming bunion derby race: form a partnership to share expenses, hire a trainer, and divide any

6. Arthur Newton, England, 1928. Source: Rob Hadgraft, private collection.

prize money between them. The two men hired an English trainer named George Barren, described by Harry Berry in his book, *From L.A. to New York, from New York to L.A.* (1990) as a former "athlete of moderate ability, but more important, a skilled mechanic and a reasonable cook."[13]

Once the men received the news that the race was on, they boarded a ship for New York and arrived with just ten days to spare.[14] In New York,

7. Arthur Newton and Pete Gavuzzi racing together in Canada, 1931. Source: Guy Gavuzzi, private collection.

they bought a one-ton Chevrolet truck, which they fitted out with two beds, an ice chest, a portable stove, a collapsible bed for Barren, a gramophone, and a couple of dozen classical records, "a foresight," Newton wrote, "which gave us a great deal of pleasure later on."[15]

While Newton and Gavuzzi waited at the start line for the beginning of the second day's race, Pyle's as-yet-untested cadre of women dancers and the all-girl band sat in the open-air compartment of his bus, watching the scene and, as Westbrook Pegler wrote, "batting their eyes at the unfamiliar brightness of the morning sun."[16] Rain clouds, however, soon appeared and drove the ladies under cover and drenched the assembled runners, who would get their first real test of long-distance running that day—46.4 miles to Trenton, the state capital and site of one of the most important battles of the Revolutionary War. On December 26, 1776, American troops under the command of General George Washington routed the Hessian garrison and gave renewed hope to the struggling Continental Army.[17] Pyle hoped his stay in Trenton would have a similar effect on the flagging fortunes of his Bunion Derby. Trenton would be the second stop on their coast-hugging southerly journey to Baltimore before the derby turned west and began to tackle the vast distance across America to Los Angeles, where sixty-thousand dollars in prize money waited for the top fifteen finishers.

At the start line, some of the experienced men, like Newton, gave the rookies friendly words of warning to slow down and forget about trying to stay with the 1928 veterans.[18] Most of the veterans knew from experience what pace to maintain for a given distance and terrain. Most had also been training for months for the race, putting in at least two or more twenty-five-mile runs or longer a week. Few of the rookies had put in anything close to that level of training.

Perhaps the rookies still clung to the old notion that training for longer than thirty miles a week strained the heart and took years off the lives of those who pushed beyond it. This arcane belief was debunked after a team of Philadelphia doctors examined twenty of the 1928 finishers shortly after the end of the race. The medical team found no evidence of enlarged hearts, abnormal bones and joints, or other ailments beyond what would be expected in a normal population. The doctors concluded that normal human beings, given enough food and rest, were capable of running the trans-America distance without damaging their bodies.[19] The 1928 veterans had adopted this new understanding into their training routines, some putting in hundreds of miles a week.

The veterans also understood the importance of taking in enough food to meet the massive calorie needs of a trans-America runner— roughly three times that of a normal man. Through trial and error, most of the 1928 runners had developed a basic formula: eat the biggest possible breakfast shortly before the start, then run slowly for twenty miles as their bodies absorbed the food. Throughout the run, they supplemented the morning meal by drinking highly sweetened drinks every five or six miles, and adding honey or cheese sandwiches for longer distances. For the evening meal, a large amount of meat was the main requirement.[20]

The director general's method of setting the daily racing distance promised to add to the burdens of his bunioneers. As the derby traveled across the country, Pyle would try to negotiate with local business groups like the Chamber of Commerce for the privilege of having the race finish in their town. If he could not reach an agreement with one town, he would push on until he found one that might make a monetary "contribution" of anywhere between two hundred and two thousand dollars, depending upon the size of the city or town. Pyle would argue that the payout would be more than offset by the economic benefit, with derby fans filling local restaurants and hotels as they packed the downtown area to see the runners finish and take in his follies show. This free market system of setting the daily racing distance, from town a to town b, would result in wildly different distances—anywhere between twenty-five to eighty miles—and would add greatly to the demands of transcontinental racing on the bunioneers in the weeks ahead, especially so for the rookies who had little or no experience with daily ultramarathon racing.

The rookies of 1929 were simply unprepared to compete against the battle-hardened veterans. The smartest course of action for the newcomers would have been to treat the first few weeks of the race as a training exercise. The new men needed to hold back until their bodies had time to adjust to the rigors of running daily ultramarathons and then race once they were stronger, but few listened to the veterans, caught up as the rookies were in the excitement of the opening days of the derby. Arthur realized that the art of transcontinental racing had "to be learnt first hand, and nothing but the active experience will convince a man that he will make better time over a long distance if he travels more slowly at the start than he feels sure he could manage."[21]

The veterans ran fast on the flat course to Trenton. Paul "Hard Rock" Simpson, a North Carolina veteran and physical education instructor from Elon College, won the stage race, covering the distance in six hours and eleven minutes, in just under an eight-minute-per-mile pace. Rookie Karl Cools of Belgium finished close behind him, with Salo in third and Eddie Gardner of Seattle close behind him in fourth. Karl's brother, Juuls, finished in the top ten.[22]

The Cools brothers and many of the thirty-four rookies had ignored Newton's warning and were sucked along in the vortex of the leaders, who kept testing the limits of speed they had established the year before.[23] In this race, the top nine finishers ran sub-nine-minute miles. In 1928, most of this year's front-runners—Pete Gavuzzi, Paul Simpson, Eddie Gardner, and Johnny Salo—had spent weeks far back in the pack,

8. Unidentified man and Leonard Lewis, #39, early dropout in the 1929 race. Source: Charles Kastner, private collection.

mixing walking and running until they had developed the speed and stamina they would show on the flat roads of Illinois, Indiana, and Ohio. During their initiation, faster, better-known, and perhaps more talented runners like the Finnish marathon star Willie Kolehmainen pushed their bodies too hard and dropped out of the contest, leaving "the shadow runners"—men who arrived in Los Angeles without international reputations and unknown to the national press—to collect the prize money.[24] The 1929 rookies needed to emulate the 1928 veterans, but few listened, and they pushed themselves to exhaustion or injury and an early exit from the race.

C. C. PYLE'S FOOTRACE

39

New York to Los Angeles

9. Official race bib, Leonard Lewis. Source: Charles Kastner, private collection.

Race director Charley Pyle seemed to be just as inept as most of his rookie bunioneers. The day started badly for him when the truck carrying his show tent skidded off the rain-slicked road and rolled over into a farmer's field, the first in a slew of problems that would haunt him that day.[25] A deputy sheriff then served him with a writ of attachment from the Thomas Deming Furniture Company of New York. After Pyle's eight-hundred-dollar check had bounced, the company had taken legal action to recover payment for the thousand chairs he had purchased for his follies.[26] The day ended with city officials refusing to allow his stage show to perform in Trenton, probably because he had forgotten to obtain the necessary permits. Syndicated reporter Westbrook Pegler wrote, "Mr. Pyle was in a temper against the commissioners of the city of Trenton."[27] Miss La Belle Rene, a baritone saxophone player from Chicago in the all-girl band, complained that the police ignored the sale of "intoxicating applejack" but would not give an artist "a permit to play the saxophone."[28]

An irate Charley Pyle then ordered his men to move his derby camp across the Delaware River to Morrisville, Pennsylvania, where he hoped to find a more receptive audience and avoid the writ of attachment issued by a New Jersey judge.[29] He thought he had made his escape until New Jersey police detained two of his late-arriving patrol cars, one driven by Andy Payne. Pyle spent the next hour trying to reason with the officers, and "young Mr. Payne," quipped Westbrook Pegler, "was in disfavor with the management of the Bunion Derby."[30] In spite of his pleas, the officers kept the cars. Charley then returned to New York City, where he hoped to straighten out what he called a simple misunderstanding with the owners of the chair company and get treatment for a severe cold. He expected to rejoin his parade the next day.[31]

A Tough Time to Be a Rookie

Day 3, 75 Men

The men would leave Morristown for Philadelphia—the cradle of the American Revolution. By 1929, Philadelphia had grown into a massive city of almost two million souls, the third largest in America.[32]

The front-runners wasted no time in getting there, with veteran runners Troy Trimble of Los Angeles, Eddie Gardner, Paul Simpson, fifty-five-year-old Australian Herbert Hedeman, and Guisto Umek of Italy setting a fast pace as they raced across the flat and well-paved 29.3-mile course.[33] Johnny Salo, running farther back, barely escaped injury when a car brushed by him. He had to leap off the road; Salo lost his footing and went sprawling on the sidewalk, but he escaped uninjured, except for a few scratches.[34]

The sweating Troy Trimble, who had dropped out in the early days of the 1928 derby, finished first and wore a red beret, which set streams of red dye running down his face until he looked like a badly beaten boxer.[35] The top eight finishers covered the distance at a pace of less than eight and a half minutes per mile, a minute and a half per mile faster than Andy

Payne's derby-winning pace in 1928.[36] The fast pace had broken scores of men who tried to keep up with the front-runners. Juuls Cools, who was among the leaders on the first day, tumbled into eleventh place in the cumulative standings, and both he and his brother were exhausted and unsure whether they could continue the race. Thirteen others dropped out after reaching Philadelphia, leaving the field at sixty-two.[37] After just 134 miles and three days of racing, 20 percent of the field had gone, including the 1928 chronicler, John Stone Jr., whose memoir of the first race, *The Hells of the Bunion Derby* (ca. 1928), gave a gripping account of the herculean effort required to race across America.[38]

The three-day survivors were just getting started. They had more than three thousand miles and two and a half months of mountain, prairie, and desert running ahead of them. This first few days of the derby were a wake-up call for the leg-dead rookies: they were competing against a cadre of steely-tough veterans who had honed their skills in the brutal 1928 race after enduring pain and suffering that few of these rookies could imagine. The men of 1928 had cut their feet to ribbons and burned themselves raw in the Mojave Desert, frozen in drafty tents in the Arizona high country, eaten miserable food, and slogged through ankle-deep mud in the Texas Panhandle. The rookies realized that they were in for the fight of their lives if they hoped to collect any prize money in Los Angeles.[39]

With so many veterans in the derby, many of the exhausted newcomers were having second thoughts about continuing the race. Philadelphia's lone entry, Ken Mullen, had already spent most of the $1,200 he had saved for the derby. After buying a car, paying the entry fee, and covering necessary expenses, he had just ten dollars to his name. He was not anxious to continue with just ten dollars in his pocket and hoped that his supporters would contribute more funds soon.[40] Other rookies, like twenty-year-old Jesse Dalzell, twenty-five-year-old Elmer Cowley, and the Cools brothers, Karl and Juuls, were simply hoping to survive until tomorrow.[41]

The Cools brothers were the most promising rookies in the race, having won several marathons in France, but they had not given their bodies time to adjust to the rigors of daily ultramarathon racing and were now on the verge of quitting the race. They took a wild gamble to get there after stowing away on a ship to reach New York, where they were discovered and interned at Ellis Island by United States customs officers until they paid a fifteen-hundred-dollar admission bond. A group of Belgian New Yorkers heard of their plight and raised enough money to pay the bond and Pyle's entrance fee, but the brothers' dreams of Bunion Derby glory seemed very much in doubt as they slept in their beds in Philadelphia.[42]

The director general had returned from New York City in much better spirits after apparently having settled his legal troubles with the Thomas Deming Furniture Company.[43] Charley claimed "there was no rubber check" but that he had stopped payment because of the poor quality of the chairs.[44] Pyle somehow "adjusted the matter" and believed that "we are getting organized now and will have clear sailing to the coast."[45] Well, not quite. Throughout the afternoon, Charley's work gang tried unsuccessfully to raise the massive tent for his cross-country follies, forcing him to cancel the matinee opening of his as-yet-unseen stage show.[46] A famous revivalist had once used the tent to good effect, packing its three thousand seats with anxious sinners ready to give their souls to God.[47] Charley's salvation came that night when his crew managed to erect his tent for the 9:00 P.M. show—his belated première.[48]

The follies' theme was aviation, playing to audiences still enamored with Charles Lindbergh's solo flight across the Atlantic in 1927. A movie screen behind the stage was filled with images of airplanes, the all-girl band was dressed in pilots' outfits, and the show opened with the movie score from *Wings* (the first movie to win an Academy Award) as Charley's twenty-one debutantes pranced across the stage performing the latest dance steps from New York. Pyle followed the opening with blackface comedy acts, a husband-and-wife acrobatic act, well-known radio singers, and vaudeville comedians. Charley also had several trucks full of lighting, props, and wardrobes and a small army of stagehands to assemble and take down the tent and sets.[49]

In the crowded East Coast cities, the Cross Country Follies may have seemed ordinary. Pyle hoped that as he went farther west into isolated hamlets and towns, few would have seen the likes of his stage show and his tent would be packed with paying customers, but his dreams of financial redemption would be challenged by what some saw as the unsavory

10. C. C. Pyle's Cross Country Follies. Source: *Official 1929 Program*, John Stone, private collection.

nature of the race: a sizable portion of Americans viewed the Bunion Derby as a dangerous aberration from the true nature of sport and would have nothing to do with the race or the follies.[50]

His detractors had forgotten their history. Less than fifty years before the race, long-distance running looked nothing like the amateur sport it had become by 1929, when athletes raced in marathons for loving cups and medals. It was much more like professional boxing, with its multiracial, working-class stars competing for prize money with often-fanatical fans betting on the likely winners.[51]

The sport reached it zenith in the late 1870s and early 1880s, when a frenzy for "six day go as you please" racing swept the United States and Great Britain. In fan-packed, smoke-filled arenas, fans cheered on their favorite competitors (commonly known as "pedestrians") as they raced around an indoor track for six days. Top pedestrians survived on less than four hours of sleep a day and slept on cots inside the track's oval.

In one legendary race in 1880, a former grocery store clerk and Haitian immigrant Frank "Black Dan" Hart smashed the world record for six-day racing by covering 565 miles around an indoor track in Madison Garden. He earned seventeen thousand dollars in prize money for his victory.[52]

Around the turn of the century, the rough-and-tumble world of professional foot racing began to fade away, replaced by amateur athletic clubs and university track and field programs.[53] By the 1920s, the sport's blue-collar past was forgotten, and the defenders of the new status quo were not anxious to see the sport return to its working-class roots—and that was exactly what Pyle did with his Bunion Derby. His bunioneers were the mirror image of the old pedestrians. They came from working-class backgrounds and competed for prize money, frequently to make better lives for their often-struggling families.

To the fans of the derby, there was something noble about Pyle's bunioneers. They were everyday men with everyday jobs. They were not wealthy. They had not attended college. They walked beats, ploughed fields, and worked in factories. They were real life examples of the potential for greatness that rested within every American.

This notion crackled through the minds of many Americans after Charles Lindbergh's solo flight across the Atlantic in 1927. Pyle's Cross

11. Frank "Black Dan" Hart, circa 1880, Charles Kastner, private collection.

Country Follies was a traveling celebration of his flight with its aviation theme, and by association, the courage and dogged determination of Charley's bunioneers. Lucky Lindy, like the bunioneers, had chased a twenty-five-thousand-dollar cash prize offered to the first pilot who flew solo between New York and Paris. Six pilots had died trying to collect it. He became an overnight sensation. In a national tour, he was mobbed by huge crowds, the likes of which had not been seen since the Armistice Day celebrations marking the end of World War I in 1918.[54] Pyle knew that Lindbergh had touched a potent and potentially lucrative nerve with the American people. He offered the young flyer a princely sum of a half million dollars for the privilege of managing his career. When Lindbergh turned him down, Charley tried to capture some of his magic by staging his two bunion derbies and by turning his follies show into a celebration of flight.[55]

Across America, business and civic leaders in towns where Pyle hoped to stage his follies show would wrestle with these two dueling images of race: an aberration from true sport or an example of courage and persistence. Each town would, in effect, hold its own referendum on the Bunion Derby. In some towns, its leading citizens—newspaper editors and civic and business leaders—dismissed it as a national joke, but in others they embraced it, and a civic or business group would collect enough money to make a "contribution" and bring the runners and his Cross Country Follies to their town.

What the citizens received in return was a chance to see a bit of the world that was far removed from the everyday life of small town America in 1929, where families huddled around the radio or went to the silent pictures for entertainment. They experienced something new and odd: a New York dance troupe, an all-girl band wearing pilot outfits, and iron tough men speaking a dozen different languages engaged in the struggle of their lives.

The director general had bet everything on the follies' success. If too many fans shunned his race and left follies seats unfilled, he had no hope of paying out the sixty-thousand dollars in prize money that he offered to the top fifteen bunioneers or of pulling himself from the brink of bankruptcy.

Charley Pyle's life had been a high-stakes poker game ever since he emerged on the national scene in 1925 when he persuaded the greatest football player of the twenties, Harold "Red" Grange, to enter into a partnership with him.[56] In a wild four-year ride, Charley went from an obscure Illinois theater owner to a force that shook the rafters of professional sports in America. Under Pyle's leadership, Grange joined the Chicago Bears in midseason after he played the final game of his senior year at the University of Illinois in 1925. Through gate receipts, endorsements, and movie deals, Pyle created a money-making machine that made each man fabulously wealthy, but Charley was not satisfied with financial success alone.[57] He dreamed of owning his own National Football League (NFL) franchise. When the Bears' owner refused to make him a part owner in 1926, Charley secured a lease on Yankee Stadium and asked the NFL to grant him his own team.

When the NFL turned him down, he formed a rival nine-team league—the American Football League—and founded his own team, the New York Yankees, with Grange as its star player.[58] The nation, however, was not yet ready for two leagues. Only Pyle's team remained by the end of the season, and he had spent most of his fortune trying to keep it out of bankruptcy.[59] That same year, Charley rattled the staid world of amateur tennis when he organized the nation's first professional tennis tour, signing six-time Wimbledon champion Suzanne Lenglen to a forty-city tour.[60] In 1927, Pyle finally fulfilled his dream when the NFL brought his New York Yankees into the league, but he continued to lose money on the team, and it became even worse when Grange suffered a devastating knee injury that kept him out of the rest of the season.[61]

Pyle then assumed the management of the first transcontinental Bunion Derby, which left Los Angeles on March 4, 1928, and finished in New York City on May 26, 1928.[62] From the start, Charley proved to be woefully unprepared to lead 199 men across the country and used most of his remaining fortune and that of his business partner, Grange, to get there.[63] After the derby, Pyle's empire dissolved around him: Grange terminated his partnership with Pyle, and Charley sold his nearly bankrupt NFL franchise.[64]

Hounded by unpaid creditors from the first derby and his NFL team, Pyle needed another moneymaker to reverse his financial decline. He thought he had found it in the second Bunion Derby. "It's different now," he told Brian Bell of the *Cleveland Plain Dealer*, "we are on a firm business basis and this [race] cannot fail to be a big success."[65] He charged each man a hefty three-hundred-dollar entry fee and took no part in feeding or housing the bunioneers during the race, as he had done in 1928.[66] All he needed to do was make the follies a financial success, but after the first two days of the derby, that seemed a very unlikely prospect. To survive, he needed to start filling his three-thousand-seat show tent with paying customers, work out the problems he had experienced in setting up and

12. Charley Pyle, 1926. Source: Library of Congress.

taking down his tent and sets, and ensure that he had the proper permits to hold his show. His bunioneers were counting on him to do so. Many had bet their life's savings that he would be true to his word and produce the sixty-thousand dollars in prize money in Los Angeles.

The strain of the past four years had taken a physical toll on Pyle, who was nearly fifty years old in 1929: he had gotten grayer; his

13. Charley Pyle, March 31, 1929. Image courtesy MPI Home Video.

once-immaculate hair had thinned, the odd hair stuck out of place; he had noticeable bags beneath his piercing blue eyes, and his tailored suits seemed a bit misplaced on his paunchy six-foot, one-inch frame.[67]

From Philadelphia, the bunioneers would hug the coast to Baltimore, following the route of the old colonial post road that had connected the city with Washington, D.C., and the southern colonies.[68] For the next three days and 199 miles, the bunioneers would retrace the path that the founders of the new American Republic—George Washington, Thomas Jefferson, and Benjamin Franklin—had followed on horseback more than 150 years earlier.[69]

Johnny Salo Regains His Racing Form

Day 4, 62 Men

The men would run thirty-eight miles under sunny skies on a paved road to Wilmington, Delaware. In these ideal conditions, Pete Gavuzzi blasted across the starting line, chasing Johnny Salo for the lead and determined to whittle away at the two-hour gap that separated him from three front-runners: Paul Simpson, Johnny Salo, and Eddie Gardner.[70] Gavuzzi had held back in the opening days of the race but now felt ready to begin the battle for first place.[71] His initial effort got off to a rough start when he took a wrong turn after running far ahead of the pack, but he soon got back on the course and caught Salo, who had assumed the lead. Then the two old rivals decided to run together and paced the field into Wilmington, tying for first-place honors in the stage race.[72] The effort moved Salo into second place overall and Gavuzzi into ninth, with Simpson in first.[73]

"The flying cop from Passaic," Johnny Salo, had returned to racing form after a difficult start. He had regained the sun-bronzed complexion acquired in the previous year's race and his stomach trouble had abated, thanks to the work of his two trainers; his wife, Amelia; and Bill Wicklund.[74] The two quickly proved themselves to be a first-class team. The fair-haired Wicklund had been the captain of the 1924 Passaic High School cross-country team.[75] Wicklund would follow Salo in Johnny's 1921 Ford, keeping him on pace and supplied with fluid and food.[76] Amelia, his Finnish-born wife, would take care of Johnny before and after each day's race. Mrs. Salo had been an athlete in her own right in Finland and had trained women athletes and provided massages at the Luxor Baths, a spa not far from Passaic.[77] Johnny was full of praise for his wife: "She's the only woman trainer in the race. And man, she's a good one. The best I've ever seen. And just learnin' too."[78] After each race, she would hustle him off to the motor home they had purchased before the race, complete with a kitchen and beds, where she would massage his sore muscles and then cook him a meal, which, a Passaic reporter wrote, "aid[ed] him greatly in keeping fit."[79] Unfortunately for Johnny, Amelia would leave the derby in Baltimore for Passaic to be with their two children, Leo and Helen, just as the race was ascending the Appalachian Mountains.[80] When she rejoined the team several weeks later in Ohio, after her husband's desperate pleas, Salo was in a very bad way, and she would need every ounce of her skills to keep him from dropping out.[81]

For now, though, Johnny was in high spirits as he spent the night in Wilmington in second place. It was the only major city in the tiny state of Delaware.[82] The city was a prosperous manufacturing center, seemingly an ideal place for Pyle to hold his follies—but once again, events did not work out as planned for the great promoter.[83] The members of his work gang refused to put up the tent until he paid them their back wages, effectively closing down the show for another night.[84]

Racing to the Bay

Day 5, 57 Men

By the next morning, five more men had dropped out of the derby, leaving just fifty-seven men to make the seven o'clock start.[85] The bunioneers left the congested, exhaust-filled roads between New York and Wilmington behind them.[86] With blue skies above, the men passed through peaceful farm country as they ran the thirty-seven miles to Havre de Grace, Maryland, a picturesque town at the mouth of the Susquehanna River on the western shore of Maryland's Chesapeake Bay.[87] They had reached "the Bay," the nation's largest estuary and a vast harbor and nursery for oysters and Maryland's famous blue crabs.[88]

The Australian Herbert Hedeman, at fifty-five the oldest runner after sixty-four-year-old Charley Hart of England, ran the distance in four hours and forty-five minutes.[89] He beat second-place finisher Johnny Salo by twenty minutes and vaulted from fourth to first place in the cumulative standings. The Australian had recently immigrated to the United States, where he had married an impoverished widow with five children. He entered the race in hopes of pulling his new family out of poverty with his winnings. Hedeman and his countryman, thirty-eight-year-old Mike McNamara, had scraped together enough money to recondition an old truck into a motor home, hire a trainer, and set out for Los Angeles. McNamara, five inches taller at six feet, one inch, was a much more powerful and consistent runner than his partner. He, like Hedeman, had come to America in the twenties and lost his life's savings in a failed business venture. Both men had bet everything on winning a share of the prize money in Los Angeles.[90]

Pyle would have no better luck staging his follies in Havre de Grace than he had in Wilmington. Charley apparently had solved his labor troubles, but he had forgotten to check the condition of his tent. His crew raised it in time for the evening show, but as the follies began to perform, torrential rains poured through tears in the canvas, putting an early end to the show and forcing the three hundred spectators to run for cover.[91] With salaries of about $2,000 a week and net receipts of about $150, Charley was once again facing a serious cash-flow problem.[92] He hoped for better luck at the next stop in Baltimore.

Wild Weather to Baltimore

Day 6, 56 Men

Another man dropped out, leaving fifty-six men to shiver in a cold, drizzling rain as they lined up for the forty-four-mile race to Baltimore—Maryland's largest city at about eight-hundred-thousand people and a thriving seaport on Chesapeake Bay—on a course that skirted the western side of the bay.[93] As the day went on, the cold gave way to unseasonable heat as warm air from the Gulf Stream collided with cool northern air. The result was violent thunderstorms that drenched the men as thunder rumbled and lightning bolts flashed in the sky.[94] As the runners finished at the old circus grounds in Baltimore, the storms passed, replaced by a steamy mugginess more typical of midsummer.[95]

Despite the weather, Gavuzzi won the forty-four-mile stage in breathtaking speed, covering the distance in a bit more than five and a half hours, a pace of seven minutes and forty-one seconds per mile.[96] He called for his tobacco pipe as he crossed the finish line and vaulted from ninth to fourth place in the overall standings.[97] Salo finished next, eighteen minutes behind him, fast enough to move him into first place.[98] Hedeman, who had run so brilliantly the day before, had pushed his aging body too hard, finishing in eighteenth place and dropping to third overall.[99] This day also spelled the end for the two brothers from Belgium, who failed to reach Baltimore by the midnight cutoff. The pair had talent, but they were simply not ready to keep pace with the 1928 veterans on the flat roads of the Eastern Seaboard.[100] They joined a growing list of talented but departed rookies who would not heed Newton's warning to slow down and had pushed themselves into race-ending injury and exhaustion.

Charley Pyle continued to seem just as inept as his rookie bunioneers. The recent rains had soaked the fairground, making it too muddy to support his show tent and forcing him once again to cancel the night's performance.[101] After this last setback, Pyle abandoned the tent altogether and sent it back to the owners with orders to send him a smaller, more manageable one. In the meantime, Pyle planned to stage his follies in local theaters along the route.[102]

The trip down the Eastern Seaboard had been nothing but a financial disaster for the director general. His moneymaking engine, C. C. Pyle's Cross Country Follies, had given only one performance since the derby left New York City. Despite teetering near bankruptcy, Charley remained upbeat. Forever a salesman and an optimist, he boldly told the press that "we'll finish in Los Angeles and next year we'll have another one," and he claimed that the "annual [C. C. Pyle] event is already one of the world's running classics. It will be even more so in years to come."[103] He called rumors that the derby was breaking up "baloney" and added, "I don't care what [the reporters] say as long as they don't misspell my name."[104]

3

Six Days of Hell—Crossing the Appalachian Plateau

Baltimore, Maryland, to Wheeling, West Virginia, April 6–April 11, 1929

SHORTLY AFTER THE FIRST BUNION DERBY ENDED, John Stone Jr. wrote his memoir, *The Hells of the Bunion Derby* (ca. 1928). It lays out in stark terms the challenges of transcontinental racing. Stone described a scene near the finish of a brutal seventy-five-mile run through the Catskill Mountains in New York in the last days of the derby, with men still struggling to the finish in the early hours of the morning. He wrote, "We were completely exhausted after three thousand miles, but it made no difference. As we went along that morning, I can well recollect seeing some of those poor boys laying along the side of the road with their faces in the grass which was wet with dew, waiting until they could get strength to get into camp. We had to pick some up and shake them to get them started down the road again. Even then some would collapse from exhaustion right in the road and we had to hold each other up to get to our control point." Once they finished, the men had, at best, a few hours of rest before they would be back on the road again.[1]

In the next six days of the 1929 race, Pyle's bunioneers would face a similar test as they headed west across the Appalachian Mountains, a vast system that stretches from Canada to central Alabama, made up of a series of north-south ridgelines and valleys that separates the Eastern Seaboard from America's hinterland.[2] Here the veterans would have to decide whether they had the stomach for another gut-busting effort that

14 John Stone, author of *The Hella of the Bunion Derby* (circa 1928). Source: John Stone, private collection.

would push their bodies beyond pain, beyond exhaustion, to a point near total collapse. They had touched that point in 1928 when they crossed the Mojave Desert, crested the Continental Divide, and finished the seventy-mile run in the Catskills that Stone described in his memoir. Over the next six days, the surviving rookies would earn the right to call themselves bunioneers as they searched for the limits of human endurance.

The men would follow Route 40 across the mountains—a road first conceived in the 1790s when a group of Baltimore bankers and business-men put up funds to build a road west to increase trade with the rap-idly developing western territories. With federal help, the road eventually

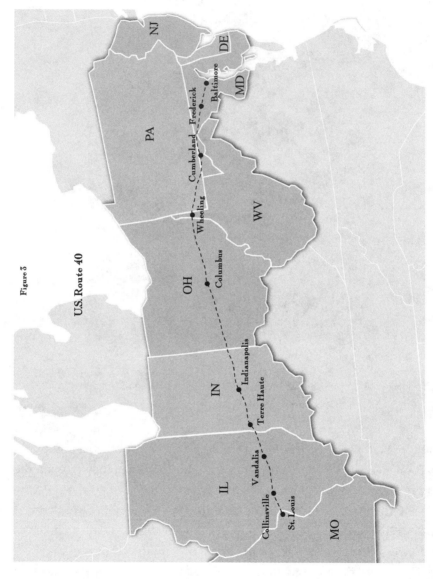

Figure 3

U.S. Route 40

Map 3. US Route 40.

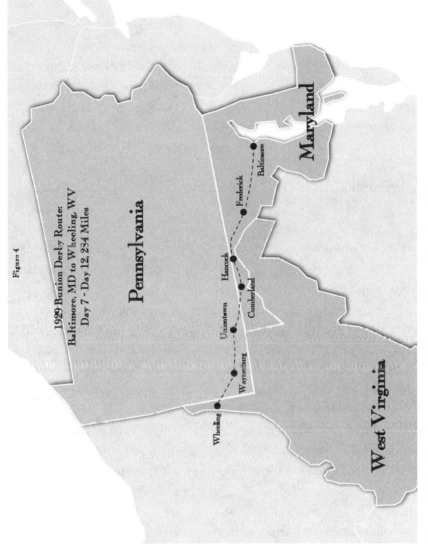

Figure 4

1929 Bunion Derby Route:
Baltimore, MD to Wheeling, WV
Day 7 - Day 12, 234 Miles

Pennsylvania

Maryland

West Virginia

Wheeling

Uniontown

Waynesburg

Hancock

Cumberland

Frederick

Baltimore

Map 4. 1929 Bunion Derby route Baltimore, Md., to Wheeling, W.Va.

stretched across Maryland, West Virginia, Ohio, Indiana, and Illinois.[3] In its heyday, the National Road was filled with stagecoaches, heavy-laden Conestoga wagons, and men on horseback or on mules, all hauling settlers, visitors, government officials, and politicians west to the new states of the Northwest Territory beyond the Allegheny Mountains[4]—a rugged part of the Appalachians extending from central Pennsylvania, crossing western Maryland, and going into eastern West Virginia.[5]

The National Road had fallen into disrepair with the coming of the railroads, but with the Federal Highway Act and the explosion in automobile use in the 1920s, the road was upgraded and designated US Route 40.[6] It once again funneled Americans over the Alleghenies to the Mississippi River and St. Louis. Pyle's bunioneers were about to run the length of it.

Into the Foothills

Day 7, 50 Men

The first day was a warm-up, a forty-five-mile trek to Frederick, Maryland, on gently rolling hills with the temperature at a pleasant fifty-two degrees at the start in Baltimore.[7] A big crowd was on hand to see the surviving fifty bunioneers start after six more men had dropped out the night before. A police escort had to clear a path for the men through the throng. Most of the veterans started off at a steady pace, but the majority of the rookies could barely move their exhausted legs.[8] Gavuzzi and Newton arrived at the start a few minutes late and passed some of these unfortunate men who, wrote Newton, "were no less than astonishingly comic in their amazing contortions to start running."[9]

As the men began to ascend the rolling hills, the temperature soared into the low nineties and it became uncomfortably hot and humid as a record-breaking, unseasonal heat wave gripped Maryland. Many of the men developed bad sunburns and heat exhaustion, leaving them, as Newton wrote, "light-headed and giddy."[10] The warm weather brought out the crowds near the finish. The *Frederick Post* reported that a holiday mood prevailed on the streets of Frederick throughout the morning as people waited for the arrival of the runners.[11] Frederick was a town of about fourteen thousand, steeped in Civil War history, with the titanic battles of Gettysburg and Antietam having been fought nearby. In July 1864, Confederate General Jubal Early rode into town and demanded a two-hundred-thousand-dollar ransom; if not received, he would burn Frederick down. Five city banks advanced the town the money, and Frederick was still paying back the banks when the Bunion Derby reached the city.[12]

Pete Gavuzzi arrived first, running with his graceful stride, and did not appear tired despite the oppressive mugginess of the afternoon.[13] He won his second stage race in a row, in just under seven hours, at about a nine-minute-per-mile pace and with Gardner and Salo thirteen minutes behind him. The three seemed to have suffered no ill effects from the run and were taken by their trainers for lunch and rubdowns.[14] The finish gave Salo a commanding one-hour and ten-minute hold on first place, with Gardner in second and Gavuzzi in third, sixteen minutes behind Eddie.[15] This matchup had the making of an epic battle for the twenty-five-thousand-dollar first prize between three extremely tough, talented, and experienced men. The cream had risen to the top in the Bunion Derby.

Though it may have seemed easy for the front-runners, it was a far different experience for the less-organized, less-trained, and less-talented bunioneers behind them. The men trickled in throughout the day, leg dead, dehydrated, sunburned, and exhausted.[16] The trek had claimed an additional four men, reducing the field from fifty to forty-six by the next morning. The Cools brothers dropped out for good following a belated effort to rejoin the race after Pyle apparently relaxed the midnight cutoff rule in Baltimore; Tom Ellis of Hamilton, Ontario, was out after being accidentally kicked in a tendon by another runner; and Arnie Souminen, the middle-aged Detroit physician who had led the derby into Texas the year before, quit, according to Newton, "due to insufficient training and overly long mileage."[17]

The men finished at the State Armory, where Pyle's race announcer gave a few facts about their lives as the bunioneers crossed the line and the official timers added the day's race time to the their cumulative totals.[18] A large crowd was on hand to greet the men. A reporter from the *Frederick Post* found the runners to be "a strange collection, drawn from all parts of the world. Some are jogging along backed by cities and clubs with cars, trainers, and the acme in equipment. Others, their life savings staked in meager supplies, scarcely know where their next meal is coming from."[19]

Charley Pyle finally managed to hold two performances of his follies, but attendance was dismal—fewer than five hundred combined attended the shows. Pyle, though disappointed, stated that he "expects to clean-up from now on."[20] The *Frederick Post* liked the show, claiming it was better than the average production that typically played in Frederick and noting that "the costumes were both beautiful and new and [with] plenty of clean comedy sandwiched between singing and the dancing numbers."[21]

Running on Historic Ground

Day 8, 46 Men

The forty-six runners faced a hellish fifty-two miles of ever-steeper hills run under a broiling sun with the temperature again pushing into the nineties.[22] Several hundred supporters left the comfort of their beds to see the seven o'clock start at the armory. The athletes stamped their feet, impatiently slapped their arms, and moved nervously about before getting under way.[23] Eddie Gardner struck out first, opening his assault on Johnny Salo's hold on first place. Salo stayed close behind him as the men toiled over a roller coaster of peaks and valleys.[24] They were running through history: over Braddock Heights, where the British General Edward Braddock had passed as his army blazed a trail into a frontier road on his way to fight the French in the Ohio Valley in 1755;[25] over the summit of South Mountain, which was bisected by the north-south-running Appalachian Trail; there, General Robert E. Lee and his men had battled Union troops at Turner's Gap in 1862.[26]

In these brutal conditions, Salo caught Gardner after about two hours of racing, and they ran neck and neck at about a nine-minute pace per mile until they were about fifteen miles from the finish line at Hancock, Maryland. In the heat, Johnny developed stomach cramps after drinking some milk, allowing Eddie to race on to victory. Gavuzzi and Newton followed close behind with their valet, Barren, squeezing the contents of a large sponge over their heads every few miles.[27]

Eddie Gardner won the lap and cut Salo's lead to twenty-one minutes. The effort left him exhausted and his body soaked in sweat.[28] Salo was in worse condition. Disabled by stomach cramps, he was without the services of his wife, Amelia, who was back in Passaic. Her home cooking and rubdowns had gotten him through the first days of the race to Baltimore. Now the entire burden fell on Bill Wicklund.[29] Arthur Newton found the hills and heat to his liking and finished third, with Gavuzzi in fifth.[30]

The rest of the bunioneers finished throughout the afternoon, with their trainers' cars following behind them.[31] They would rest at the night's control point in the small western Maryland town of Hancock, located at the narrowest point of the state where less than two miles separated its northern neighbor, Pennsylvania, from West Virginia to the south.[32]

Eddie Gardner Takes the Lead

Day 9, 45 Men

The men faced another day of weary slogging up and down increasingly steep mountains, with no letup from the oppressive heat that enveloped them like a blanket. They would run thirty miles to the manufacturing town of Cumberland in the far western portion of Maryland.[33] The first four miles of the road were pleasant as they ran over rolling hills planted in apple orchards before they ascended a series of mountain ridges on steep grades and tight turns that caused many car engines to overheat or break down—and that ensured steady work for local towing and auto repair shops.[34] In these conditions, the derby leader, Johnny Salo, held back; fearing shin splints, he took most of the long, winding hills at a walk and finished in a tie for second with Pete Gavuzzi in just over an eleven-minute-per-mile pace.[35] Salo wasn't concerned about losing his grip on first, noting that "there will be plenty of opportunities in this race. It is too early to think about getting a lead and holding it."[36]

Eddie Gardner did not show a similar level of caution and won the lap in six hours and thirty-six minutes, beating Johnny by over an hour and moving into first place overall with a thirty-six-minute lead.[37] Eddie won the admiration of the *Cumberland Daily News*, which called his victory "quite a feat when one takes into account the mountains east of this city."[38] Gardner raced down Baltimore Street to the finish in Cumberland at about one thirty in the afternoon, where thousands of fans had crowded around the finish to get their first view of the bunioneers.[39]

The twenty-nine-year-old Eddie "the Sheik" Gardner was a child of the South. After his birth in Birmingham, Alabama, his family escaped the state's all-pervasive racial discrimination for the West, moving first to Colorado and then to Seattle, Washington. At age fifteen, Gardner returned to Alabama to attend Tuskegee Institute, then a technical school for black students run by Booker T. Washington. At Tuskegee, Eddie learned a skill as a steam-boiler repairman and joined the school's track team, where he showed amazing talent as a distance runner. In the 1920s, he returned to Seattle as a stylish runner who won the state's ten-mile championship three times.[40] His Seattle fans had nicknamed him the "the Sheik" for the white towel he tied around his head when he ran. In the 1928 Bunion Derby, he had been a beautiful but erratic runner. He matched Gavuzzi in style but was more powerfully built, like Salo, at five feet, four inches tall and 145 pounds.[41] In 1928, he wasted his talent with flashy stage wins from which it took him a day or two to recover. Although finishing with more stage wins than any other runner, he claimed only eighth place and one thousand dollars for his efforts.[42]

Gardner returned in 1929 as a more polished and mature transcontinental runner. He told a reporter from the *Afro-American* that "this race is not going to the one who runs the fastest but to the one who has the endurance to stick it to the end."[43] Eddie Gardner was deeply religious. He did not smoke or drink. He was quiet, tough, and extremely brave, using his faith as a shield against the bigotry and hate he had faced in the first race when the derby crossed the segregated states of Texas, Oklahoma, and Missouri.

The Sheik had come back ready to race and prepared to deal with the barrage of racial slurs and death threats that he knew awaited him in the South. He told the same reporter that "just from New York to Baltimore, I have all manner of things said to me along the road so you can only imagine what it was like farther south. Last year there were verbal threats of violence but no one put their hands on me during the entire race. They say

15. Eddie "the Sheik" Gardner, circa 1926. Source: *Seattle Post Intelligencer* Collection, Museum of History & Industry.

nigger, I hope you drop dead, and other remarks much worse than that, but I am used to them now and they don't cause me any worry."[44]

Gardner's trainer, George Curtis, a middle-aged African American tailor from Seattle, had joined Eddie for another trip across America. He came equipped "with all things necessary for such a grind," including army cots they could use to camp out in western deserts and prairies and in towns without African American communities where no hotel would give them a room. Even in the North, most hotels were reluctant to have Gardner as a guest, and when they did, he was often relegated to the boiler room, basement, or other less-than-ideal accommodations. Together, Gardner and Curtis were ready for the ordeal that awaited them.[45]

As the men finished in Cumberland, a reporter was pleased that "all of the puppy pounders" (feet were often called "dogs" in the 1920s) wore numbers giving those who purchased programs "great delight" when they matched a name to a number. England's Charley Hart, the senior runner at age sixty-four, was the last to cross the finish line at nine that night and was almost done in by the hills and heat.[46]

Crossing the Rugged Alleghenies

Day 10, 40 Men

The next day's run would be the worst yet encountered, a brutal, gut-busting sixty-three miles to Uniontown, Pennsylvania. The course crossed four spurs of the rugged Alleghenies, putting the men on another leg-numbing roller coaster where they gained and lost thousands of feet of elevation.[47] In the 1920s, dozens of car companies tested their models for brakes and power on this winding, hilly road.[48] Record-high temperatures mixed with heavy rain added to the misery. Rookie runner Jesse Dalzell, a former bellhop from Springfield, Missouri, called it the worst day of the entire race.[49]

After leaving Cumberland at about eight hundred feet, the bunioneers climbed and descended three mountains in quick succession, all near three thousand feet in elevation: Big Savage Mountain, Little Savage Mountain, and Negro Mountain. At 3,075 feet, the last was the highest point on the National Road between Baltimore and St. Louis.[50] From there, the men continued to dip and climb until they reached Uniontown, a coal-mining town of about twenty thousand and the county seat of Fayette County, Pennsylvania.[51] To add to the misery, many of the men drank contaminated water, causing an epidemic of stomach trouble.[52]

Given this hellish combination of heat, hills, bad water, and extremely long distance, the middle-aged Guisto Umek from Trieste, Italy, seemed remarkably fresh when he reached the city limits of Uniontown paced by his young New York trainer, who followed behind him in his car. Umek had been a champion race walker before becoming a bunioneer. As a runner, the Italian had a powerful and elegant style, which he used to take fourth place in the 1928 derby. He was one of a handful of men with the talent and knowledge to challenge the three front-runners for the twenty-five-thousand-dollar prize in the second derby. With fire alarms wailing in a victory salute, Guisto crossed the finish line after ten hours of running, having beaten his nearest challengers, Gavuzzi and Granville, by over an hour. Eddie Gardner finished fourth in a tie with New Yorker and 1928 veteran Sammy Richman and retained his overall lead. Richman would join Umek in the race for the top prize money in the coming weeks. Salo finished in fifth.[53]

The sportswriter for Uniontown's *Daily News Standard* understood what the bunioneers had accomplished, calling it "the longest hardest day's run in all history."[54] After the race, an epidemic of vomiting and diarrhea broke out among the finishers as men trickled in throughout the night.[55] The midnight rule was relaxed to allow the last finisher, Sweden's Karl Apelquist, to complete the distance after staying on his feet for more than eighteen hours.[56] The day's run to Uniontown had reacquainted the veterans with the full meaning of what it meant to be a bunioneer. For the surviving rookies, they were reborn into a brotherhood of ironmen with a clear understanding of what it would take to reach Los Angeles.

That day, the hills proved too much for two 1928 veterans: Niels Nielson of Chicago was disqualified after a race official caught him riding in the back of a truck, and Troy Trimble dropped out from exhaustion.[57] These men would later claim that they had given Pyle their personal funds, which they could draw upon for meals as the race progressed. For whatever reason, Charley would not return the money, and they left empty handed, angry, and vowing revenge. When the derby finished in Los Angeles, the men went to the city prosecutor and asked him to file charges against Pyle for stealing their money.[58]

One person who seemed unaffected by the day's run was the thirty-one-year-old Jamaican-born tailor Philip Granville of Hamilton, Ontario. He gave a short talk to a group of young athletes at the local YMCA. A reporter covering the event admired Granville's muscular body at six feet and 180 pounds and the easy manner he displayed when speaking to the boys after running his grueling race over the mountains. He had a light complexion and referred to himself as Jamaican Indian rather than Negro. As had happened in 1928, audiences were struck that a person of color could speak with such ease and appeared remarkably well educated with his British-sounding accent. Granville stressed the importance of exercising and working out at the YMCA. He credited his good health to his training sessions at his hometown's Y in Hamilton, Ontario, which allowed him to avoid having to visit a medical doctor for treatment.[59]

He was also brash and often arrogant, frequently holding interviews with reporters in bed while he smoked a cigar and ate a pint of ice cream. He matched his brashness with talent, having been the national race-walking champion of Canada before he entered the first Bunion Derby, where he proved to be an equally talented runner. His third place in 1928 had earned him five thousand dollars in prize money.[60]

Granville had come to the second Bunion Derby with a well-organized and well-financed racing team that included his manager, Tom Crompton, who had been with him in 1928, and his trainer, Ben "Red" Arnold, a former Hamilton boxer, who was a competent trainer, expert driver, and mechanic. He also brought along an automobile and two thousand dollars worth of equipment, including three camp beds, a cooking outfit, a gasoline lamp, mosquito netting, refrigerator, radio, phonograph, fishing rods, rifles, several pairs of handmade shoes, and "twenty-four changes of costume to suit climate conditions and a bicycle." The reporter added that "it has been said that all he lacks is the Encyclopedia Britannica." He had brought four hundred dollars worth of fine brandy, but having forgotten about America's Prohibition laws, he was relieved of it at the border.[61]

Charley was also in fine spirits that day. He held two showings of his follies to sold-out houses and rave reviews at Uniontown's West End Theater. Though suffering from a cold, he was onstage and introduced the lead runners to the audience. Pyle finally believed he had turned his follies into the moneymaking machine he had envisioned at the start of the race, but there was a serious problem with Charley's hope for financial salvation.[62] By jettisoning the three-thousand-person show tent, he had dramatically reduced the number of seats he could potentially fill at each performance—now, at best, that meant a thousand seats per show because of the smaller size of most theaters he would use as the derby traveled across the country. To cover the sixty thousand dollars in prize money, he had counted on filling his show tent for two performances each day. Unless Pyle could find additional sources of revenue, his promise to pay the bunioneers their hard-earned money seemed seriously in doubt.

Off the Beaten Path

Day 11, 36 Men

Over the previous two days, the derby had lost nine men, reducing the field to thirty-six; forty-one men had already dropped out after just 414 miles, with more than 3,000 miles left to go.[63] The day's run to Waynesburg, Pennsylvania, in the far southwest corner of the state, threatened to add more names to the list of the departed. To get there, the men had to leave the well-maintained and hard-surfaced Route 40 and race over rough and partly unpaved dirt roads that turned to mud in heavy rain. They would rejoin Route 40 two days later in Wheeling, West Virginia— exhausted, sick, and cursing Pyle for the detour.

Despite pouring rain, more than a thousand people turned out near the start at the West End Theater as the thirty-six survivors equipped themselves with all manner of rain gear to ward off the elements.[64] It was a rather forlorn scene at the start, with the constant rain and a misty landscape of logged-off hills dotted with coal mines and abandoned coke ovens.[65]

On a slippery brick road that Arthur Newton called "nothing less than an abomination," the men were thankful, at least, that most of the big hills were behind them, but the majority of them were miserable, stricken by stomach trouble that continued to plague them from the unclean water they had drunk the day before.[66] Cramps forced Johnny Salo to stop more than a dozen times during the race. He was probably suffering from diarrhea, and he could not eat any food, which was a death sentence for an ultramarathoner, who had to consume massive amounts of calories to keep his body functioning.[67]

Johnny finished in a dismal thirteenth place that day. Paul Simpson took first-place honors and Gavuzzi and Gardner tied for third. Like Umek and Richman, Simpson was another of the potential challengers to the three front-runners. The results widened the gap between derby leader Eddie Gardner and Salo to almost two hours, while third-place holder Pete Gavuzzi came within four minutes of knocking Johnny out of second.[68]

The day's slippery roads claimed three more bunioneers, one unnamed but possibly the senior runner Charley Hart, who had struggled for the past few days, along with Apelquist, who had taken more than eighteen hours to finish the previous day's grind, and Bill Downing of Bedford, Iowa. Apelquist and Downing were out with shin splints, leaving the field at thirty-three.[69]

Several thousand people braved the incessant rain to greet the runners in Waynesburg, where enthusiasm for the runners and for Charley's Cross Country Follies was running high.[70] Three days of favorable reviews from Frederick, Cumberland, and Uniontown sparked interest in the show, which prompted the local Chamber of Commerce to sponsor it. The chamber promised two hours of family-friendly entertainment with tickets a dollar for adults and fifty cents for children.[71]

Muddy Misery

Day 12, 33 Men

The thirty-three leg-weary runners would pay dearly for Pyle's detour to Waynesburg as they began the fifty-two-mile run to Wheeling, West Virginia, a town of about sixty-two thousand. It was once the center of a movement to secede from Virginia that persuaded the inhabitants of the surrounding region to break away from that state and form a new, pro-Union state during the Civil War.[72]

With most of the mountains behind them, the men had been expecting an easy time. And it was easy for about an hour, until the paved road ended and the men faced eighteen miles of ankle-deep mud in a steady downpour. Newton remembered that "that mud was bad, very bad and many inches deep."[73] The muddy roads made it impossible for the trainers to follow. Most men could not get any kind of footing to run, making for agonizing hours of sloshing through shoe-deep mud without any support from their trainers.[74] Wet, cold, and exhausted, the bunioneers finally found salvation three miles short of the West Virginia line when they reached a paved road.[75] Salo told a reporter from the *Wheeling Register* that "outside of the tough grind over the mountains from Cumberland to Uniontown, today's race was toughest so far."[76]

In Wheeling, excitement was building for the arrival of the runners. The Chamber of Commerce had paid five hundred dollars for the privilege of hosting the bunioneers, and a large crowd had gathered to watch the finish. Most fans expected the first runners to arrive around one in the afternoon, but the muddy roads had delayed their arrival by several hours. The main thoroughfares in Wheeling were jammed with an immense throng waiting for the overdue bunioneers to arrive.[77] This was the largest gathering since the town had welcomed Charles Lindbergh after his solo flight across the Atlantic.[78]

Tiny Pete Gavuzzi showed his lion-sized heart when he won the race, covering the 52.3 miles in just over eight hours, running at the remarkable pace of nine minutes and fifteen seconds per mile, mostly in ankle-deep mud.[79] The little Englishman was splattered with mud when he crossed the line shortly after three in the afternoon and then called for his beloved tobacco pipe. Afterward, Pete went with his valet, Darren, to the Windsor Hotel, where he shaved before returning to watch the rest of the men finish.[80] He had humbled front-runner Eddie Gardner, beating him by one hour and forty minutes and second-place Johnny Salo by two hours and forty minutes. He bumped Salo out of second place and put himself within about an hour of passing Eddie. Johnny finished in a distant fifth-place tie with Guisto Umek after wallowing in the mud for almost eleven hours.[81] Umek had been grazed by a car the day before, slightly straining his right leg, which was made worse by the horrible conditions.

By six that evening, only seven of the thirty-three men had reached the finish line.[82] The rest of the bunioneers were still on the course, many gutting through old injuries or suffering through new ones aggravated by the muddy conditions.[83]

Rumors swirled around the derby that Johnny's stomach troubles might force him out of the race. Salo was, in his own words, "very weak," and he attributed much of his stomach troubles to the absence of his wife, who had cooked his meals until she left the race in Baltimore. He told a *Wheeling Register* reporter that "I have been having considerable stomach trouble caused undoubtedly by the change of food." Johnny had written Amelia the day before, asking her to rejoin the race as soon as possible.[84] Passaic's *Daily News* reporter Arthur McMahon downplayed predictions of Johnny's imminent collapse, believing in the legendary toughness he had shown in the 1928 race. McMahon thought he had already begun to recover and would improve in the next few days.[85]

At his vaudeville show, Charley Pyle praised his bunioneers: "The race is the most remarkable marathon in the present day history. I don't see how the boys keep up the pace, which forced many internationally known stars out of the race." Those that are left, he boasted, "are the cream of distance marathoners from all over the world."[86]

Charley was right on all counts. The surviving thirty-three men were the elite of the distance-running world. They had shown unbelievable toughness and determination over the preceding six days. Mud, bad water, mountains, and heat had not stopped them. The survivors were all veterans now, the new ironmen of 1929. They would soon reach better ground as they rejoined Route 40 on the flat and well-paved roads across Ohio, Indiana, and Illinois. Here, for the next twelve days and 583 miles, the battle for the twenty-five-thousand-dollar first prize would begin in earnest. The gap between the three front-runners—Gardner, Gavuzzi, and Salo—and the rest of the pack was growing daily. Salo's status was questionable. It was unclear whether other men would cast caution aside and challenge the front-runners. Exciting times lay ahead in the Old Northwest.

4

Fast Times in the Old Northwest

Wheeling, West Virginia, to Collinsville, Illinois,
April 12–April 23, 1929

FOR THE NEXT TWELVE DAYS, the front-runners would test the limits of speed and distance on the flat roads of Ohio, Indiana, and Illinois. Each day, they would need to determine if the distance Pyle set for the stage race would allow the front-runners to race competitively, without pushing themselves to exhaustion or risking a race-ending injury. Since the daily distance could vary wildly depending upon where Pyle decided to end the race for the night, each man had to decide where that safe distance was and hold back if Pyle forced him to run beyond it. Charley Pyle was on a quest of his own as he tried to find towns with receptive audiences that would fill theaters and transform his follies into a moneymaking enterprise that would allow him to pay his bunioneers their hard-earned prize money.

The thirteenth stage of the race would take the men to Ohio, the first of three states they would cross in the former Northwest Territory, the name for the vast tract of land between the Alleghenies and the Mississippi River ceded by the British to the fledgling American Republic after the end of the Revolutionary War. The new nation's leaders had organized the Northwest Territory with an enlightened hand, forever outlawing slavery and guaranteeing religious freedom.[1]

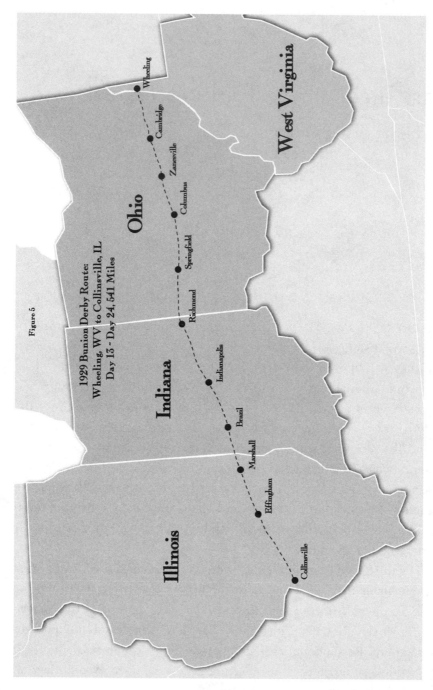

Figure 5

1929 Bunion Derby Route:
Wheeling, WV to Collinsville, IL
Day 13 - Day 24, 541 Miles

West Virginia

Ohio

Indiana

Illinois

Wheeling

Cambridge

Zanesville

Columbus

Springfield

Richmond

Indianapolis

Brazil

Marshall

Effingham

Collinsville

Map 5. 1929 Bunion Derby route, Wheeling, W.Va., to Collinsville, Ill.

No Respite for the Weary Men

Day 13, 33 Men

After the men had conquered the mountains, Pyle gave them no respite when he forced them to run an exhaustingly long fifty-nine-mile stage run to Cambridge, Ohio.[2] Considering what he had just come through, Pete Gavuzzi turned in an amazing performance when he covered the miles at a nine-minute-per-mile pace to win the stage. He cut Gardner's lead to just two minutes and won his third stage race in a row. Paul Simpson finished second, Gardner third in a ten-minute-per-mile pace, and Salo a distant sixth.[3]

The run to Cambridge only added to the misery Johnny Salo had endured in the Appalachians. Along the course, he was racked by nausea, vomiting, and diarrhea and seemed on the verge of dropping out of the contest entirely.[4] He had fallen more than five hours behind Eddie and had three runners trailing him by less than an hour and a half.[5]

Johnny needed to recover quickly, for he could not keep going without taking in the enormous quantities of food necessary to meet the needs of an ultramarathoner—at least three times the calories of an average adult. His chance for redemption came when his wife, Amelia, rejoined the derby in Cambridge. After Baltimore, she had returned to Passaic to care for their two children, Leo and Helen. With her husband on the verge of quitting the derby, she abandoned that plan and would stay with him until the finish in Los Angeles.[6] The dream team was back together—and just in time. Bill Wicklund would follow him on the course, while Amelia would cook his meals, tend to his injuries, and massage his sore muscles in their motor home at the end of each day's race.

Like Salo, most of the other bunioneers were still hurting after their ordeal in the Appalachians, and Pyle's brutally long run did nothing to improve their spirits. To a Cambridge reporter, the thirty-three bunioneers appeared to be a rough-looking bunch, with "sore and aching legs" and only a handful of men in "good physical trim."[7] Some of them apparently tried to escape their misery by accepting rides from passing motorists.

Two local deputy sheriffs who were patrolling the road claimed that they saw at least a dozen runners accept rides. An indignant Charley Pyle dismissed the charges offhandedly, maintaining that the "hick officers" had confused runners with trainers who were getting in and out of their cars while tending to their men. He stressed that his patrolmen were out on the course constantly, and any man accepting a ride would be caught and dismissed from the derby, but the rumors persisted.[8] A local reporter wrote that a trainer told him that he had seen several runners accepting rides that day.[9]

There probably was some cheating in the derby, especially by those struggling to remain in the race, often far from the public eye and finishing hours behind the front-runners. For the leaders, however, it was a different story. Followed by reporters, rival trainers, and fans, they would have found cheating to be a very risky venture. As Gavuzzi said years later, "Some would steal rides on cars to catch up a few hours," but most of the cheaters eventually dropped out, leaving the racing to "a bunch of very hard" and, he might have added, honest men.[10]

Gavuzzi's Charge

Day 14, 33 Men

The next day, the men had an easy twenty-five-mile run along the National Road to Zanesville, Ohio, once the capital in the early days of the state.[11] Pyle let the men start at ten o'clock, three hours later than usual. Most of the bunioneers considered the race more or less a holiday, given the shorter race distance. The rain, however, returned to depress the happy mood.[12]

The course, run on a brick road over shallow hills and valleys, was made for speed, and Pete Gavuzzi used it to wrest first place from Eddie Gardner. Racing through the course at a seven-and-one-half-minute-per-mile pace, Gavuzzi whisked past Zanesville's courthouse just as the clock struck one. Gardner could not keep pace and finished in third behind a reenergized Johnny Salo.[13] Salo's stomach problems had disappeared, and he gave full credit for his recovery to his wife.[14] With his team back together, Salo seemed ready to reopen his assault on the front-runners.

Gavuzzi's display of speed seemed lost on the citizens of Zanesville. Columnist Alan J. Gonder of the *Zanesville Signal* thought the race was "about as attractive as a sneeze on a cold, wet morning" and "devoid of color."[15] Charley Pyle hoped for a better reception at the end of the next day's fifty-five-mile run to Columbus, the state capital and home of Ohio State University, where Pyle had briefly been a student before he dropped out to begin his entrepreneurial career.[16]

Lawsuits and Bad Press

Day 15, 32 Men

With the fifty-five-mile run, Charley had put his men on a roller coaster of distance running: one day short, the next day unreasonably long. Arthur Newton was not pleased: "Those short laps were far too few for our liking, and to make sure we didn't get used to them we were sent off for a fifty-five miler next day to Columbus."[17] To add to their misery, the traffic was terrible. It was Sunday, and drivers came out in droves to catch a glimpse of the bunioneers, tying up traffic for miles along Route 40.[18] With idling cars turning the air blue with smoke, Gardner ran fast, determined to stop his slide in the standings. He matched Gavuzzi stride for stride, finishing in a tie for first place in an eight-and-one-half-minute pace per mile. Salo finished in third, fifteen minutes behind them.[19]

Like Zanesville, Columbus seemed to dismiss the derby as a stunt. The *Columbus Evening Dispatch* called the bunioneers a "motley assemblage" of men, and few attended Pyle's follies.[20] To make matters worse, local deputies seized three of his patrol cars and the bus he used to transport the cast of his cross-country follies as an attachment in a lawsuit filed by the New York Chevrolet dealership. It alleged that Charley owed the company $2,100 for six cars he had purchased before the start of the race. Pyle claimed it was merely a misunderstanding and that an agreement had been reached with the company, but local law enforcement did not concur.[21] The cars and the bus remained in Columbus under police guard, stranding many of Pyle's entourage. The next day, the sheriff allowed Charley to use the bus to haul the cast of the follies to the next stop in the race, Springfield, Ohio, but it returned to Columbus late in the afternoon under police guard.[22] One commentator from Toronto's *Globe and Mail* worried that "if some of these law suits amount to anything, it may develop that the present Bunion Derbyists are merely getting a lot of exercise."[23]

Wet and Miserable

Day 16, 32 Men

Pyle's plunging fortunes were matched by the weather. A cold north wind and rain made conditions miserable as they ran to Springfield, Ohio, a city of about sixty-nine thousand and the county seat of Clark County.[24] Pete Gavuzzi, now nicknamed the "bearded wonder from Southampton" because he hadn't shaved since the race started sixteen days before, ignored the weather and won his fifth straight stage race. He finished in about six and a half hours and extended his lead over Eddie Gardner to a half hour.[25] The Sheik finished second in just under seven hours with Salo a distant fourth. Despite his wife's cooking and care, Salo's stomach trouble had returned. He was struggling once again, and the gap between him and first place had stretched to more than five and a half hours.[26] Johnny's team had more work to do.

After the run to Columbus, bunioneer Mike Joyce of Cleveland received a visit from his wife. She told him bluntly, "Mike, you either got to start running or else you got to come back home to Cleveland and go to work." In 1928, this tiny Irish immigrant, at barely five feet tall, had led the derby through Cleveland in the final weeks of the race. Before that race, he had left the city an unknown factory worker and father of five. His gutsy performance had made him a city hero and front-page news in the *Cleveland Plain Dealer*. He went on to win fourth place and used his $2,500 prize money to help his struggling family make a better life.[27] This year, Mike had fallen far behind the front-runners and was using up what was left of the Joyce family savings to stay in the race. With a family to feed and a job waiting for her husband at the Fisher Auto Body plant, Mrs. Joyce seemed less than enthusiastic about his continuing the race.[28] Before the next day, however, she had softened, telling his trainer, Harold Jinks of Houston, to "be sure to look after him."[29] Another 1928 veteran, Seth Gonzales of Raton, New Mexico, dropped out of the race. Gonzales, who was buried in the pack, grew tired of the rain and simply said he "didn't feel like running any more." His exit left the field at thirty-one.[30]

Happy Times in the Hoosier State

Day 17, 31 Men

The next run would take the men to Indiana. Pyle was glad to see the last of Ohio. His native state had been nothing but trouble for him: sheriff's deputies had seized his cars and bus and accused him of allowing widespread cheating, and local newspapers had given scant attention to his Bunion Derby. When they did, they belittled the bunioneers and his vaudeville show. Amid the whirl of lawsuits and bad press that Charley had generated, no one seemed to have noticed the monumental battle that was taking place between Gavuzzi, Gardner, and Salo as they vied for first-place honors.

The bunioneers hoped for a better reception in Richmond, Indiana, at the end of another brutally long run. The men were fortunate that the sixty-three-mile trek was run on a flat, paved road and in cool temperatures with a stiff wind at their backs.[31] On the long, cold, windswept course, Johnny Salo made another attempt to challenge Gavuzzi and Gardner. This time, he destroyed his competition, setting a blistering pace of eight minutes and twenty-two seconds per mile to win the stage in eight hours and forty-seven minutes.[32] Gavuzzi finished a distant second, a full fifty minutes behind him, with Gardner twenty minutes after that. Mike Joyce, perhaps in response to his wife's scolding, finished in fifth place, his best performance in the derby so far.[33]

Daily News reporter Arthur McMahon, who traveled with the derby across the country, was giddy over Johnny's performance, writing that "if anyone has any doubts about that feat being one of the greatest accomplishments of the 1929 athletic season in any branch of sports, let him come out here and tell it to the residents of this Hoosier state community."[34]

Salo had had a rubdown and a meal and had dressed in his street clothes before Gavuzzi entered Richmond. McMahon credited the return of Mrs. Salo with her husband's revival and thought Johnny had regained the running form he had shown in the last two weeks of the 1928 derby when he had chased Andy Payne for first place.[35]

The race to Richmond also seemed to revive the derby's fortunes. The runners were given a great reception when they finished at the Lawrence Theatre, where large crowds attended both sessions of Pyle's Cross Country Follies.[36] The *Richmond Palladium* called the show "exceptionally good," citing Madame Duval's Dancing Debutantes and Claire Stone, a popular radio singer, as being very "well received."[37] The rival *Richmond Item* was also impressed by the health of the bunioneers after they had run more than seven hundred miles: "Contrary to natural opinions, the runners all appeared in good physical condition. The men made a picturesque sight as they plodded their weary way toward the finish line, wearing small woolen caps and heavy union suits under their regular track suits, to protect their bodies from the cold."[38] Arthur Newton, who had dropped from fourth to eleventh place during the Appalachian crossing, echoed this sentiment. After shaking off a bout of stomach troubles, he began to regain his appetite and, despite the distance, "felt distinctly better."[39]

The fortunes of Philip Granville, in sixth place, seemed to be going in the opposite direction. Granville's business manager, Tom Crompton, had antagonized Phil's trainer, Benny "Red" Arnold of Hamilton, into quitting the race, leaving Crompton to fill Arnold's shoes until a replacement could be found.[40] Back in Hamilton, Arnold told a reporter that he did not mind tending to Granville's needs on the course but drew the line at being forced to carry Crompton's heavy trunk up to his hotel room every night. He told the *Hamilton Spectator* that he was engaged as a trainer, not as a porter.[41]

In his Hamilton interview, Arnold gave his opinion on the three front-runners: "Gavuzzi," he stated, has "a long stride and runs easy and has lots of strength," but Arnold did not like his stride, claiming he "lifts his feet so high that they hit hard when they come down." He had high praise for both Eddie Gardner and Johnny Salo, complimenting Eddie on his steady performance and toughness and Salo for his courage and determination.[42]

Johnny Salo Makes His Move

Day 18, 31 Men

The three men would have a chance to test each other's mettle on a thirty-five-mile course to Knightstown, Indiana, on the eighteenth day of the race. The conditions were perfect: cool temperatures; no rain; a flat, well-paved road; and a gentle headwind.[43] Johnny took full advantage of them. With hundreds of fan-filled cars lining Route 40, he covered the distance at a seven-minute-and-forty-second-per-mile pace, the equivalent of running a marathon in three hours and twenty minutes.[44] Gavuzzi and Gardner did not give chase and finished fifty minutes behind him.[45]

Johnny reached the finish at the Alhambra Theater a few minutes after two in the afternoon, having run through a great crowd that lined Knightstown's main street. As Salo trotted up to the theater, a reporter asked him why he ran so fast. He replied, "I felt like running, so why hang back?"[46] In two days of extraordinary racing, he had almost halved the deficit between himself and front-runner Pete Gavuzzi and had opened a seven-hour lead over fourth-place Guisto Umek. Salo was no longer looking over his shoulder.[47] He had his eyes firmly set on capturing first place. The speed he had shown in the last weeks of the 1928 race was back. It remained to be seen whether Gardner and Gavuzzi were up to the challenge of staying with him.

Day 19, 31 Men

On the next day's thirty-five-mile run to the state capital in Indianapolis, the two front-runners changed tactics. Salo was for real. Gavuzzi and Gardner could not hold back and count on another bout of stomach trouble to erase the time he had gained on them. They would try to limit the damage by sticking close to him, conceding their time advantage slowly and making him work for every minute he might cut from their lead.

For the first twenty miles, the three front-runners paced each other across the pancake-flat, cornfield-lined road, but in the last stages the Finn stepped away from his rivals "as if," Arthur McMahon wrote, "he were trying to reach Los Angeles before the sun dipped in the West."[48] Johnny again raced fast at a pace of about seven and a half minutes per mile.[49]

As he approached the finish at the Colonial Theater in downtown Indianapolis, mounted police had to clear a path for him. He was going so fast that he ran right past the timer's table at the finish, but for all his effort, Johnny gained just eleven minutes on first place.[50] Gardner and Gavuzzi had picked up the pace and were close behind him at the finish. Years later, Pete stated his strategy for staying with the front-runners: "Course you knew who your rivals were, the people within a few hours of you, and if one of those made a break you just had to stick near them."[51]

Salo's resurgence was pushing his two rivals to run at or below an eight-minute-per-mile pace, dangerous territory that often resulted in race-ending injuries for those who stuck with it day after day. At this pace, each man's support team had to be up to the challenge of keeping its charge fed, rested, hydrated, and injury free. Johnny had Bill Wicklund and Amelia; Gavuzzi had George Barren and the wise counsel of his racing partner, Arthur Newton; and Eddie had George Curtis.

During the 1928 race, George had followed Eddie across America in his classic touring car, called a Hupmobile, and faced down white mobs and death threats as Gardner raced across Texas, Oklahoma, and Missouri. Curtis was nearly fifty years old, an African American who, like Gardner, had experienced the brutality of the South firsthand as a young man before moving to Seattle.[52] He was part father figure and part trainer, a man who shared with Eddie the pain and danger of competing against whites in 1929 America.

Along the way, Curtis had developed some novel ideas about preparing Gardner for the next day's race. He would rub Gardner's feet with a compound of double-strength witch hazel, arsenic, and liniment and would rub the soles with a mixture of mutton suet and powdered resins.[53] George got the idea from watching cowboys use the mixture to keep the hooves of burros from splitting in western deserts.[54] Curtis would soon need all the tricks he had to keep his runner in the derby during the coming days.

On these flat roads, the three front-runners were widening the gap between themselves and the rest of the field. The gap between Salo in third and Umek in fourth had grown to an almost unbridgeable eight hours, with Sam Richman close behind in fifth, Paul Simpson in sixth, and Phil Granville in seventh. Phil was now more than twenty-three hours out of first place and out of the running for the top prize money.[55]

This fact did not deter Teddy Oke, a millionaire Toronto businessman and sports promoter, from announcing that he would fund Granville for the remainder of the trip. As Granville was the only Canadian left in the contest, Oke hoped that he would somehow win the Bunion Derby for Canada.[56] With this new backer, Phil hired Frank "Sully" Sullivan as his trainer. Sullivan had worked as a trainer with Pyle's professional football team and would look after Granville for the remainder of the race.[57]

Wonder Man

Day 20, 31 Men

The next day's fifty-six-mile race to Brazil, Indiana, posed a problem for the three front-runners: after days of hard racing, should they test already-sore muscles by racing over such a long distance? The head referee, Steve Owen, a three-hundred pound former All-American and New York Yankees professional football tackle, was not concerned about the effects of such a long run on the health of the men.[58] His job was to start the race, and he didn't need a gun to get his men's attention. At seven o'clock, he simply shouted to the assembled runners once the roll had been called: "All right, let's get going. Stop in Brazil. It's only fifty-six miles."[59]

Conditions were good for racing: a flat concrete road, no rain, and mild weather.[60] Johnny Salo ran hard, racing through the fifty-six miles at about eight minutes and twenty seconds per mile and finishing in just under eight hours, with Gavuzzi just minutes behind him.[61] A reporter gushed that Johnny's nickname of the "flying cop" should be changed to "Wonder Man, Iron Man, Mystery Man, or what have you."[62]

The pace was too much for Eddie Gardner. He pulled a leg muscle and finished in eighth place. He lost more than two hours of hard-earned time against Gavuzzi and Salo, with Johnny now just twenty-five minutes away from taking second place from him.[63] Gardner had gambled and lost. George Curtis needed to work fast to get him back in racing form for the next day's stage.

Charley Pyle was far away from the battle for first place. He was off in Columbus, trying to free his cars and his bus from the writ of attachment. Pyle sent back confident telegrams that he would soon rejoin the derby with the bus, but he did not return that night.[64]

In Charley's absence, his deputies left essential things undone. At each stop, Pyle had agreed to reserve hotel rooms for the men where they could take a shower and change clothes after the race. This did not happen in Brazil. After finishing the fifty-six-mile race, the sweating and exhausted bunioneers were forced to stand around the finish line for more than an hour until Pyle's agents finally made arrangements for them to shower and change clothes.[65] As they stood there, chilled and stiff, a local reporter wrote that the runners "made public their opinion of Pyle and his crew."[66] When Granville's trainer tried to put a blanket around his shoulders, "He threw it on the ground and 'cussed' Pyle and his agents for their failure to make arrangements."[67]

Johnny Salo was not part of the unhappy cast of bunioneers. As soon as he finished, Amelia hustled him off to their motor home, where she laid him on a cot and massaged his sore muscles.[68] Gardner, too, escaped the confusion. Joe Leggett, an old classmate of Eddie's at Tuskegee Institute, took Gardner and George Curtis to his house for the night, where they had dinner, comfortable beds to sleep on, and a hearty breakfast before the next day's race.[69]

This incident only added to Arthur Newton's growing disenchantment with the director general. Newton was getting increasingly angry with Pyle over the length of the daily runs. The long run had claimed another bunioneer, reducing the field to twenty-nine. "There is no doubt," he said, "that the absurdly great distance[s] we were called upon to cover were the cause of many of the best runners dropping, just as they prolonged the suffering of others who could have recovered much more quickly from temporary injuries if they could have run no more than thirty or thirty-five miles a day to negotiate."[70]

Into the Land of Lincoln without Mr. Newton

Day 21, 30 Men

Perhaps Newton's pleading did some good, for the next day's run of thirty-three miles was within his thirty- to thirty-five-mile sweet spot for sustained long-distance racing.[71] This day's race would be the last in Indiana, a state whose people embraced the run at a very gut level, looking past Charley's ragtag organization and mismanagement into the heart of an amazing test of courage and endurance by superbly trained athletes.

At about the halfway point in the race, the derby passed through Terre Haute, Indiana, where many of its sixty-eight-thousand inhabitants had packed downtown streets to catch a glimpse of the runners.[72] A local reporter could not understand why thousands of people stood around for several hours to see a "straggling group of men" shuffling down the street.[73] He found the trainers' cars that accompanied the runners much more interesting, being plastered with signs and festooned with flags from the particular runner's home state or country.[74]

Eddie "the Sheik" Gardner led the race into Terre Haute, having apparently recovered from the leg injury he had suffered the day before in the long run to Brazil. Six minutes later, Gavuzzi and Salo arrived, jogging side by side. The three men were not running fast by recent standards, cruising along at about eight minutes and forty-five seconds per mile. The pace was about a minute slower than the pace maintained by the front runners in recent races at similar distances.[75]

When they reached the finish in Marshall, Illinois, the three front-runners crossed the line together in a tie for second place. They left first-place honors to Paul Simpson, who was mired in sixth place overall.[76] In effect, they had called a truce, the first in twenty-one days of racing. They seemed to be echoing Newton's word that sustained racing was not possible at Pyle's "extended distances." The men had decided that the race to Marshall would be a recovery day, a chance for them to rest before renewing the battle for the twenty-five-thousand-dollar first prize.

As the bunioneers crossed the finish line in Marshall, named in honor of John Marshall, the fourth and most influential chief justice in

U.S. history, anxious words were exchanged between runners and trainers about the fate of Arthur Newton.[77] A car had struck him seven miles from the start line. He had broken a bone in his shoulder and wrenched his leg. The specifics of the accident are unclear. The local *Terre Haute Star* reported that a car driven on the wrong side of the road came up behind Newton, knocked him down, and ran over him.[78] A more detailed account of the accident was published weeks later in California's *Calexico Chronicle*. It claimed that a car driven by a minister's wife ran into him from the side. The woman was arrested and taken to a justice of the peace, where she was fined for reckless driving.[79] Whatever the version, Arthur Newton was out of the race and in pain.

Newton was taken by ambulance to a Terre Haute hospital, where a doctor set his broken bone and encased his shoulder and upper arm in plaster. The physician advised him to stay in the hospital for three weeks while the bone set, but Arthur hoped to leave much sooner than that, since he believed he would recover much "better in the open air."[80] For the time being, he was stuck in a Terre Haute hospital, leaving Gavuzzi and Barren to continue on without him.

With Newton out of the race, the Bunion Derby had lost a man with the experience, reputation, and temperament to stand up to Charley Pyle and speak on behalf of the bunioneers. The derby had also lost the greatest ultramarathoner of his generation. Even in 1929, when he was nearly fifty, he had stayed close to the front-runners during the hellish Appalachian crossing and was always ready to use his vast knowledge to help the younger, inexperienced men stay in the race. Always optimistic, Newton was anxious to return to the derby.[81] The men would sorely miss his advice and counsel in the coming days.

For the next few days, the men would run across the flat prairies of Illinois, the land of Abraham Lincoln. In 1929, Illinois was a large and prosperous state, blessed with rich farmlands that produced vast amounts of wheat, corn, and soybeans, and its bustling cities made it a manufacturing powerhouse second only to New York and Pennsylvania.[82] Route 40 would take the men south of the colossus of Chicago and across the state through farm country dotted with neat, well-established towns.

A Rocky Start in Illinois

Day 22, 29 Men

The derby got off to a rocky start on its first day in Illinois. When Charley arrived in Marshall after his fruitless stay in Columbus, he found his derby near bankruptcy. The members of his vaudeville troupe discovered the next morning that Pyle had not paid their hotel bills. The cast had done its part, playing to packed houses at the city's Sourwine Theater the night before. The hotel was holding the baggage until all accounts were paid. The *Terre Haute Tribune* noted that "Pyle's derby appears to be running along on its feet without any head."[83] He was, indeed, in a very difficult position. Charley had no cash reserves to speak of after he lost his fortune on the 1928 derby and on his professional football team. No one would lend him money while he was pursued by lawyers trying to seize his property for unpaid debts. Pyle, for all his brilliance as a marketer and motivator, was an inept manager who seemed to lack any qualms about leaving bills and salaries unpaid. The tragedy, of course, was that his bunioneers were spending their own hard-earned dollars to chase their dream of winning a share of the sixty thousand dollars in prize money. These men were trusting Charley to live up to his promise, which seemed, at the moment, a very risky proposition.

The weather did nothing to lift the gloom that hung over the Bunion Derby on the twenty-second day of the race as thunderstorms drenched the men with rain and lighting bolts flashed around them. As the men ran, Newton wrote that they "cursed at the weather, laughed at each other and ambled along."[84] Pyle had made things worse by forcing the bunioneers to run another of his extended distances, this time 52.4 miles to Effingham, a town of about five thousand noted for making fine church pews.[85] In better weather, the men might have enjoyed the well kept fields and farm houses they ran by, "but none of these things," wrote Arthur Newton, "helped to keep a fellow warm and dry while he was hoofing it to the next control."[86]

Johnny Salo seemed to take no notice of the weather as he raced along the wet road to Effingham. He was not a graceful runner, but he could plow through mud, rain, and lightning and keep going far beyond what Newton thought was a reasonable racing distance. Gavuzzi and Gardner had style, gliding over the miles with godlike perfection, but in these conditions, bulldog tenacity trumped form. And Salo had the edge on that score. He knew it, and he used it to cut every second he could off Gavuzzi's lead.

As lightning flashed and thunder rumbled, Salo raced through the terrible weather, running at a pace of eight minutes and fourteen seconds per mile, a mile-pace equivalent to running a marathon in three hours and thirty-five minutes.[87] He was far ahead of the pack until Guisto Umek caught up with him five miles from the finish. Johnny was in no mood to be passed. With a burst of speed, he left the Italian far behind him as he raced to the finish.[88] Passaic's *Daily News* crowed, "The Finnish gentleman known to his Passaic friends as Johnny Salo, of Spring Street, did a bit of running today."[89] His rival, Eddie Gardner, could not keep pace. Nagged by a recurring leg injury, Gardner finished in sixth place, vaulting Salo into second by over an hour. Salo still trailed front-runner Pete Gavuzzi by three and a half hours. Despite Umek's second-place finish, he was still mired in fourth in cumulative time, buried eleven hours behind Eddie.[90]

Gardner was not in a good mood that night as he lay in the basement of an Effingham hotel nursing his injured leg while the white runners were upstairs in their comfortable rooms in a town whose slogan is "Heart of the U.S.A."[91] From Gardner's boiler-room accommodations, a reporter from Oklahoma's *Black Dispatch* asked him if his race "had handicapped you to an extent." Eddie replied: "Sure, here I am—down in the basement, [with] no place to take a bath and prepare for the hardships of the day ahead of me."[92] He said that in some towns, the "colored people" would take him in, but for the most part "this is the general fare with which I have to put up."[93] Gardner's trainer, George Curtis, thought Eddie's race had spurred the white runners to keep pace with him, since "everyone of the 'ofays' [derogatory term for whites] would break their necks trying to catch the 'coon' [derogatory term for an African American]."[94] To add to the disillusionment, Curtis complained in a letter to Seattle's black newspaper, the *Enterprise*, that Eddie had not received a single note of support from his hometown fans in Seattle, unlike the year before when he had been flooded with telegrams and letters of encouragement.[95] The *Enterprise* responded by urging its readers to send cards and letters and provided a list of cities and addresses to send them to.[96]

Eddie, for all his talent, had come face-to-face with the bitter reality of being black in 1929 America. The experience had left both him and Curtis increasingly angry and embittered. For three weeks, the Sheik had either led or stayed with the two greatest ultramarathoners of his age. For his efforts, he had received a daily barrage of catcalls and racial slurs from white fans and resentment from many of his white competitors. After the race, he was relegated to hotel boiler-room basements and largely ignored by his Seattle fans, who seemed to have lost their fascination with trans-America racing. And the worst was yet to come. The derby was just days away from entering the Jim Crow South, where white opposition to Eddie's participation in the Bunion Derby could turn still uglier and even deadly.

Bunion Derby Fever

Day 23, 29 Men

The twenty-third day of the race seemed filled with hope for the struggling derby. The rain had stopped and the sun had returned to warm the runners' aching bodies.[97] The men would race on a flat, well-paved road at what Newton thought a reasonable distance—31.8 miles to Vandalia, the last town at the end of the Old National Road and a place that one author called "quintessentially rural and American."[98]

The bunioneers raced through farm country under a warm sun and blue sky.[99] The improved weather did nothing for the spirits of second-place holder Johnny Salo, who came down with another bout of stomach trouble. He finished in fourth place, twenty-five minutes behind Pete Gavuzzi and Eddie Gardner, who raced through the course at a pace of seven minutes and forty-five seconds a mile. Johnny had simply pushed too hard in the previous day's fifty-six-mile race. Gardner and Gavuzzi had not. In near-perfect conditions, the duo put their graceful strides into high gear. With their first-place tie, Pete erased all the gains Johnny had earned in hard running the day before, and Eddie had cut Salo's hold on second place by half. Paul Simpson finished third, hoping to knock Sammy Richman out of fifth place.[100]

As the men finished, Vandalia was in a holiday mood; its streets were lined with people waiting to see the bunioneers.[101] Pyle's street vendors were selling programs, and cast members from the follies were performing acrobatic and juggling acts. Even the mayor was on hand to greet the men as they finished.[102] That evening the townspeople turned out in droves at the Liberty Theater to attend Pyle's vaudeville show.[103] This was a far cry from the follies' reception in Effingham, where there were two poorly attended performances.[104] This town of four thousand had breathed new life into the ailing Bunion Derby.

The derby, in return, breathed new life into Vandalia. The idea that men could run across America stirred the athletic passions within some of its townspeople. For weeks after the derby left town, the *Vandalia Union* wrote that "many of the younger generation were seen trotting up and down the streets in characteristic running style and postures, swinging their arms and imitating the champions that passed through here Tuesday."[105] To the *Vandalia Union*, it looked like the "running 'bug,' bacilli, or germ, or whatever it was" had infected local citizens and "nothing but running will cure it."[106] A week after the race, thirty local Boy Scouts planned to hold a ten-mile derby of their own. Delmar Appleby, an employee at the Deal Barber Shop, seemed particularly affected by the race. He bet his friends twelve dollars that he could run four miles to nearby Hagerstown and back and covered the distance in forty-eight minutes without any training. "He was not a youngster," wrote the *Vandalia Union*, but he came back to town "as frisky as he left."[107] Appleby went on to organize a fourteen-mile run from St. Elmo to Vandalia, with at least forty people pledged to run the race.[108]

Vandalia was not unique. Pyle's two trans-America races had inspired a slew of towns to host local distance races. In places like Conway, Missouri, and Port Angeles, Washington, seemingly sane men with everyday jobs—teachers, farmers, construction workers, and mail carriers—lined up with little or no training for a twenty-five- or fifty-mile race for a small cash prize.[109] Usually more than half the runners dropped out, with the survivors limping across the finish line with blisters the size of half dollars and shoes stained with blood.[110]

The Bunion Derby had opened the minds of everyday people to the hidden, almost godlike potential that lay within each of them and had brought the sport back to its working-class roots. Like the pedestrian runners who came before them, they were common men who left factories and farms to use their athletic talents to make better lives for their often-struggling families.[111]

Those who ran the mini-Bunion Derbies had the chance to grasp the courage it took to unlock such effort, something the bunioneers had to do on a daily basis as they raced across America. These one-day bunioneers had discovered that the derby was not, as its critics claimed, an aberration from the true nature of sport; it was, at its heart, a celebration of the common man and his potential for greatness.

The tragedy for these ironmen—the godfathers of modern ultramarathoning—was that Pyle should have told them by Vandalia that he would never be able to pay the prize money. Instead, he continued the race and allowed them to spend the last of their savings to stay in the derby.

The bunioneers had good reason to take him at his word. In 1928, he paid his prizewinners despite an army of naysayers who said he was bankrupt. In 1929, he claimed to be in better shape financially than he had been at a comparable time in the 1928 race. He also claimed to be planning a third Bunion Derby in 1930 and annual races thereafter.[112] This opened the tantalizing possibility to men like Salo, Gavuzzi, Granville, Richman, Umek, and Gardner that they could become professional, full-time bunioneers and make their fortunes in the sport.

There was also, of course, much to doubt about Pyle's comforting assurances that he would pay his men and his rosy predictions for trans-America racing. After two years with the director general, the bunioneers knew that he was an often inept and unscrupulous businessman who left a trail of unpaid bills and bounced checks in his wake. They had seen a parade of deputy sheriffs seize his vehicles for unpaid debts and had listened to the grumbling of the often-unpaid follies cast. Even the most optimistic runner must have had his doubts about the wisdom of trusting the director general to keep his word.

After the race finished in Vandalia, Charley dined with *St. Louis Post Dispatch* reporter Robert W. Safford. As he munched on a biscuit dripping in butter, Pyle explained that his biggest mistake of the race had been purchasing the massive show tent. Even after he jettisoned it in Baltimore and started holding his follies in local theaters, he knew his vaudeville show would never be the moneymaking machine he had envisioned at the start of the race. He candidly told Stafford that "it will take about four years to put the cross-country marathons on a paying basis."[113] At best, the money he made from the follies barely covered his derby expenses. He was putting nothing aside to fund the sixty thousand dollars in prize money, and he had no outside sources of cash or money of his own to make up the difference. Like the *Titanic*, the Bunion Derby was sailing on to oblivion. Pyle had to have known what the end result would be, but he was still caught up in his own rhetoric. The master salesman was lying to himself and to his men. His bunioneers were chasing a mirage, the proverbial pot of gold that lay at the end of the transcontinental rainbow in Los Angeles.

The Business of Ballyhoo

Day 24, 29 Men

The next morning, Safford watched the surviving twenty-nine bunioneers line up for the start of another gut-busting extended distance that Newton despised.[114] This time they would run sixty miles to Collinsville, Illinois, the last stop before the derby crossed the Mississippi River into Missouri. Safford found the start to be a very drab affair, with the referee shouting orders to begin the race and the men painfully forcing their battered bodies to move.[115]

The reporter blamed their lack of spirit on the presence of money. "There is none of the sporting spirit," he wrote. "It is a business based on ballyhoo."[116] Safford, of course, missed the fact that these "businessmen" had endured injuries and pain that the reporter could barely comprehend or that the front-runners had pressed the limits of human endurance to the breaking point as they raced each other across Ohio, Indiana, and Illinois. These bunioneers were running for profit, but along the way, they had opened the eyes of often-sleepy and insular townspeople to the untapped potential of the human spirit.

These "businessmen" at least had pleasant scenery as they ran through farm country on the way to Collinsville on a flat, well-paved road under clear skies.[117] In a repeat performance of his brilliant, long run to Effingham, Johnny Salo regained his form. He ran the sixty-mile course at eight minutes and twelve seconds per mile and finished in eight hours and thirteen minutes. He beat Gavuzzi and Gardner soundly, cutting Pete's lead to three hours and extending his lead over Eddie to an hour.[118] Johnny had to sprint the last few miles. "A dog chased me," he panted as he crossed the finish line. "Airedale dog off a farm. I had to run."[119] Paul Simpson finished six minutes behind him and succeeded in bumping Sam Richman out of fifth place in the cumulative standings, potentially earning Paul an additional $250 in prize money if he held the position to Los Angeles.[120]

After almost one thousand miles of racing and twenty-four days, just twenty-nine runners remained since the derby had left New York City on Easter Sunday. They had left forty-nine of their brothers scattered along the thousand-mile course. Those who were unprepared had left quickly; the Appalachians tested the mettle of the rest. The twelve days in the Old Northwest showed the survivors that the race for the top-prize money was a three-way affair between three unbelievably tough and gifted men: Gavuzzi, Salo, and Gardner. Barring injury, they had a lock on first, second, and third place, respectively—forty-one thousand of the sixty-thousand dollars in prize money. The rest of the pack would fight for the remaining nineteen thousand dollars spread out between fourth and fifteen places. It was also clear that Pyle didn't have the money to cover the prize money, but he lacked the courage and grace to tell his men. He hoped for a miracle, but he had used up all his wishes long before. Finally, the race had lost its senior statesman, Arthur Newton, who had railed against Pyle, saying he should think of his men before forcing them to run more of his extended distances.

Ahead lay the Mississippi River and a return to familiar ground, US Route 66 across Missouri to Chelsea, Oklahoma (the 1928 race had followed the length of Route 66 from Los Angeles to Chicago), before the derby headed south to Dallas and then west across the vast western prairies and deserts to Los Angeles. Along Route 66, Eddie Gardner would face special danger as a black man competing against whites in the Jim Crow South. Gardner knew what to expect after the previous year's harrowing run. He was prepared for it. He was ready to face the firestorm of hate that awaited him across the Mississippi.

5

On Familiar Ground

Collinsville, Illinois, to Chelsea, Oklahoma,
April 24–May 3, 1929

Eddie Gardner: Unsung Hero

Day 25, 29 Men

Eddie Gardner was the first man to cross the Mississippi River, running across the Free Bridge to St. Louis, a mammoth city of more than eight hundred thousand souls.[1] He was running fast on the short twenty-two-mile course from Collinsville, Illinois, to Maplewood, Missouri. None of the other bunioneers tried to stay with him. Newton wrote, "We all knew Gardner meant to win this lap even if it 'bust[ed]' him." Eddie took off, "and after one or two had given a sidelong glance at his speed, they left him alone and said goodbye to him."[2] He was flying, averaging six-minute-and-forty-six-second miles, which translates into about a two-hour-fifty-minute marathon pace.[3]

The *St. Louis Post Dispatch* took a photo of Gardner as he crossed the bridge. He looks determined, calm, and stone-faced, much like Johnny Salo during one of Pyle's extended runs but with more to prove. Eddie wore his trademark "Sheik" headwear, a white towel tied around his head and a white sleeveless shirt and shorts with his number 165 pinned on the shirtfront. A few inches below the number, he had sewn an American flag. It was about six inches wide and was put there for all to see.[4] Poignantly, without words, Gardner announced his return to the Jim Crow South as an American and, on that day, as the finest distance runner in the world.

75

First Into St. Louis in Cross-Country Race

—By a Post-Dispatch Staff Photographer.

16. Eddie Gardner crossing the Free Bridge into Missouri. Source: "First into St. Louis in Cross Country Race," photo from *St. Louis Post Dispatch*, April 24, 1929.

His performance mesmerized St. Louis's African American community, which turned out in droves to see him. They packed the bridge. As he passed them, many black youths hitched rides or hung on the sides of passing trucks to keep pace with Eddie until the finish in Maplewood.[5]

He had returned to a divided and wholly unequal world where blacks adored him and most whites despised him. In the next three states he would pass through (Missouri, Oklahoma, and Texas), either state or local laws or custom relegated blacks to being a permanent underclass with separate but woefully inferior schools and basic services, with few legal protections, and with little or no access to the voting booth. Whites had the legal, political, and economic power, and they used violence and intimidation to keep it exclusively for themselves. Missouri, for example, had an infamous reputation for lynching black men suspected of committing crimes against white women. Between 1900 and 1931, white mobs hanged seventeen black men, and in one notorious case, they left the body of a school janitor hanging under a bridge a quarter mile from the University of Missouri.[6]

In this world, blacks did not compete against whites, or if they did, "Negroes" did not win, especially in distance racing. It was common wisdom that whites had a clear advantage, since African American men were thought to be childlike and easily distracted, especially by women and gambling, which made them unfit for anything longer than the sprint distances.[7]

In 1929, Eddie Gardner entered Missouri with a clear understanding of what was ahead—day after day of intimidation and death threats—but he was determined to race in spite of the dangers. He had learned to fight segregation at his alma mater, Tuskegee Institute in Alabama. The school taught its students a trade and the dignity of physical labor, be it plumbing, carpentry, or competitive running, and expected them to perform it so skillfully that even the most racist whites would have to take notice and perhaps, in turn, change their attitude toward segregation.[8]

Eddie, however, had changed the nature of the struggle from passive to active, into something that looked strikingly modern and dangerous: he was applying nonviolent resistance by running in an integrated footrace in the segregated South to challenge injustice, and he was willing to risk his life to do so. Death could await him at any crossroad or from any passing car, but he kept going, unbowed by fear. Whites might kill him, beat him, or threaten him, but they could not change the fact that on this day he was running as the leader of the greatest footrace of his age and challenging deeply held preconceptions of black men as he went—and giving hope to millions of his fellow African Americans who saw him race or who read about his exploits in the black press. In the birth year of Dr. Martin Luther King Jr., Eddie had returned to the South with an American flag on his chest, a man willing to die for his cause.

For Gardner's two rivals, Johnny Salo and Pete Gavuzzi, crossing the Mississippi River represented just another stage race into just another state on the long transcontinental trail to Los Angeles. The men were grateful, however, for the shortened twenty-two-mile course, a rare break from the daily grind of racing in the thirty- to sixty-mile range, which would give them a blissful afternoon to rest after the day's run. The duo crossed the Free Bridge together eleven minutes after Gardner, "smiling broadly," wrote Arthur McMahon, "when their feet touched Missouri soil." Then they paced each other to the finish in Maplewood at a sub-eight-minute-per-mile pace, leaving Gavuzzi's lead over Salo untouched at three and a half hours.[9]

After the race, Pete called for his pipe, took a puff, and found his senior partner, Arthur Newton, there to greet him. Newton had returned with both shoulders heavily braced in a plaster cast after having spent the preceding week recuperating at the country house of some American friends. For the last week, George Barren had served as Gavuzzi's man Friday, coach, cook, driver, and trainer. Pete would once again have the greatest racer of the age by his side. Newton, though banged up, would stay with Gavuzzi for the remainder of the race.

Johnny headed back to his wife, Amelia, and his motor home, where he could let his aching body heal a bit before facing the return to the longer distances. Reporter E. A. Fetting interviewed Salo there while he rested in his bed "unclothed," looking to Fetting as if he were "a mass of bandage, iodine and adhesive that reminded one of the World War." Johnny told him, "I lost two nails yesterday and I guess I'll lose another one tomorrow" as he unwrapped one of the bandages on his feet and sliced open a

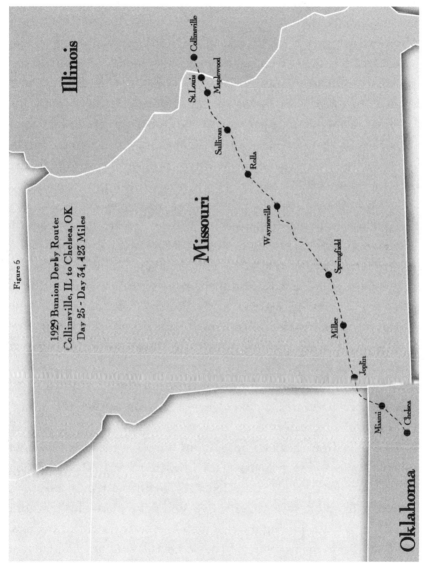

Figure 6

1929 Bunion Derby Route:
Collinsville, IL to Chelsea, OK
Day 25 – Day 34, 423 Miles

Illinois

Missouri

Oklahoma

St. Louis
Collinsville
Maplewood
Sullivan
Rolla
Waynesville
Springfield
Miller
Joplin
Miami
Chelsea

Map 6. 1929 Bunion Derby route, Collinsville, Ill., to Chelsea, Okla.

blister with a penknife. Salo told him that his left hip and leg muscles hurt and had been giving him much pain over the previous three days. Amelia was there with him, holding him together as his trainer, confidant, cook, lover, and friend, a "devoted wife," wrote Fetting, "ready to work as the man works—all the time."[10]

Such support was crucial as the three front-runners battled for the lead. Despite a seemingly endless array of pulled muscles, blisters, stomach problems, and near misses from passing cars, Gardner, Gavuzzi, and Salo kept getting faster. The rest of the competitors watched in wonder as they slipped farther and farther behind the front-runners yet remained convinced that the three would soon break at the faster speeds and vindicate their decision to run slowly. As derby runner Guy Shields of Baxter Springs, Kansas, put it, "I can't keep up the pace that Gavuzzi, Salo, and Gardner set. Nobody else in the race can. The main question the runners discuss is whether those three will 'crack' before we reach Los Angeles."[11]

The men, however, were discovering that their waiting game had a price. Most were short on cash, and they were having trouble persuading their hometown supporters to send them more as the gap between them and the front-runners grew. For example, Elmer Cowley of Clifton, New Jersey, sent urgent telegrams to his fans to send more funds. When none came in, he was forced to borrow money from other runners to buy new shoes and fix his trainer's car. Most of the men faced the same problem and appealed to all they knew for an infusion of funds.[12]

Charley Pyle had cash flow problems of his own as his Cross Country Follies continued to sputter. In most of the towns where it stopped, his show received rave reviews but seldom filled the theater or brought in enough money to cover its expenses. One frequently asked question among the cast was, "Have you eaten yet?," with the typical response being "No."[13] To add to the indignity, Pyle had not replaced his bus after it was seized in Ohio, forcing the cast members to beg rides in trainers' cars or hitchhike to the next town.[14] The *St. Louis Post Dispatch* wrote that this state of affairs caused the follies cast to "grumble more than [the bunioneers] who are picking 'em up and setting 'em down along the highway for twenty-five to sixty miles a day."[15] For whatever reason, most of the troupe stayed on, allowing Pyle to earn just enough cash to keep the derby staggering forward. Perhaps the cast members, like the bunioneers, were caught up in the grand adventure of racing across America.

Pyle needed something to shake up the derby. He thought he had found it by hiring Jim Thorpe as the follies' new master of ceremonies. Thorpe's name was once spoken with awe and respect in Missouri and Oklahoma.[16] He was born in Oklahoma to mixed white and Indian parentage and had left to attend the Carlisle Indian School in Pennsylvania. He had captained the school's football team and won All-American honors as a halfback as Carlisle had beaten such powerful teams of the day as Harvard and the University of Pennsylvania. In 1912, he was heralded as the greatest all-round athlete in the world after winning gold medals in the 1912 Olympic Games in Stockholm in the decathlon and the pentathlon.[17] The next year, his world unraveled when the United States Olympic Committee stripped him of his Olympic medals after it learned he had played semipro baseball for two summers during college. For the next seventeen years, he scratched out a living as a professional football and baseball player before finally retiring in 1928 at age forty-two to sell cars in Ohio.[18]

Burly, hard drinking, blunt, and often arrogant, Thorpe had squandered most of the goodwill earned in the early days of his career, but he still had name recognition and longed for a chance to return to the national spotlight. He wanted to try his luck in Hollywood and become a film star. Charley offered him the vehicle to get there: he could work his way to Los Angeles while he honed his acting skills in the Bunion Derby. Both men hoped the new partnership would turn their fortunes around.[19] Thorpe would become a shadowy figure in the race. He never gave interviews and was seldom quoted in the press. He seemed content to perform on stage but did nothing to grab headlines. Thorpe would remain an uncharacteristically silent member of Pyle's follies show as it made its way to Los Angeles.

The director general could have picked a better stretch of road to begin Thorpe's tenure. For the next five days, the men would run through the Ozark highlands, ancient, eroded mountains covered with oak, hickory, and other hardwoods, crisscrossed by fish-filled streams and dotted with small towns and farms. It was a place for tourists and fishermen but lacked the large population centers that might help him fill his depleted coffers.[20] If the weather cooperated, it promised to be a pleasant place to

17. Jim Thorpe. Source: Library of Congress.

race except, of course, for Gardner—white fans in the region had yelled obscenities, racial slurs, and death threats at the black bunioneers in 1928.[21]

Into the Ozarks

Day 26, 28 Men

The first day in Ozark country opened with a sixty-one-mile run to Sullivan, a shoe-making town of about twenty-five hundred.[22] This was familiar ground for the veterans, who had followed the same road, Route 66, east across Missouri in 1928—but much of it this time was shrouded in mist. Strong headwinds and cold rain made for miserable racing conditions,[23] especially so for Eddie Gardner, who had reinjured his leg in the previous day's display of speed. He lamented the weather: "Rain, rain, rain, all the time the incessant tattoo of rain in the face."[24] Johnny Salo, however, reveled in it, since he knew that Gavuzzi hated running hard in the rain. With his steely-eyed gaze, Salo plowed through the mist to win in about an eight-and-a-half-minute-per-mile pace and cut Gavuzzi's lead by a third to three hours.[25]

The duel between the front-runners was far from the minds of the rain-soaked fans who jammed the finish. They were there to see Sullivan's own Pat Harrison cross the line in fifth place in the day's stage race.[26] He was the town's hero, a tough and relentless runner who had hobbled across the Mojave Desert in 1928 on lacerated feet and had survived to reach Sullivan as the derby made its way to New York City.[27] In 1929, this quiet, unassuming schoolteacher returned to familiar faces and cheers. Though mired in seventeenth place, he had given the townspeople a chance to bask briefly in the national spotlight and lift their focus from the hard, everyday world of work and family as they followed his progress across the country. Its grateful citizens raised five hundred dollars to keep Pat in the derby.[28]

Hours later, Gardner crossed the line—dripping wet, exhausted, and sore. Eddie had raced far too fast the day before, reinjured his leg, and limped along while he absorbed a hail of death threats and catcalls.[29] He must have had second thoughts about his decision to race in the South. George Curtis would later tell the *Chicago Defender* that the experience "took the heart" out of Eddie. Curtis recalled that "along the line across Oklahoma and parts of Missouri reference was shouted at [Gardner] regarding his color and daring him to finish first for that day." He added that "many times, the little fellow would be forced to get into a car and go some twenty miles beyond to get a resting place, and then come back in time in time to start off with the others."[30]

Rough Roads and Solitude

Days 27, 28, and 29, 27 Men

On the second day in the Ozarks, the beauty of the land revealed itself and a warm spring sun caressed the aching bones of the twenty-seven men who had survived the ordeal of the day before.[31] The long run had claimed one of their brother bunioneers, Olli Wanttinen. This tough Finn had been one of the front-runners in 1928 before a car hit him and broke two of his ribs near the finish in Chicago.[32] This year, he had risen to twelfth place before stomach cramps forced him to walk for the last two weeks and left him too weak to finish the sixty-one-mile grind.[33] Newton had scolded Pyle in the past for forcing his men to run beyond the thirty- to thirty-five-mile range, believing that longer distances aggravated injuries that might have healed at lower mileage and unnecessarily forced great runners like Wanttinen out of the derby.[34]

In the morning light, few of the bunioneers could have imagined that Route 66 had been a battleground less than a lifetime before, where Union and Confederate soldiers fought and died for what had been a strategic road between Union-controlled St. Louis and the lead mines to the west near Joplin, Missouri, an important source of lead for bullets for Union troops.[35] The night's control point, the former Union fortress town of Rolla, lay forty-five miles west through beautiful countryside that had long since erased the scars of war.[36]

After the previous day's exhausting run, neither Gavuzzi nor Salo was in any mood to race on a loose gravel road and in hot conditions. They pulled back into the nine-and-a-half- minute range and ran with Gardner, who had recovered enough to pace them to the finish.[37] The trio ran easily over gentle, rolling hills dotted by small farms and isolated hamlets like Bourbon, Hofflins, Cuba, Fanning, and St. James.[38] Their quiet mood was broken when a motorcycle lost control in the still-muddy road and swerved into them. Gavuzzi jumped out of the way and wrenched his back in the process. As the motorcycle regained control and went by, Salo made a grab for the driver, missed, and then picked up a rock and flung it at him. Passaic reporter Arthur McMahon wrote that the rock "was low and on the outside and the wild rider took his base."[39] The trio of Gavuzzi, Gardner, and Salo left the racing to Paul Simpson and Guisto Umek. Simpson, in fifth place, ran at an eight-minute-per-mile pace to win the stage and cut Umek's hold on fourth to just an hour.[40]

On their third day in the Ozarks, Pyle finally let the men run at what Newton called a reasonable distance: thirty-two miles to tiny Waynesville, in the heart of the Ozarks, a place, Missouri's *WPA Guide* reported, where farmers come to town to "buy their blue denim and flour, their coffee, salt, and sugar with unhurried deliberation."[41] Gavuzzi reached Waynesville first, racing over a hilly gravel road in a seven-minute-forty-seven-second pace and adding eleven minutes to his lead over Salo. Despite the best efforts of his trainer, Gardner's nagging leg injury returned; he finished in seventh place and fell four hours behind Johnny.[42]

Sunday, April 28, was a day of rest for the God-fearing inhabitants of Waynesville, but it was not so for the weary bunioneers, who were off on another of Pyle's despised "extended" runs, this time fifty miles to Conway, for another day of brutal running on a rough, gravel road run beneath a hot Missouri sun.[43] Newton wrote that the road surface was "uncomfortable for running [but] the scenery almost made up for it" as they ran through the Mark Twain National Forest and tiny Hazelgreen, with its small hotel for fishermen and vacationers.[44] Salo and Gavuzzi again decided to call a truce to their duel and spend a bit of their hard-earned lead as Umek and Richman tied for first-place honors. The two front-runners were making a statement: if Pyle forced them to run an unreasonably long distance, the two would not race each other and risk injury.[45] They would jog along together and resume the battle when they felt it was safe to do so. After a month of racing, the two knew roughly where the limit of human endurance lay—somewhere near fifty miles—and they would not push past it to appease Charley Pyle.

The course was also trying the patience of Arthur Newton as he bounced along in the back of his truck and sweated in his plaster cast. Barren tried to avoid the many potholes that dotted the road, but he could not miss them all. Newton winced in pain each time he hit one, a reminder of how quickly fortunes could change in the Bunion Derby.[46] Newton, with his typical English "stiff upper lip," still remained upbeat and relished the chance to be part of this great footrace, and he happily dispensed advice to Gavuzzi and to any other runners who sought his help.[47]

Jesse Dalzell's Bittersweet Homecoming

Days 30 and 31, 27 Men

On the thirtieth day of the Bunion Derby, the men would leave the rough roads and solitude of the Ozarks behind them and reach better ground for racing: a fairly flat concrete road through open farm country on the forty-one miles to Springfield, Missouri, the state's fourth-largest city, with a population of fifty-seven thousand.[48] Gavuzzi announced his intention to go on the offensive by putting on a display of running power. Pete crushed the forty-one-mile course in four hours and fifty-one minutes, running in just over a seven-minute-per-mile pace, the equivalent of running a marathon at just over a three-hour pace.[49] Salo tried to stay close, running in the mid-seven-minute-per-mile range, and lost only twenty minutes.[50] Pete claimed he had set a world record for forty miles after beating the amateur record by nine minutes. Record or not, it was an amazing run.[51] Gavuzzi had pushed into the danger zone, racing at or below the seven-minute pace that had spelled doom for those men who had raced there in 1928. Both Salo and Guisto Umek thought Gavuzzi would soon join the ranks of the departed if he maintained that pace in the next stage race.[52]

Eddie Gardner could no longer race at anything near that speed and was rapidly dropping out of contention for first-place honors. His leg injury had no time to heal. The rough gravel roads and Pyle's extended runs had done their work. He limped through the course to finish in a distant fifteenth place, Gardner's slowest lap of the entire derby, and saw his gap between second and third grow to six hours.[53] Eddie needed more than George Curtis's attention to stay with the front-runners; he needed a miracle. But he did have a plan B, a chance at least to hold on to third place. He could use the seven-hour cushion between him and Guisto Umek in fourth place. He could slow down and jog along for a week or two and give his leg a chance to recover. All he needed to do was keep Umek close and return to a faster pace after his leg healed. Eddie needed to decide: risk it all for first or settle for third?

The stage race to Springfield would be a homecoming celebration for twenty-year-old Jesse Dalzell, one of the youngest runners in the Bunion Derby.[54] Dalzell's story seemed more appropriate for 1928, when most of the runners were unknown men with little training or money chasing a wild dream of beating a cadre of international stars for the twenty-five-thousand-dollar first prize.[55] Dalzell, who arrived in New

York woefully short on funds and on knowledge of transcontinental racing, had come from the humblest of backgrounds as a bellboy at a Springfield hotel.[56] While the veterans headed west with trainers and support cars, he started out alone. Against all odds, he eventually found a trainer, survived the Appalachian crossing, slowly began to run with more confidence, and had moved up to fourteenth place by the time he reached Springfield.[57] Though Dalzell was one hundred hours out of first place, his story had made him a hero to his hometown fans. When he reached the city in fourth place in the stage run, the crowds cheered and fire sirens wailed in greeting. His face was deeply tanned and he wore a clean white tracksuit, with the city's motto, "Springfield, Mo., Heart of the Ozarks," printed on the front. That night Jesse and his family stayed free of charge at Springfield's Colonial Hotel, where he had worked as a bellboy.[58] Jesse Dalzell had taken a page from Andy Payne's 1928 story: he had left the city unknown and penniless and had returned an iron-man and hero.

A runner's status could change quickly in the Bunion Derby. Many things could go wrong—a misstep, an accident with a passing car, a tainted bite of food, and hundreds of other variables—all with the potential to end a man's dreams of glory. Jesse would learn this lesson on the thirty-first day of the race. It began with a violent thunderstorm that forced several carloads of his fans to abandon their plan to follow him on Route 66. With the rain falling and the thunder booming, hundreds of well-wishers milled about the start as the race began. A police motorcycle escort flanked him, trying to clear a path through the crowded street. In the confusion, a car swerved into him. As he jumped to the side, he lost his balance and sprawled on the road as one of his legs slipped under the wheel of one of the police motorcycles, which ran over his ankle. After a brief pause, the crowd held its breath as Jesse got up and tried to walk. After a few steps he found the pain to be unbearable.[59] A doctor examined the leg and, fortunately, found no broken bones, but it was extremely sore. Jesse set off again, painfully walking the entire thirty-four miles to the finish at Miller.[60] That morning, Dalzell's trainer, Robert Oakes, quit, probably believing Jesse now had no chance to stay in the

Bunion Derby. Jesse was also low on funds, with just enough to cover nine more days of racing.[61]

Despite the disasters that had just struck him, Dalzell remained upbeat, showing the bunioneer's spirit that had gotten him through the first brutal one thousand miles. He told a reporter that "I'll keep on if have to crawl. I'm handicapped now for my trainer quit me when I was hurt this morning coming out of Springfield so I'll have to fight it out alone."[62] His spirit earned the respect of the sports editor of the *Springfield Leader*, who urged his readers to contribute to a fund to keep Jesse in the race.[63]

Among the front-runners, Gavuzzi ran hard for a second day, covering the thirty-four miles in four hours and fifteen minutes, or at a seven-and-a-half-minute-per-mile pace. He was going so fast that he pushed his cumulative mile pace to under nine minutes per mile for 1,324 miles— more than a minute per mile faster than Andy Payne's winning pace in 1928.[64] Salo lost an additional twenty minutes as his deficit neared four hours. The day had not gone well for him. He had eaten an especially heavy dinner and felt sluggish when he started the run.[65] On the course, a snake wiggled across the road in front of him, frightening him so badly that he could not breathe easily for ten minutes. "I'm scared of snakes," he told a reporter, adding that he planned to buy a gun and ammunition to deal with any serpents that might cross his path again.[66]

Eddie Gardner had decided to risk it all. He ran fast, shutting out the throbbing pain in his leg and finishing in third place. At least temporarily, he kept his deficit with Johnny Salo at about seven hours.[67] He would not drop back and concede the battle for first place to Gavuzzi and Salo. Eddie had entered the race to win for himself and black America. He would press on at a fast pace, putting his faith in God and George Curtis to keep him in the Bunion Derby.

After a day of rain and thunder, the men rested in the tiny hamlet of Miller. Arthur Newton was not impressed with the local inhabitants, whom he found to be both uncouth and unwashed. When he asked several residents where he might get a bath, he was met with blank stares. He wrote that the citizens of Miller "could not understand anyone needing what had always been unnecessary to them."[68]

Johnny Salo: Beast of the Bunion Derby

Day 32, 27 Men

May 1, 1929, opened with clear skies and mild temperatures, a day fit for
May Day, when schoolchildren celebrated the coming of spring by giving
baskets of flowers to their families. The nice weather brought out throngs
of spectators along Route 66 until a cold front with high winds and heavy
rain rolled through the area and drove them away.[69] This was perfect Salo
weather, and he used it to his advantage, knowing that Pete was unlikely
to chase him in these conditions. As the storm hit in the late morning,
he picked up the pace and charged through Carthage, a prosperous little
town of about ten thousand that had been burned to the ground by Confederate soldiers during the Civil War.[70] He averaged seven-and-a-half-
minute miles until he reached the control point in Joplin at the end of the
forty-seven-mile course. Salo "was literally blown into town while hail
stones bounced all over him," wrote Arthur McMahon of Passaic's *Daily
News*.[71] He was the undisputed beast of the Bunion Derby, an all-weather
ironman. He cut forty-five minutes off Pete Gavuzzi's lead and quashed
any rumors that he was not up to the challenge of running at a sub-eight-
minute-per-mile pace.[72]

The talented but erratic Australian Herbert Hedeman finished next. He
was followed by Eddie Gardner in third in just under an eight-minute pace,
giving hope to his fans that his leg had recovered and that he would soon
be back in the battle for first place. Gavuzzi finished in sixth, in an eight-
and-a-half-minute pace, which was now relatively slow by Bunion Derby
standards.[73] Salo and Gavuzzi had been pushing the pace for days and had
pulled the injured Gardner, Sam Richman, Guisto Umek, Paul Simpson,
and Philip Granville along with them. These men had reset the limits of
speed as they chased the pot of gold at the end of the transcontinental rainbow in Los Angeles. Charley Pyle had it right when he told the *Joplin Globe*,
"The race this year is better than the first derby despite the fact that our
ranks have been cut down greatly. The main thing is, we have no tourists
along this year. They're all runners and they are setting a real pace."[74]

Pyle's bunioneers would spend the night in Joplin, a city of about thirty-four thousand near the center of a thirty-mile-long lead- and zinc-mining belt.[75] After the Civil War, Joplin had become a boomtown as miners poured into the region. By the 1880s, the city was filled with gaudy saloons, dance halls, and gambling rooms. Over the decades, Joplin had lost its rough edges and by 1929 was a prosperous financial hub for the surrounding mining region.[76]

Many of its citizens flocked to a local theater to watch Pyle's follies. The show opened with introductions from Jim Thorpe, followed by music from the all-girl six-piece band, Cleo Balcolm's Girl Syncopators. The band leader, Miss Balcolm, was dressed in a shimmering sequin jacket and skirt with gleaming silver slippers; her female musicians were in aviators' suits with Sam Browne belts and boots. After the opening song, two burlesque-circuit comedians entertained the crowd before Madame Duval's Dancing Debutantes pranced across the stage attired in what Miami, Oklahoma's, *Miami News Record* called "clever costumes" and performed the latest dance steps from New York City. Next came blackface comedy acts; songs from blues singer Clara Stone; and novelty acts like Louise and Mitchell, a husband-and-wife team that performed balancing stunts and feats of strength with, the *Record* wrote, Louise "lifting Mitchell over her head and tossing him around in the Amazon style."[77] Fans packed the theater to see what the paper called "a cracker-jack good show," acknowledging that there was a glimmer of hope that the follies might keep the derby afloat until it reached Los Angeles, still more than two thousand miles and a month and a half away.[78]

Things were also looking up for Jesse Dalzell, who had seen his hopes and dreams crushed the day before. Jesse's brother, O. B. Dalzell, had taken over as his new trainer, the Yellow Cab Company of Springfield had lent him a Dodge touring car, the Zeppelin Oil Company would pay for his gas and oil, and the Karchmer Tire Company gave him a new set of wheels.[79] Dalzell had, once again, defied the odds and would continue to race as a bunioneer.

Jesse's story, though inspiring, was a sidelight to the main story line of the race: the brilliant fight between Gavuzzi and Salo for first place. Each move by Gavuzzi was answered by one from Salo. Each man had his style:

Pete loved flat roads and warm weather, and Johnny preferred storms and hills. There were enough of both for each man.

Into Oklahoma

Day 33, 27 Men

The conditions favored Salo on this day—rain and a slippery clay road—and he used them in classic fashion, blowing through the mud and rain in a seven-and-a-half-minute pace on a thirty-five-mile course to Miami, Oklahoma, on the western end of the tri-state mining area anchored by Joplin to the east.[80] He tied for first place with Sam Richman and cut twenty minutes more off Pete's lead, reducing it to about three hours, where it had stood before Gavuzzi made his two-day charge in Missouri.[81]

The duo had again moved the bar of pace and endurance and left the rest of the field struggling to catch up. Both could run as long as fifty miles at a seven-and-a-half-minute pace per mile for days, but they would not race hard beyond that distance. They had now arrived at the boundary between racing and survival, and they refused to go beyond it.

Eddie Gardner could not stay with them. His runs in recent days had aggravated his injury to a point where every step became a test of courage, an exploration of pain. Gardner, who had entered Missouri with so much hope, was staggering, like a punch-drunk fighter in the fifteenth round. He was for all practical purposes dead on his feet—waiting for his mind to tell him what his body was screaming at him to do: drop out of the race.

Local interest was not focused on the titanic struggle between the front-runners or on Gardner's sad end but, rather, on bunioneer Guy Shields of Baxter Springs, Kansas. In 1928, Shields had proven to be a better dancer than bunioneer when he set a world marathon dancing record in New York City.[82] But as Route 66 took the men through the extreme southeast corner of Kansas, thousands of people lined the road to greet the thirty-eight-year-old hometown hero.[83] When Shields reached Baxter Springs in fifth place for the stage run, hundreds of schoolboys jammed the road and tried to pace him through the city. They were soon joined by eighty-one-year-old D. S. "Dye" Chubb, a colorful local pioneer. Chubb

18. Eddie Gardner a year earlier on Route 66, Oklahoma, 1928 race. Source: El Reno Carnegie Library.

was clad in a sweater and a white cap, and the *Baxter Springs Citizen and Herald* wrote that he "dashed at a sprightly rate down the street between lines of spectators."[84] Pyle had almost bypassed the town after the Chamber of Commerce refused to pay him one hundred dollars for the honor, but Shields's trainer apparently persuaded him to let Guy have his moment in the sun.[85]

As long as his money held out and his trainer stayed with him, Shields was content to keep to his schedule: run at a ten-to-eleven-minute-per-mile pace, eat "plenty of good food . . . and get at least eight hours of sleep each night." He said he didn't think much about the race and daydreamed a lot about such things as building castles or going to Europe. "It's all in a day's work," Guy claimed, "and it's not a bit hard when you become accustomed to it. Jus' stepping it off, that's all."[86]

Back to Andy Land

Day 34, 27 Men

On their first full day in Oklahoma, the bunioneers would endure another extended run, fifty-five miles to Chelsea, the last stop on Route 66 before the derby headed south to Texas. The bearded and sun-blacked men ran on a mostly dirt road under cool, clear skies amid a country dotted with farms.[87] Guisto Umek led the field, taking the miles at a seven-minute, forty-five-second pace. Gavuzzi and Salo finished forty-five minutes later. It was Guisto's victory lap, his celebration as he took over third place with its potential six thousand dollars in prize money from an ailing Eddie Gardner.[88] He was telling the world that he had the legs to be there as he pushed beyond Gavuzzi's and Salo's self-imposed fifty-mile limit to serious racing. With Eddie on the verge of dropping out, Umek would soon be in a class by himself, separated from second place by fourteen hours and from fourth place by eleven.[89] Barring a miracle, he would never catch Salo, and if he could stay healthy, no one could catch him. For all practical purposes, Guisto Umek had won third place in the Bunion Derby.

Eddie was in the final days of his agony. He had to temporarily drop out of the race and travel seventeen miles before he could find a doctor who would treat him. He then resumed the ordeal, painfully walking near Jesse Dalzell, the injured Springfield entry, limping badly in last place in a parade of the walking wounded.[90] Both men were hanging on by a thread in the Bunion Derby.

Johnny Salo nearly joined their ranks when he narrowly avoided being struck by a car on the course. With little shoulder to run on, Salo jumped to the centerline to avoid being hit by a speeding car racing up behind him and barely missed being struck by another car traveling in the opposite direction.[91] Johnny seemed to be blessed with nine lives, but he was using them up fast on narrow and dangerous Route 66.

Along the road, thousands of farm families waited to a catch a glimpse of the bunioneers and "their Andy,"[92] Andy Payne, the local farm boy who had defied all the odds and won the 1928 Bunion Derby and its twenty-five-thousand-dollar first prize. In 1928, he had set about the task of racing across America in a businesslike way and methodically "kept stepping along." He was rail thin, curly haired, and part Cherokee, a son of a hill farmer from nearby Vinita. He was shy, humble, and resolute—qualities that endeared him to hard-working Oklahomans.[93] As the Bunion Derby went east across the state in 1928, school was let out, bands played, and firehouse sirens wailed in a salute to Andy Payne.[94]

In 1929, his Chelsea fans soon discovered that Andy was not the country boy who had won the 1928 derby.[95] As a cast member in the follies, "He has changed a lot and taken on city airs," wrote a reporter from the *Muskogee Daily Phoenix*.[96] In newspaper photos, Andy looked nothing like the skinny, sunburned kid who had led the race to Chelsea the year before. He had put on weight and adopted what the Muskogee reporter called "city ways": "he wears knickers and taps his cigarette on his thumb nail."[97] Asked about his future plans, he told a reporter that, like Thorpe, he might enter the movies, claiming he had already been offered a movie contract. He brought one of his younger brothers along with him. When asked if he had "bunion ambitions," the younger Payne said he had enough bunions to start with.[98]

From Chelsea, the derby would leave Route 66 and head south to Dallas and then west across the vast Texas plains. In these broad, open spaces, Johnny Salo would make his bid to unseat his English rival. Guisto Umek, though fifteen hours behind him, harbored the notion that he could catch Johnny despite the long odds. Eddie Gardner would not be with them. His opening run into Missouri had been a triumph, a gutsy challenge to the Jim Crow South, but it had also been his undoing. By Chelsea, he was a broken man and would soon be out of the contest. The remaining miles to Los Angeles would be a duel between two of the greatest ultramarathoners the world had ever known. There would be fast times ahead in the Bunion Derby if Charley Pyle could keep his rickety race going. He hoped for better times in oil-rich Texas.

6

Heading to the Promised Land

Chelsea, Oklahoma, to Dallas, Texas,
May 4–May 10, 1929

CHARLEY PYLE'S day of reckoning was coming closer. Each stage race brought the derby a bit nearer to Los Angeles, where he would be called upon to pay his bunioneers their hard-earned prize money. With a month and a half to go, Pyle was a man with few options: his follies had contributed nothing toward covering the debt, he had no money left of his own, and he could not borrow the prize money with his history of lawsuits and attachments for unpaid debts. He had to earn the prize money, but the math was not working in his favor. When Charley began the derby, he had brought along a three-thousand-seat show tent and planned to hold at least two performances a day.[1] He had, in effect, been counting on six thousand paying fans a day to generate the sixty thousand dollars he would need when he reached Los Angeles. Once Pyle abandoned the tent in Baltimore, he had to rely on local theaters, which typically held no more than a thousand seats.[2] Even with two sold-out performances a day, which seldom happened, his revenues were drastically lower than what he had envisioned when he launched his show in New York City. No matter what he did, he could never escape the inevitable: Charley could not pay his bunioneers their prize money, and he hid that fact from them.

In the face of impending doom, Pyle clung ever more tightly to his vision, looking for better times over the next horizon. He abandoned any hope of making money in Oklahoma and turned his sights south to Dallas, Texas, and the oil-rich cities and towns sprinkled along the 467-mile road to Pecos at the end of the west Texas plains. These were isolated

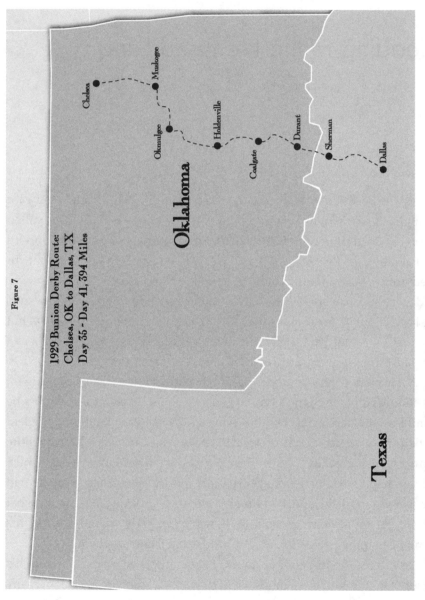

Figure 7

1929 Bunion Derby Route:
Chelsea, OK to Dallas, TX
Day 35 - Day 41, 394 Miles

Map 7. 1929 Bunion Derby route, Chelsea, Okla., to Dallas, Tex.

places with vaguely familiar names like Breckenridge, Sweetwater, Big Springs, and Midland, where cowboys and roughneck oil workers might pay to see his follies and where town fathers might make a monetary contribution to bring his derby show to town.

Pyle's promised land of Dallas was still four hundred miles south of Chelsea, and he wanted to get there in a hurry. In a series of brutally long runs, averaging fifty-six miles a day, he pushed his men to the brink of physical and mental exhaustion and shamefully used them as pawns in his desperate attempt to keep out of bankruptcy.

Goodbye to Eddie

Day 35, 27 Men

The first day began with a 73.4-mile run to Muskogee, Oklahoma, a distance, Arthur Newton wrote, that "was greatly in excess of a reasonable figure."[3] This race followed the fifty-five-mile run to Chelsea that had left most of the bunioneers leg sore and exhausted. Pyle's official starter, his burly football star Steve Owen, gave the starting command and the tired men started down the road to Muskogee.[4]

Third-place holder Guisto Umek seemed unfazed by the long distance. He had just passed Gardner to assume third, and now he set his sights on Salo in second, fourteen hours ahead of him. Umek opened his campaign in spectacular style by setting a new standard for speed and endurance: nine hours and forty-two minutes for 73.4 miles, or seven minutes and fifty-six seconds per mile. In effect, Guisto ran almost three successive marathons, each in under three hours and thirty minutes.[5] No one had ever run that fast over such a long distance before, and few, including Gavuzzi and Salo, believed he could sustain that effort for very long. The two front-runners were content to lose an hour and a half of their lead and let the Italian have his victory.[6]

The extreme distance was the death knell for Eddie Gardner. He fought back the aching pain in his leg for twenty-five miles and refused to listen to George Curtis's pleas to drop out of the race. Finally, though, as his pain built to a crescendo, he stopped and sought treatment from a physician in

Muskogee. He returned and started again, but after a few strides he found it impossible to continue. "I'm through," he said, and dropped out of the race after 1,536 miles of brilliant racing.[7] Though some of the white runners resented the idea of having an African American in the race, none of them doubted Eddie's talent and courage. The white runners had sweated with Gardner while they crossed the Appalachian Plateau and marveled at his graceful form and blazing speed as he ran across Ohio, Indiana, and Illinois. Despite his skin color and more than three hundred years of racial stereotyping, Gardner had proven himself. He was one of them—a bunioneer. Arthur Newton gave the eulogy on behalf of Eddie's fellow bunioneers: "We lost a good man on account of the [excessive distance]. . . . We are all sorry at Gardner's demise, for we all liked him."[8]

To Eddie "the Sheik" Gardner, the Bunion Derby had been far more than a footrace; it had become a crusade, a vehicle to fight the endemic racism he encountered every day he raced across America, and Eddie had committed his body and soul to the cause. He apologized to his fellow African Americans for dropping out of the race. "I hope they understand," he told a reporter, "that I stayed in the [Bunion Derby] as long as my physical condition would allow. I did my best. That is all anyone can do."[9] "I am sorry," he added, "I wanted to keep on running and win—FOR YOU, my people." Bill Gibson of Baltimore's *Afro-American* spoke for all of black America when he thanked Eddie for his gutsy effort and asked his readers to contribute to a fund established in his honor at his alma mater, the Tuskegee Institute in Alabama.[10] Pyle asked Gardner to remain with the derby as an advisor to the bunioneers, but Gardner declined, telling Oklahoma's *Black Dispatch*, "I had to get away and nurse my sorrow in the silence of my best friends."[11] The Bunion Derby had lost an immensely talented and extremely brave bunioneer.

Umek's Amazing Race

Days 36 and 37, 26 Men

On the second day to Dallas, the tired survivors lined up for a brief return to shorter distances on a forty-four-mile run to Okmulgee, the capital of the Creek Nation when Oklahoma was Indian Territory.[12] Umek again reached the finish line first in eye-popping style, running at seven minutes and forty-five seconds per mile, winning his third consecutive stage and leading Newton to call the Italian's last three stage wins as "perhaps the most astonishing performance in the race."[13] Umek accomplished this feat in horrible conditions, plowing through hail and rain to cut the gap between third and second to twelve hours.[14] This caused both Pete and Johnny to, in the words of the *Miami News Record*, "cast anxious eyes" at their new rival, who had quickly become the star of the Bunion Derby.[15]

Guisto Umek had been a champion race walker in Trieste, Italy, before he entered the first Bunion Derby in 1928. He quickly converted to running and showed both talent and endurance by finishing fifth in the race.[16] He spent the summer in Clifton, New Jersey, where he learned some halting English and became a popular figure in the town.[17] Umek had star quality: a handsome, bronze-colored face; a full head of wavy black hair; and sculpted legs. He was a slightly taller and more muscular version of Pete Gavuzzi, with the same continental flair and elegance to his stride but a lifetime older.[18] Runners in their midforties and older had been able to sustain only brief forays into the extended distances at racing pace before their exhausted bodies made them pay for their imprudence; it remained to be seen whether Umek would soon join the ranks of the departed or whether he was that rare phenomenon who would force the front-runners to push even harder at the borders of endurance and pace.

The Italian's string of victories forced fourth-place holder Paul Simpson to search for a countermove as he fell farther and farther behind him. Paul "Hard Rock" Simpson was a man brimming with potential—a twenty-four-year-old physical education instructor at Elon College in North Carolina.[19] Like Gavuzzi, Simpson had youth and talent on his side, having shown speed and tremendous endurance in the final weeks of the 1928 race after overcoming a brutal initiation into transcontinental running.[20] He had earned the nickname "Hard Rock" when the derby crossed the Mojave and the Arizona high country, where he endured pain and injuries that forced scores of his brother bunioneers out of the race.[21] "As rapidly as disabilities [were] heaped upon him," a reporter wrote, "he broadened his grin and carried them . . . [and] won the admiration of everyone for his grit."[22] Simpson had returned to the 1929 race as a much more polished and mature runner along with a support car and his trainer, fellow North Carolinian Wesley Williams, but he was mired in fourth place, eleven hours behind the new shooting star of the Bunion Derby and falling farther behind each day.[23]

Simpson turned for help to Charley Hart, the sixty-four-year-old English sage of long-distance running who had entered both Bunion Derbies and been forced out of both due to exhaustion.[24] Hart was a predecessor of Arthur Newton, who was himself the father of modern ultramarathoning. Charley had held the one-hundred-mile speed record before Newton eclipsed it.[25] Short, squat, and tough, this wise-cracking London boot maker was the sentimental favorite in both Bunion Derbies, a man whose chance at transcontinental racing glory had come too late in life for him to reveal his talent. However, he was also an excellent coach,[26] and in 1928, after he quit the race in the Arizona mountains, he became the coach for Pete Gavuzzi. With a Union Jack tied across the trunk of his support car, he paced Gavuzzi across the country to almost-certain victory before an infected tooth forced Pete out in the waning days of the race.[27] Paul Simpson now had the senior member of the English running elite on his side.

For most of the men, who plodded along at an eleven-to-twelve-minute-per-mile pace, the maneuvering of the front-runners seemed suicidal. Most were merely trying to survive, to cross the finish line, shower, eat, and then sleep before they repeated the process again. For some, the extended distances were simply too much to bear. Two bunioneers, Herman Kester of Sawtelle, California, and one unnamed runner found the forty-four-mile race too much for them and withdrew. The long runs of the previous several days had left them exhausted and unable to continue. Both men were many days out of first place with little hope of winning prize money, yet they had remained for thirty-six days and 1,581 miles of running.[28] They survived injuries and pain that few individuals outside of this select group of men could comprehend. They had earned their Bunion Derby laurels. The field now stood at twenty-four bunioneers.[29]

For all but the top six runners, it made no financial sense to stay in the contest. The bunioneers were not men of means with independent wealth to bankroll their race across America.[30] They relied on contributions from hometown fans and family or the generosity of those they met along the way to supplement their meager budgets. Most were blue-collar workers—farmers, laborers, factory workers—who had joined the derby to chase a dream of grasping the twenty-five-thousand-dollar first prize and making a better life for their often-struggling families.[31] As the likelihood of significant prize money dimmed, they stayed on anyway, perhaps caught up in the grand adventure of racing across America in the company of tough and committed men. "The long trail" had cast a spell on them, clouding their reason, pushing them to continue despite pain, despite injury, despite all that Pyle could throw at them. Those out of contention slogged on, hoping, like their fumbling leader, for a miracle and redemption.

That night in Okmulgee, Umek's ability to race at these longer distances must have set off discussions in Salo's and Gavuzzi's camps. Johnny, at any rate, seemed to conclude that the limits of endurance were a bit farther than he thought. In the next day's race to Holdenville, he ran at near an eight-minute pace for sixty miles to finish first in eight hours and six minutes and received,[32] according to Passaic's *Daily Herald*, a "tremendous ovation as he checked in by the thousands that lined the streets," but the effort left him looking "thin and worn," a bad sign for his chances in the next day's run.[33] Umek finished thirty-five minutes later, followed by Gavuzzi twenty minutes after that. Salo's gutsy run had cut fifty-two minutes off Pete's lead, reducing it to just under two hours and increasing his lead over Umek to twelve hours.[34]

That night, Johnny and Amelia celebrated his victory at a banquet held in his honor by the American Legion.[35] Most of the men, however, were, in Newton's words, "miserably tired" after days running at "these terrible distances" and thought only of rest, including forty-four-year-old Guisto Umek, who was suddenly beginning to feel his age.[36]

Long Miles through Dreary Country

Days 38 and 39, 24 Men

The men faced another day of extended distance on the fifty-four-mile run to Coalgate, in the heart of Oklahoma's coal-mining region, as they followed Route 75, the main north-south road to Dallas.[37] Arthur Newton was not impressed by the scenery or the people he met along the way: "big dumps of refuse, smoky chimneys, coke ovens. . . . This is the sort of country we had now reached, a land where many of the girls, both large and small, wore mechanics' overalls all day."[38]

In this bleak land, Pete Gavuzzi responded to the preceding day's drubbing by Salo. Like a counterpuncher in a boxing match, he abandoned the old fifty-mile limit they had both followed and ran fast, winning the stage in about an eight-minute-per-mile pace and gaining back most of the time he had lost to Salo the day before.[39]

Umek finally paid for his days of speed: he broke down under the strain of the last few days and lost two hours to Johnny. This pushed the deficit between second and third place to fourteen hours, just about where it was before he opened his assault on second place.[40] Umek had succeeded in making the front-runners go faster at longer distances, but he had gained nothing by it and had pushed his middle-aged body to the breaking point.

In Coalgate, the townspeople packed downtown streets to watch Pyle's bunioneers finish the race.[41] A few days before, a man named W. M. A. Downing had arrived in town, announced that he was Pyle's agent, and began negotiating with the Chamber of Commerce for a cash payment to bring the derby to Coalgate. It was soon discovered that Downing was an impostor and was wanted for embezzlement in Missouri. He was arrested and returned to Missouri for trial.[42]

The bunioneers were exhausted, but Pyle pushed them even harder the next day. He sent them on a fifty-mile run down a muddy dirt road lashed by thunderstorms to Durant, a farming community in the Red River Valley—perfect conditions for Johnny Salo.[43] In Salo's game of tit for tat with Gavuzzi, a reporter joked that Johnny ran "faster than a sheriff chasing Charley Pyle."[44] Salo seemed impervious to the heavy rain and thick mud that mired cars like flies on flypaper along the road.[45] Arthur Newton was awed by Johnny's ability to use his powerful body to run hard in the worst of conditions.[46] Salo won the stage, arriving in Durant in the middle of a downpour after running at just over an eight-minute-per-mile pace, and cut Gavuzzi's lead to about two hours.[47] A recharged

Paul Simpson finished second, ten minutes later, announcing his intent to challenge Umek for third-place prize money.[48]

After the race, Johnny and Amelia were taken in hand by the Durant chapter of the American Legion, fed, and put up in a nice hotel for the night at the Legion post's expense.[49] Salo, as a World War I veteran and legionnaire, was a source of great pride to the organization. In any town he stopped that had a Legion post, his fellow legionnaires were there to help him with offers of a meal, a shower, and a hotel room for the night.

Across the Red River to Texas

Day 40, 24 Men

On the sixth day of the race to Dallas, Pyle's exhausted band of runners finally had an easy run, a thirty-mile race that took them across the Oklahoma-Texas border at the Red River into Sherman, Texas. It was a town of about sixteen thousand people, built along the old St. Louis-to-San Francisco stagecoach line.[50] The bunioneers continued to follow Route 75, then a red clay road made slippery and muddy by recent rains. It took the men across the broad, fertile valley of the Red River, passing lush fields of cotton, corn, and wheat.[51]

Paul Simpson won first-place honors, followed by Phil Granville in second and Pete Gavuzzi in third, all running at nearly an eight-and a half-minute-per-mile pace, a relatively slow pace for the distance.[52] Pete did not have to run hard to push his lead back to two and a half hours. Johnny Salo did it for him. He finished a distant sixth and earned a rebuke from his wife for his poor performance. She blamed it on overeating, telling a reporter, "He eats all day and all night. How can he run?"[53] His wife was wrong. Johnny's problem was not food but simple exhaustion after running fast for fifty miles on muddy roads the day before.

Charley Pyle was in a much better mood than Mrs. Salo that night. He bragged to a reporter that he was seventy-five thousand-dollars better off than he had been at a comparable point in the 1928 race and brashly added that he planned to make the Bunion Derby an annual event "despite," he joked, "all the writs of attachments that were ever issued."[54] The last comment was the only one with a ring of truth. The real, desperate financial picture became clear the next morning, when he had trouble finding enough cash to pay his cast's hotel bill in Sherman. The hotel held the luggage until he paid the bill later in the day.[55]

"Mighty Little Short of Criminal"

Day 41, 24 Men

Pyle's final push to Dallas added to his well-earned reputation as an unscrupulous and uncaring leader of his Bunion Derby parade. He sent his men on a 79.9-mile run to Dallas—the longest leg ever run in both Bunion Derbies. "They [the runners]," Newton wrote, "knew too well that there was a hideous time in store for them on the morrow, though exactly how bad they were to find out." "Say what you like," he said, [forcing already overworked men to run such a distance] "was mighty little short of criminal."[56]

The weather added to the misery: a broiling Texas sun combined with the distance left the men "absolutely dog-tired and bone-weary" when they reached Dallas, wrote Newton.[57] The last indignity happened in sight of the finish line and the official timing table at the Oak Cliff School near Southern Methodist University, where Pyle detoured the men around the city for four miles to give the citizens of Dallas a chance to see them. Newton wrote that the men were furious.[58] Until midnight, the bunioneers were still "dragging themselves in," some with their spirits broken, others spitting oaths and curses at Pyle, and all but a few utterly exhausted.[59]

Johnny Salo seemed set apart from his fellow bunioneers. Perhaps stung by his wife's comments, he set a grueling pace, pausing only to eat, and finished the distance in eleven hours and twenty-two minutes, much of it run on muddy roads, in an eight-and-a-half-minute-per-mile pace. He cut Gavuzzi's lead to an hour and a half and increased his lead over Umek to sixteen hours.[60] At the finish, Salo seemed like a man possessed as he jumped up the steps of the Oak Cliff School with a broad smile on his bronzed face.[61] He seemed to be hardly breathing and was anxious to talk to reporters after his long run on the red clay roads. He noted that he got lost and even ran a mile out of his way "but that's all right," he added, "sure it was a pretty tough grind but here I am."[62] Arthur McMahon wrote, "The pace which Salo set yesterday from Sherman would have run the best cow pony into the ground."[63] Johnny had broken his own rules on pace and distance. He had entered uncharted territory. He had crossed the threshold from a great runner to a legendary one with a frenzied drive and talent that left his competitors shaking their heads in wonder. At that moment, he was in a class of his own, arguably the greatest runner of his generation, perhaps of all time.

Thousands of fans flocked to see Johnny finish.[64] Pyle hoped many of them would buy a derby program for five cents and a hot dog or cotton candy from his vendors and, above all, see his stage show. If he ever hoped to turn his derby into a moneymaking machine, this was the place to do it. Dallas was a city of commerce: the nation's foremost inland spot-cotton market and an important center for buying, selling, and refining oil.[65] The city had wealth, and its citizens were fascinated by Pyle's bunioneers but not by his follies. Few came to the show, and two shows the next night in Fort Worth brought in just $137 in receipts despite an advertising bill that was twice that much; furthermore, "similar small crowds greeted the troupe in other places."[66] Members of his vaudeville cast told reporters that most threatened to quit because Charley had not paid them in four weeks.[67]

Pyle had fatally miscalculated the earning power of his Bunion Derby. Revenue from his follies and other sources—selling programs and food and contributions from cities and towns—would never amount to more than pocket change that might, at best, get his derby to Los Angeles. Through it all, he kept up a steady stream of lies and half-truths, making comforting statements to the effect that he would have the money to pay his bunioneers. And he made them while pushing his men to the brink of exhaustion with his backbreaking runs.

For the front-runners, the brutal race to Dallas evolved into a high-stakes poker game. Guisto Umek made the biggest bet, racing for days at an eight-minute, thirty-second pace per mile or faster at the extended distances, and he lost badly. After Dallas, he was sixteen hours behind Salo, buried deeper in third than he was when he opened his campaign to overtake the front-runners. In hindsight, it was a foolish adventure that risked his lock on the six thousand dollars for third place. In Dallas, he was exhausted and had a reenergized challenger, Paul Simpson, on his trail. Salo was the biggest winner. His gutsy, almost insanely bold race to Dallas had put him within one and a half hours of first place and had broken his challenger, Umek.[68]

For the next twelve days, the bunioneers would race across the west Texas plains to Pecos at a much more leisurely pace than they had just endured: forty miles a day on average, fifteen miles less than the Chelsea-to-Dallas leg. At around forty miles, Gavuzzi had run at a seven-minute to seven-and-a-half-minute-per-mile pace for days. Salo would have to recover fast if he hoped to cut more time off his rival's lead.

7

Under Western Skies
Dallas to Pecos, Texas, May 11–May 22, 1929

FROM THE COUNTRY'S EARLY DAYS as a collection of colonies, the western frontier has been a beacon of hope to Americans searching for a better life and a new beginning. "Go west" has always been a hallmark of the American character. In the California Gold Rush of 1849, thousands of easterners quit farms and office jobs to stream west, braving Indian raids and desert heat to reach the gold fields. Legions of pioneers followed, many taking the southern route from St. Louis to Dallas, then west to El Paso and across New Mexico, where they hugged the Mexican border to avoid the towering Rockies before crossing the Sonora Desert to the promised land of California.[1]

The bunioneers would retrace the southern route to California, first making the 467-mile journey from Dallas to Pecos across the vast, open spaces of West Texas.[2] In the late 1920s, the state was rich in natural resources, including more than 50 percent of the proven oil reserves in the United States.[3] With demand for gas and oil products skyrocketing, oil money had injected new life into many of the once-sleepy agricultural towns that the bunioneers would pass through on their twelve-day trip to Pecos before they ascended the barren and mostly unpopulated high-desert lands to the west. Pyle hoped these towns had ready cash to spend on his follies show. The bunioneers held no such dreams. Most were exhausted. Newton called them "a listless and fagged out crowd" after a week of brutal racing to Dallas.[4]

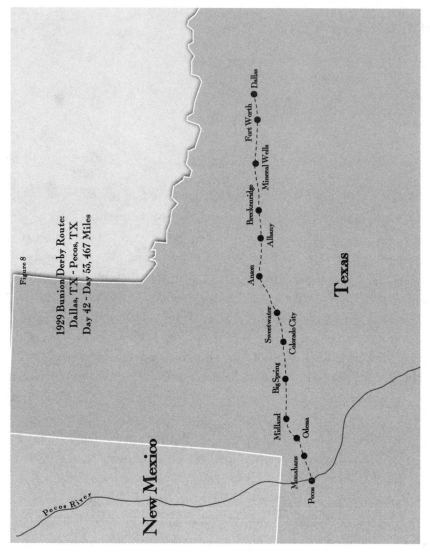

Figure 8

1929 Bunion Derby Route:
Dallas, TX - Pecos, TX
Day 42 - Day 53, 467 Miles

New Mexico

Texas

Pecos River

Dallas
Fort Worth
Mineral Wells
Breckenridge
Albany
Anson
Sweetwater
Colorado City
Big Spring
Midland
Odessa
Monahans
Pecos

Map 8. 1929 Bunion Derby route, Dallas, Tex., to Pecos, Tex.

Searching for Pyle's Redemption

Days 42 and 43, 24 Men

The men set out for Fort Worth, thirty-three miles to the west. The shorter distance helped cheer them up. Some of the racers had been on the road for eighteen hours on the run to Dallas, and they were grateful for the chance to rest. The front-runners—Gavuzzi, Salo, and Umek—declared a holiday and quietly jogged along together as they ran past orchards and truck gardens nurtured in the rich soil bordering the road to Fort Worth, "where," the masthead of the city's *Star Telegram* proclaimed, "the West begins."[5]

Forth Worth had vast cattle stockyards and the world's largest system of oil pipelines, which connected the surrounding oil fields with the city's refineries.[6] Despite its wealth, the city's residents spurned Pyle's derby. His follies played to a nearly empty theater that left Charley even deeper in debt. Big cities such as Dallas and Fort Worth had their own thriving theater scene, and their citizens were not willing to take a chance on Charley's traveling road show.[7]

Pyle pushed on, this time fifty-three miles to the resort town of Mineral Wells across sparsely populated and semi-arid desert country in hopes of finding a more receptive audience for his follies show.[8] Salo and Gavuzzi would not lead Charley's quest. Both men were exhausted and needed rest after racing beyond fifty miles in recent days, spurred on by Umek's three-day string of victories.[9] The Italian, however, had proven himself all too human, and they returned to their singular focus on each other. Each man knew that the key to victory was building a sizable lead over the other, and each was determined to stop the other from doing so. The Chelsea-to-Dallas leg had shown both men that racing hard at the extended distances offered a chance to make lead-changing gains if the runner could recover fast enough to hold off the inevitable charge of his opponent in the following days. The rules of the game were changing as the competition between the front-runners intensified.

Guisto Umek led the derby to Mineral Wells as he resumed the frantic approach to racing that he had used on the Chelsea-to-Dallas leg of the derby—run fast regardless of the distance—and finished an hour ahead of the front-runners.[10] Along the course, sixth-place Philip Granville had a narrow escape when a drunk driver swerved into him, forcing him to leap over a culvert to avoid being run over. He tumbled down a dry riverbank, breaking a bone in his toe, bruising his heel, and wrenching his hip. A surgeon informed Granville that he would need to drop out of the race, but Granville thought otherwise and limped to the finish line in a performance typical of the courage shown by Eddie Gardner and Jesse Dalzell.[11] Phil may have soaked his injured foot in the mineral baths at the night's control point at Mineral Wells, a resort town with about four hundred wells reported to cure, noted Texas's *WPA Guide*, "hysterical manias" and many other ailments.[12] Sadly for Pyle, those tourists who were there to "take the waters" did not seem to hold a similar desire to attend a performance of his follies show.

Entombed in Plaster

Day 44, 24 Men

Charley, angry and frustrated after three days of half-filled shows, headed deeper into the west on a 54.4-mile race to Breckenridge.[13] The men did not share his missionary zeal as he searched for the proverbial Promised Land where townspeople would pack his follies show. Newton lamented that they were all tired men, "absolutely dog-tired and leg-weary," as a result of the tremendous distances.[14] Salo and Gavuzzi again refused to race. They spent most of the time joking with each other as they jogged along the road and finished in a fifth-place tie.[15] As long as Pyle tried to push them to run these long distances, the two front-runners would give their fans nothing to cheer about.

Sammy Richman lacked the front-runners' caution. Like Guisto Umek, he was an immensely talented bunioneer who had emerged in Texas as a runner of tremendous strength, speed, and endurance.[16] In the 1928 race, Sammy and his three brothers, Arthur, Morris, and Ben, bought an old Ford sedan for twenty-five dollars and left New York City for the start of the race in Los Angeles. All had visions of winning the twenty-five-thousand-dollar first prize, but one of them needed to drive the car along the course. They drew straws, and Ben lost. Remarkably, each of the three brothers finished the race: Arthur in twenty-ninth place, Sammy in forty-fourth, and Morris in forty-eighth, a tribute to the work ethic of this tightly knit Jewish family from New York City.[17] In 1929, Sam and Morris entered again, but after each paid the three-hundred-dollar entrance fee, they had little cash left and could not afford a trainer or a car to follow them on the course. Through sheer force of will, the two veteran runners survived, perhaps sharing food and a trainer with other runners. Along the way, Sam got faster and kept rising in the rankings while Morris remained mired in the back of the pack.[18]

On the road to Breckenridge, Sammy held fifth place and opened a hell-bent drive to reach the top ranks of the Bunion Derby, first bridging the four-hour gap that separated him from Paul Simpson in fourth and then trying to close the massive seventeen-and-a-half-hour gap between him and Umek in third.[19] In the 54.4-mile race, he covered the course at an eight-minute pace per mile and cut Simpson's hold on fourth to three hours.[20] Richman, like Umek, believed the limits of pace and endurance were by no means settled. And he would run hard at any distance as long as he was able to do so. He was risking all he had gained in a long-shot drive to move into the top ranks of the Bunion Derby.

Pyle had been pushing his men relentlessly in search of the Promised Land, and he finally found it in Breckenridge, one of the many Texas towns transformed by the discovery of oil.[21] People streamed into the town from surrounding farms and towns to see the finish, almost tripling its population. The *Breckenridge American* estimated that twenty thousand people lined city streets near the finish line at the Stephens County Courthouse in the town center, where buildings were decorated with red, white, and blue bunting; American flags flew over the road, strung by ropes between light poles; and Pyle held three sold-out performances of his Cross Country Follies.[22] He had finally found the paying customers he had longed for in Texas.

The town was also a godsend for the Richman brothers. The duo faced crossing the vast, open spaces of the West without a support car or a trainer to supply them with water and food, a prospect both were reluctant

19. Runners finishing in Breckenridge, Texas, Photo 1, May 13, 1929. Source: From *Breckenridge American* files. Photo taken by Basil Clemons.

to face.[23] As a military veteran and a legionnaire, Sammy appealed to the American Legion post in Breckenridge for help. The Legion was proud of Richman's plucky race and rewarded him with the use of a Ford roadster for the remainder of the run and the services of a local boxer to be his trainer and driver for a cut of the prize money.[24]

Breckenridge had been a bright spot in the derby's often-gloomy march across Texas. In the late afternoon, Pyle left town headed west in a rented cab, searching for similar towns that might host his men over the coming days.[25] As the cabbie drove, Charley must have felt a bit of his old confidence coming back as he looked out on a treeless landscape and dreamed of better days to come.

In 1929, road maintenance was in its infancy in the West. Most rural roads were dirt, potholed, and dangerous. West of Albany, Texas, Pyle's cab hit a bad patch of road, overturned, and dumped him into a ditch. He broke his right arm at the elbow and shoulder and was lucky to have survived without suffering more serious injuries.[26] The fate of the cab driver is unknown. Charley was taken to a local hospital with his arm terribly mangled. "Because of the peculiarity of the double-break," a reporter noted, "it [was] necessary to have his entire upper torso encased in plaster of paris."[27] Pyle claimed the doctors told him to stay in bed for six weeks, but he was horizontal only long enough for them to set his broken bones. He returned to Breckenridge the next morning, wishing he had driven

20. Runners finishing in Breckenridge, Texas, Photo 2, May 13, 1929. Source: From *Breckenridge American* files. Photo taken by Basil Clemons.

the car himself and "terribly handicapped" with his chest and right arm encased in plaster.[28] For the next month, he would head west entombed in plaster, sweating and itching in his cast and wincing in pain at every bump on the last thousand miles to Los Angeles.

Racing to the Next Oil-Rich West Texas Town

Days 45, 46, and 47, 24 Men

The next day, their wounded leader sent the bunioneers on a twenty-five mile run to Albany, Texas, a distance that would give them the afternoon to recuperate from the long runs of recent days.[29] At the start in Breckenridge, thousands of fans milled around the start line, excited about the special race Charley had arranged with local sports promoters: a head-to-head match between the town's best distance runner and Arthur Newton on the day's course to Albany. The town's choice, a young African American distance runner named Tiger Flowers, seemed an odd one in this time of Jim Crow segregation. In Breckenridge, however, skin color seemed not to matter at all as white fans cheered Flowers on when the special race began several minutes before the bunioneers got under way.[30]

The challenger quickly discovered that he was seriously overmatched when he took on Newton, a distance-running legend. Arthur's shoulder had almost healed, and he had been running with the men for about a week, helping pace the weaker ones along the course.[31] Flowers soon realized that he had, at best, a vague idea about the physical demands of long-distance racing. After the first mile, Flowers was a hundred yards behind, and by three miles the gap had stretched to a mile. At that point, Newton abandoned the race and ran back to Flowers, who was "badly winded" and barely running. Arthur then became the teacher, "giving [him] useful tips to help him along" before picking up the pace and leaving Flowers to stagger across the finish line about five hours later.[32]

On this short course, Sammy Richman resumed his assault on Paul "Hard Rock" Simpson's lead, finishing first and cutting the deficit between them to two and a half hours.[33] Simpson seemed unable or unwilling to stop Richman's relentless advance. Perhaps his coach, Charley Hart, had told him to ignore the challenge, assuming Sammy would soon break down after running for days at what many considered a suicidal pace. Guisto Umek had done just that on the road to Albany. After exhausting himself the day before, he finished far in the rear and lost most of the time he had gained in his hard running over the previous few days, while Pete and Johnny jogged along together for another day.[34]

The next day, May 15, the two front-runners reopened their long-delayed battle on the thirty-nine-mile race to Anson, a farming community set amid fields of cotton.[35] Salo made the first move, covering the distance in just over five hours while running at a seven-minute-and-forty-five-second pace per mile. Gavuzzi did not give chase and saw his first-place lead cut to an hour and ten minutes. Sam Richman finished second and cut Paul Simpson's hold on fourth place by a half hour.[36] That night, as the last men straggled in, a windstorm lashed them with prairie sand as they crossed the finish line.[37]

The men received a welcome bit of good news that night when Pyle announced that he had hired Arthur Newton as a technical advisor for the bunioneers. For the rest of the race, Newton would become a shepherd to his flock of runners. After the start of each day's race, Arthur would run up to each man, check on his status, and offer advice when required, an exercise that would take him about twenty to thirty miles of running to complete. Then he would stop by the roadside and recheck each runner as he passed by. As the lead bunioneers finished, Newton would drive ten to fifteen miles back along the course to meet and cheer up the men who were strung out for miles along the road, giving comfort to runners like Jesse Dalzell, who was still fighting gamely to keep racing despite an injured foot.[38] Charley Pyle had inadvertently given the men a voice that would keep urging Pyle to cut back on the long runs if he wanted to make the Bunion Derby a race rather than an ordeal.

The director general of the Bunion Derby, however, was not listening to reason on this day. He wanted to get to the next profitable town quickly and pushed the men back into the longer distances on a fifty-six-mile run to Sweetwater, Texas, an agricultural town injected with new wealth by refining oil from surroundings wells.[39] On this day, the skies cleared and the broiling Texas sun returned to bake the men and dry the muddy roads.[40] For whatever reason, Gavuzzi decided to run fast on the extended course and raced in blazing heat at a seven-minute-and-forty-five-second-per-mile pace with Guisto Umek, Salo, and Richman all close behind. By the seventeenth mile, Johnny had caught up with Gavuzzi and raced ahead to win by seven minutes.[41] An exhausted Guisto Umek could not keep up and staggered through the last miles of the course to finish an hour and a half behind Salo, with Umek seeing his deficit between second and third grow to fourteen and a half hours. Sammy Richman proved to be a more formidable opponent, finishing in a tie with Gavuzzi and closing to within a half hour of Simpson in fourth.[42]

Thousands of fans had flocked to town from refineries, city shops, schools, farms, ranches, and oil fields to see the runners finish and to pack Pyle's follies.[43] Charley seemed to have finally found his audience in the prosperous towns strung along the road to Pecos.

Wild Weather on the West Texas Plains

Days 48–52, 24 Men

The director general next sent the men on a short, twenty-eight-mile run to Colorado, another West Texas oil town. The men were running in very unstable spring weather: bands of thunderstorms rolled through the area as warm Gulf air collided with cold air from the north. The storms turned the road between Sweetwater and Colorado into muck, trapping the trainers' cars in town until the roads dried out.[44] The poor footing tormented Phil Granville, who ran with a broken bone in his foot, and forced two midpack runners, Joe Spangler and Elmer Cowley, to run barefoot because the thick mud made it impossible for them to make any headway in their heavy shoes.[45]

Sammy Richman seemed to defy reason. He set off at a fast pace to capture fourth place from Paul Simpson. Newton, as the new technical advisor, thought it was a bad idea and raced after him to slow him down. Arthur chased Sammy for seventeen miles before he caught up with the mud-spattered leader and had a chat, but Richman was not following Arthur's counsel. He raced on and led the derby to the finish, winning the stage race and bumping Simpson out of fourth by twenty minutes.[46] The man from New York now set his sights on catching Guisto Umek, who held third place by thirteen hours.

Johnny Salo was content to jog through the mud with Gavuzzi until the two barefoot runners tried to pass them. At the sight of them, Johnny increased his pace and beat Pete to the finish, capping three days of victories over his English rival that brought him within a half hour of taking the lead in the Bunion Derby.[47] Salo, however, was in no mood to celebrate. After fifty days of racing, he had nearly used up the fund his Passaic fans had raised for him and what remained of the ten thousand dollars in prize money he had earned in the 1928 race. Salo sent a telegram to his Passaic fan club, the Turner League, claiming that if he did not receive additional funds, he would quit the Bunion Derby. The club's president and its namesake, Police Commissioner John Turner, voted to give Johnny an infusion of five hundred dollars from its treasury.[48]

Much of the money went to buy food to replace the massive amount of calories he burned on each day's run. He was literally eating his way to an early exit from the Bunion Derby. Salo usually ate three times the amount of normal men and at all hours of the day and night. A reporter wrote that Salo would eat any kind of high-calorie food he could get, such as raw hamburgers, steaks, and sweets.[49] All of the bunioneers had similar caloric needs, but most were not as well financed as Salo and struggled

21. Muddy road in Texas, circa 1926. Source: John Stone, private collection.

to buy enough food to keep them in the race, all except Philip Granville. Thanks to his millionaire sponsor, sports promoter Teddy Oke from Toronto, Phil ate first-class meals. According to his hometown newspaper, the *Hamilton Spectator*, a typical dinner consisted of "two [bowls] of soup, two steaks, five kinds of vegetables with two dishes of dessert"; and for breakfast, "two plates of porridge, a grapefruit, four eggs and some meat" before he arrived at the start line by seven.[50]

Another day of mud and rain awaited the bunioneers on the forty-one-mile course to Big Spring. Most of the men tried to avoid the mud by running along an adjacent rail line with raised beams that, in Newton's words, "gave the men plenty of trouble"[51]—everyone, that is, except Johnny Salo, who seemed to thrive in the worst of conditions with his companion, Guisto Umek. This course brought Johnny's strengths to the forefront: a steely focus and sheer physical power. With Umek by his side, he plowed through a "veritable quagmire" at a nine-minute pace to win the stage race and push Gavuzzi out of first place, something he had tried to do since Pete had taken the lead in Ohio.[52]

The muddy roads tormented Philip Granville's ailing foot. The constant slipping and sliding aggravated his injury, pushing the pain to mind-numbing proportions and making every step an agonizing exercise in endurance. His gutsy performance won the hearts of his fellow Canadians, who by the thousands followed his progress in their local newspapers, and that of Arthur Newton, who called him "as tough as they make 'em."[53] Jesse Dalzell, the young Missouri runner, was in a similar hell. Since the motorcycle ran over his foot in Springfield, he had struggled through each day's race in excruciating pain, and the mucky road to Big Spring only added to his torment.[54]

After a day of racing through ankle-deep mud, the men arrived in Big Spring, which had long been a haven for buffalo hunters and legions of pioneers following the southern route to California.[55] The townspeople gave Pyle and his bunioneers an enthusiastic welcome, packing downtown streets to see the finish and later packing the local theater to see the follies show.[56]

The next day, a blazing Texas sun returned to dry the road on a forty-mile course to Midland, Texas, named for its position halfway between Fort Worth and El Paso. The bunioneers were following the Emigrant Road to California, where settlers in covered wagons headed west to face Indian raids and desert wastelands in New Mexico and Arizona.[57] The road was taking them deeper into the Old West of cowboys and the open range, leaving the farm fields behind and entering a sparsely populated region of vast cattle ranches on flat, dune-colored plains.[58]

On this lonely road beneath a hot Texas sun, Salo and Richman raced together at a seven-minute-and-forty-five-second pace and finished in a first-place tie, with Gavuzzi fifteen minutes behind them.[59] Arthur G. McMahon of Passaic's *Daily News* wrote that most of the town's citizens "turned out in their Sunday-go-to-meeting best to cheer the stolid Finn" and Richman as they crossed the line "hand in hand."[60]

Wealth came to Midland in 1923, when oil was discovered in the region's lucrative Permian Basin. The new oil money, according to the *WPA Guide to Texas*, gave Midland's citizens "wealth and sophistication combined with breezy western characteristics."[61] They seemed to have a special appreciation for Pyle's follies, packing the Grand Theater to see his "big time" show, which one local newspaper called the "best ever seen in Texas."[62]

Arthur Newton was not pleased about the late eleven o'clock start time that Pyle had set for the next day's race to Odessa, Texas. By that time, the Texas sun would be beating down on the men and pushing temperatures into the eighties and nineties.[63] He could not, however, complain about the 21.7-mile distance. In spite of the warm weather, Sammy Richman and Guisto Umek dueled at a nearly suicidal pace—six minutes and forty seconds per mile—as they chased each other at a sub-three-hour marathon pace.[64] Umek held a massive, insurmountable thirteen-hour lead over Sammy, yet he felt the need to fight Richman for every second the New Yorker might gain and risk a race-ending injury that might endanger his hold on the six-thousand-dollar third-place prize money. Twenty minutes later, Gavuzzi and Salo finished together after holding what Passaic's *Daily Herald* called "a merry battle along the lonely stretch of road with only tall birds and bewildered cattle to witness it."[65] The lead shifted back and forth between them for eighteen miles until they called a truce and finished in a tie.[66]

Conditions were perfect for the next stage race. "Just the right sort of weather for the runners," wrote Newton, with a light rain cooling the air as they ran on a paved road over a thirty-eight-mile course to Monahans.[67] The route would take them through what the *WPA Guide to Texas* called "a country of vast distances," unpopulated rangeland with rolling hills going north to south and dotted with sagebrush, greasewood, cat claw, yucca, and prickly pear and broken by occasional deposits of white sand.[68]

Along this lonely road, Richman and Umek began a second day of their pell-mell duel, both men pushing each other at a six-minute-and-forty-five-second pace.[69] Salo and Gavuzzi pushed each other, too, but at around a seven-minute-and-forty-second pace—each man taking the lead only to be passed by the other before they called a truce and finished together in third place.[70]

The men finished in Monahans, founded as a water stop by the Texas and Pacific Railroad between Big Spring and the Pecos River to the west. The town had been another sleepy farm community before the discovery of oil had brought it prosperity, and that meant more profit for C. C. Pyle, who had been on a five-town winning streak in his drive to stave off bankruptcy.[71]

Running to the End of the Civilized World

Day 53, 24 Men

The next morning, a reporter from the *El Paso Times* watched "a motley crew of . . . dust begrimed, unshaven men" line up for the race to Pecos.[72] They looked more like weary combat veterans than distance runners. These men were a weather-beaten, somber, and hard-hearted lot after surviving a test of endurance that few of them could have imagined when they had fought their way through the crowds in New York's Columbus Circle fifty-three days before, a journey that had left fifty-three of their brothers broken and scattered along the twenty-three-hundred-mile course. The sun-blackened men at the start line in Monahans were the elite of the long-distance running world.

The wild Texas weather returned on the thirty-nine-mile run to Pecos as morning thunderstorms pounded the men while they raced on a loose gravel road. Richman and Umek seemed untroubled by the tough terrain or the driving rain and chased each other until Guisto tired near the finish. Then Sammy broke away to win the stage in about a seven-minute-per-mile pace and cut Umek's lead to thirteen hours.[73] Gavuzzi and Salo ran slower, pushing each other for the lead as "a heavy rain fell on them, lighting flashed and thunder rolled." The two front-runners seemed to revel in the storm, laughing and joking with each other as they ticked off the miles at a seven-minute-and-forty-five-second-per-mile pace and finished together.[74]

The townspeople in Pecos were enamored of the bunioneers but not of Pyle's follies. The *Pecos Enterprise and Gusher* called the show "a flop" after it played to a half-filled theater.[75] Charley's road show had had a brilliant run over the preceding five days, but the streak ended at Pecos—an omen of days to come. Across the Pecos River, the men would leave the oil fields behind and enter a rugged, arid, and unfriendly land. For the next four days, the derby would stop at tiny outposts of civilization that dotted the road until the race reached the irrigated farming communities along the Rio Grande near El Paso. The follies would not perform in this sparsely populated land and so added nothing to the coffers of Pyle's derby parade.

8

West of the Pecos

Pecos to El Paso, Texas, May 23–May 27, 1929

A Disgruntled Band of Bunioneers

Days 54 and 55, 23 Men

The bunioneers had seen the last of the oil-rich Texas towns. For the next 219 miles, the twenty-three survivors would race across the barren desert uplands that separated them from El Paso, Texas, at the far western edge of the state.

They began the journey with a fifty-six-mile run to the tiny hamlet of Kent.[1] They had left brave Jesse Dalzell behind in Pecos after, the *Pecos Enterprise and Gusher* wrote, he was "completely crippled with sore feet."[2] His gutsy effort to stay in the race in spite of his extremely painful foot had earned him the admiration and respect of his fellow bunioneers.

For the next two days, the men would gradually climb to about four thousand feet, gaining about fifteen hundred feet in elevation after leaving Pecos. As they ran higher, the rolling plains gave way to the high desert, featuring more rugged terrain, with sagebrush and yucca dotting this windswept and sun-baked land.[3] In this arid country, the temperature can rise quickly under a Texas sun, but this day it was cold as bands of thunderstorms rolled through the region.[4] Along the course, the runners were pelted by hailstones, drenched by rain, and peppered with desert sand blown by the fierce winds as lightning bolts crashed around them— a crazy quilt of weather that forced most runners to run slowly on the wet, slippery roads.[5]

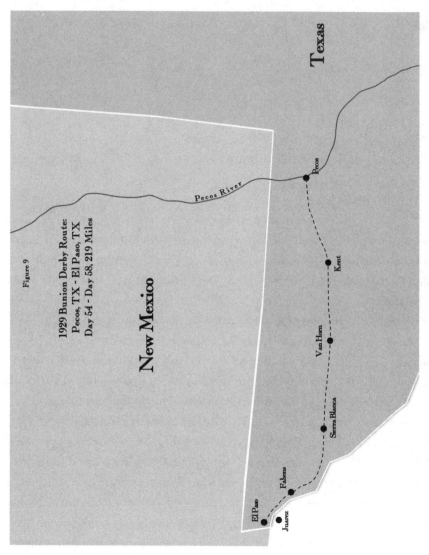

Figure 9

1929 Bunion Derby Route:
Pecos, TX - El Paso, TX
Day 54 - Day 58, 219 Miles

New Mexico

Texas

Pecos River

Pecos

Kent

Van Horn

Sierra Blanca

Fabens

El Paso

Juarez

Map 9. 1929 Bunion Derby route, Pecos, Tex., to El Paso, Tex.

Sam Richman thumbed his nose at the elements and raced through the tempest at a seven-and-a-half-minute pace per mile to win the stage. He had run, in effect, two continuous marathons at a three-hour-and-eighteen-minute pace in the middle of a thunderstorm while racing mostly uphill.[6] His constant shadow, Guisto Umek, finished thirteen minutes behind him, hanging tenaciously on his heels and refusing to relinquish much of his thirteen-hour lead.[7] These two gifted and gutsy men had thrown away the rulebook and entered a new world of their own making, an enticing world of stage-race glory that did nothing to help them win the Bunion Derby and that put them at a greater risk of injury.

Despite a string of stage wins over the preceding thirteen days, Umek had succeeded in cutting the gap between second and third by only an hour since Dallas, which left him a massive fifteen-hour lead to overcome.[8] Richman had managed to reduce Umek's lead by three and one-half hours in the same period, but the gap still stood at an unbridgeable thirteen hours. With less than a month to go in the race, both men were effectively locked in to their positions. They might have been better served by slowing down to avoid injury and "just . . . [kept] stepping along" at a consistent pace, as Payne had done in the 1928 race.[9] They did not listen to reason, however, and simply ran as fast as they could go every day. Both men were ill served by their trainers, who should have tried to temper their competitive zeal.

The battle for first place had become a stalemate for now. Pete tried a dozen times to break away from Johnny on the lonely road to Kent, but Salo clung to him like a limpet, and they finished together in fourth, leaving Salo's lead unchanged at twenty-one minutes.[10]

The derby spent the night in tiny Kent, whose population of about twenty hardy souls scratched out a living tending to the travelers who passed along the road.[11] The town had no facilities for the runners and the follies cast, which forced them to stay at a nearby campsite for the night.[12] In this forsaken place, the bored members of Pyle's follies had no audience to play to. They were twenty-four hundred miles away from the bright lights of Broadway that they had left almost two months before. Along the way, these seldom-paid actors had probably performed their show a hundred times in fifty different theaters, sometimes to packed houses and rave reviews, sometimes to nearly empty theaters and scathing ones. None of the cast members gave interviews that might have explained their extraordinary devotion to the follies. They had every reason to quit. Perhaps they had been caught up in the grand adventure of racing across America or hoped, like Payne and Thorpe, to launch their film careers in Hollywood. Tonight they were free to sit by the campfire and think about all they had seen and done, to breathe in the smell of wood smoke and sagebrush scenting the cold night air, or to look up at a million stars twinkling in the vast Texas sky.

The bunioneers were not in such a carefree mood. Most were at an emergency meeting of runners and trainers called to demand that several unnamed runners be eliminated from the race for accepting rides. The heated meeting went on for an hour, with head referee Steve Owen telling the men that he could not disqualify anyone until he or someone from his race patrol caught the violator in the act. His statement seemed to satisfy no one, and the bunioneers left disgruntled and unsatisfied.[13] The likely culprits were probably not among the top six runners. Salo, Gavuzzi, Umek, Richman, Simpson, and Granville simply had too much to lose and were too much in the public eye to risk instant disqualification if they were caught. The offenders were probably further back in the standings, with little hope of winning much prize money—these were the forgotten bunioneers who usually finished hours after the front-runners had crossed the line. The ranking of the perpetrators made little difference to the exhausted men who ran on their own two feet, especially after a day of being pelted by hailstones and drenched by torrential rains. These men resented any runner who cheated.

The fifty-fifth day of the race found the bunioneers headed deeper into the wild, lonely Texas highlands, running thirty-nine miles on a rough gravel road to Van Horn at four thousand feet, another barren watering hole on the road to El Paso.[14] There was no cloud cover to block the sun, and the temperature soared into the low nineties with only the occasional steer grazing on sparse grass to bear witness to their torment.[15] Umek and Richman braved the heat and hills to pace each other over most of the course before Umek went ahead to win the stage in about five hours.

Gavuzzi and Salo postponed their duel in these conditions and jogged along together—the sixth tie in as many days.[16]

The bunioneers and follies cast spent another chilly night in this high desert land. Perhaps some of the cast members sat around a campfire with the bunioneers, grumbling about Pyle or talking about what they would do when they finally reached Los Angeles, still more than eleven hundred miles and three weeks away.

Happy Birthday, Johnny

Day 56, 23 Men

On the fifty-sixth day of the race—May 25, 1929—Johnny Salo turned thirty-six on a lonely desert road to Sierra Blanca, an isolated supply town for the surrounding ranches at forty-five-hundred feet.[17] The year before, he had celebrated his birthday by leading the derby into his hometown of Passaic, New Jersey, with a solid hold on second place and its ten-thousand-dollar prize money on the second to last day of the 1928 race. In Passaic, fans were packed ten deep, firehouse whistles blew, and the town was draped in red, white, and blue bunting in his honor. At the finish, the superintendent of police announced Johnny's appointment as a Passaic police officer, a job given him by a grateful city for the goodwill and publicity he had brought to Passaic. He had previously found spotty employment in the nearby shipyards; now he had a permanent job. Johnny called it the happiest day in his life.[18]

In 1929, his birthday was much more subdued. He was running slowly on a poorly graveled road that dipped and climbed for thirty-four miles between four thousand and five thousand feet until it reached Sierra Blanca.[19] He was not among the lead runners in this stage race. No one lined the course to cheer him on or shout his name. The only sounds breaking the silence were the howling wind and his rhythmic footsteps along with those of his constant companion, bearded Pete Gavuzzi, who paced him, waiting for his chance to regain his front-runner status. Johnny had the lead by the narrowest of margins, twenty-one minutes after more than twenty-five-hundred miles of racing.[20]

While the bunioneers celebrated Salo's birthday in Sierra Blanca, Pyle was in El Paso, a city of one hundred thousand on the Rio Grande and the last stop in Texas. He was trying to persuade city leaders to make a cash contribution for the privilege of hosting his Bunion Derby.[21] Charley, his upper body encased in plaster from the accident, seemed more serious than before. He looked to *El Paso Times* reporter Mike Corona "like a different kind of a promoter. No brilliant silk tie or bandana, no checkered suit that catches the eye, and no salesmen talk. His short . . . silvery-white hair and conservative dress belie his profession. He looks more like a senator than a promoter."[22] Corona added, "He's reserved to the point of modesty. He doesn't rattle off lurid tales as most promoters do. He has his say and wastes little words."[23]

In El Paso, the master salesman had finally run out of "ballyhoo," that much-used word in the 1920s for sensational advertising and promotion. For the last two months, Pyle had kept up a constant banter about how he was seventy-five-thousand dollars ahead and planned to hold a third derby the next year.[24] In El Paso, he was uncharacteristically quiet. Even Charley had lost faith in his vision. He would scrape together enough money to get his derby to Los Angeles, but he knew that he could never pay his bunioneers, and he didn't have the guts to tell them.

Gentleman Johnny Ups the Ante

Day 57, 23 Men

The men returned to the extended distances with a 59.4-mile run that would take them to the western edge of Texas. From Sierra Blanca, the road climbed to a low pass before descending to the Middle Valley near the Rio Grande River, an area of extensive irrigated cultivation where, the *WPA Guide to Texas* said, "fields of alfalfa, orchards, patches of melons, gardens of roses, dahlias, and chrysanthemums, and vineyards" almost magically appeared out of the desert wastes and filled the air with the scent of growing things.[25]

With temperatures hovering near one hundred degrees, Johnny opened a new chapter in his battle with Gavuzzi. He ran hard, racing at an eight-minute-per-mile pace with Guisto Umek by his side.[26] The lead changed back and forth between them until Umek's trainer's car broke down, leaving the Italian without access to water. Salo would not abandon him, even though he lost precious time he might have gained against Gavuzzi. They paced each other for the rest of the race, stopping every mile to take food and water from Johnny's car.[27] Despite his noble gesture, Salo destroyed Gavuzzi, much as he had on the long leg to Dallas, adding fifty-five minutes to his lead, which now stood at one hour and sixteen minutes.[28] The effort, however, left him exhausted and complaining of stomach problems, the same ailment that had been the bane of his running before.[29] Salo had tempted fate by racing at the extended distances. It remained to be seen whether Pete would give him time to recover.

Pyle's follies finally had a chance to perform again at the night's control in Fabens, a prosperous little farm town that practiced its own form of frontier justice.[30] "They tried a fellow for killing his wife and lover," wrote Passaic's *Daily Herald*. The trial lasted a day and a half before the jury acquitted the killer "with honors." The *Herald* lamented, "You are a criminal if you steal a horse but just a bad egg if you shoot anybody."[31] The director general had not rejoined the derby that night but had continued west to Las Cruces and Deming, New Mexico, making arrangements for the derby's arrival there. He would rejoin the derby in El Paso.[32]

Tit for Tat. Gavuzzi Races to El Paso

Day 58, 23 Men

At 3,762 feet, El Paso is located at the lowest natural pass in this region of mountains and upland deserts, a funnel for western immigrants at the westernmost tip of Texas where it touches the borders of Mexico and New Mexico.[33] About 60 percent of the population was of Mexican descent, giving the town an international flair, with street signs in both English and Spanish.[34]

Pete Gavuzzi planned to get there in a hurry. Surrounded by irrigated fields with the sweet smells of alfalfa and the perfume of pear and apple flowers in the air, Pete answered Johnny's challenge. Newton wrote that he "took the bit between his teeth and bolted . . . and that was all any of the others saw of him till they [reached El Paso]."[35] The Englishman led the men up the valley highway along the banks of the Rio Grande with a steady downhill and dry heat hovering around one hundred degrees. With a wind at their backs and shade trees bordering the road, Pete could cope with the heat for the length of the thirty-mile course.[36]

Gavuzzi arrived at the control point in three hours and thirty-two minutes after averaging a six-minute-and-forty-seven-second-per-mile pace. He had run the distance at a sub-three-hour marathon pace and cut Johnny's lead to forty-two minutes.[37] The finish line was at the American side of the International Bridge across the Rio Grande that separated El Paso from Juarez, Mexico.[38] Pete was looking forward to crossing the bridge that night to buy a beer at a smoke-filled Juarez bar, away from the dry Prohibition America of 1929. That night, United States border agents spoiled his plans when they refused to allow non-Americans to cross into Mexico without a proper visa. This was much to the annoyance of Gavuzzi, who greatly missed his English beer.[39] That night, Newton wrote that his partner's archrival, Johnny Salo, "had a gay time" in Mexico, while Pete and the other non-Americans had to be content with "near beer" on the American side. Arthur quipped that the drink's inventor "was a mighty poor judge of distance."[40]

During his first visit to El Paso, Charley Pyle had taken full advantage of Mexico's close proximity to that Texas city. After the city's business community refused his request for a cash contribution, he decide to move his follies to a Juarez supper club, where he sipped "his first Manhattan cocktail in months and voiced a growing liking for the border country."[41] To an *El Paso Times* reporter, Charley looked peaceful but uncomfortable, with the upper part of his body, except for his left arm, encased in a cast. When asked about his arm, Charley replied, "It still hurts like hell" and lamented that that he hadn't driven the cab.[42]

The citizens of El Paso crossed the border in droves to see Pyle's show. One can imagine the scene: Jim Thorpe on a smoke-filled stage introducing the dancing debutantes before they performed the latest dance steps from New York; Spanish and English filling the air; the American bunioneers and their trainers scattered throughout the club; the beer and liquor flowing freely; and Pyle sitting at a front-row table, Manhattan cocktail in hand, sweating in his plaster cast twenty-five-hundred miles from New York City and dreading his inevitable reckoning in Los Angeles with a thousand miles more to go.

9

Across a Rough
and Unforgiving Land

El Paso, Texas, to Yuma, Arizona,
May 28–June 10, 1929

FOR THE NEXT FOURTEEN DAYS, the men would cross the arid wastelands of southern New Mexico and Arizona as they followed the old stagecoach route to Yuma—486 miles to the west. This section would challenge the men to the utmost and demand careful coordination between the runners and their support teams. Any mechanical breakdown or disruption might leave a bunioneer stranded without water in desert heat far from any town or help. Three unnamed bunioneers thought better of making the desert crossing and dropped out, leaving the field at twenty men.

The *El Paso Times* doubted that any of the runners would complete the journey with "hundreds of miles of arid lands of New Mexico and the burning deserts of Arizona and Southern California" still ahead of them.[1] This brutal land also offered an opportunity for those runners with well-organized teams and the guts to race in desert conditions. For Johnny Salo, it was his best chance to win the twenty-five-thousand-dollar first prize. With his power and bulldog determination and his wife, Amelia, and Bill Wicklund by his side, he had a chance to build a substantial lead before the derby reached the flat, coastal roads between San Diego and Los Angeles, where Pete Gavuzzi's speed and style would come into play.

Two other runners in the top ten were close enough to the man above them to have a realistic chance of advancing in the final weeks of the race. Paul Simpson trailed Sammy Richman in fifth by just five hours. While

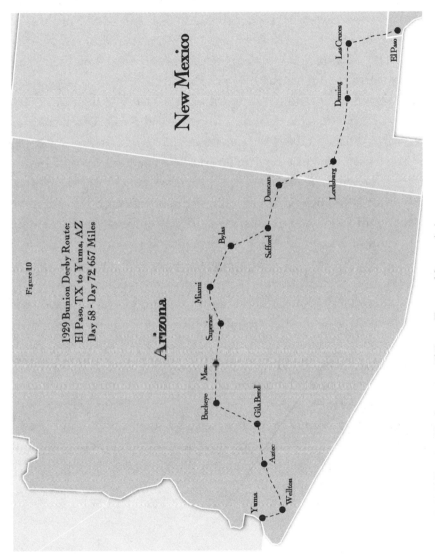

Figure 10

1929 Bunion Derby Route:
El Paso, TX to Yuma, AZ
Day 58 - Day 72 657 Miles

Arizona

New Mexico

Miami

Superior

Mesa

Buckeye

Gila Bend

Aztec

Wellton

Yuma

Bylas

Safford

Duncan

Lordsburg

Deming

LasCruces

ElPaso

Map 10. 1929 Bunion Derby route, El Paso, Tex., to Yuma, Ariz.

Richman and Guisto Umek had grabbed headlines in Texas with their stage wins, Simpson had kept methodically racing at a steady pace and cutting the gap between him and Richman, thanks in large part to the coaching skills of Charley Hart. The senior member of the Australian contingent, Herbert Hedeman, trailed the eighth-place holder, New Yorker Harry Abramowitz, by just three hours.[2] For Richman and Abramowitz, it meant casting a wary eye over their shoulders and not letting their challengers whittle away at the gap between them.

The rest of the top runners were already locked into their positions. Their goal was to avoid injury and run a conservative race. Umek, in third place, had no chance to breach the massive fourteen-hour gap that separated him from second place and had no possible challenge from Richman, who was fourteen hours behind him. Sixth-place holder Phil Granville was twenty-three hours behind Simpson in fifth and fifteen hours ahead of McNamara. Mike Joyce of Cleveland was firmly anchored in the top ten, twenty-eight hours behind Hedeman and nineteen hours ahead of eleventh-place Guy Shields of Baxter Springs, Kansas.[3] For these men, it was now a question of simply staying healthy until they reached Los Angeles.

Logic should have forced the remaining ten runners to drop out of the race. At least three did not have trainers, and all had little or no money left and no prospects of earning sufficient prize money.[4] To their hometown fans, most were a forgotten memory. All the ten had were each other and their commitment to finishing the race. These men were the shadow runners, far from reporters and the adoration of fans, enduring pain and suffering together while pushing themselves beyond what they had thought possible to emerge as ironmen. Each man had invested a piece of his soul in the race, and each was determined to see it through to the end, regardless of cost, regardless of pain.

Running in an Unfriendly Land

Days 59 and 60, 20 Men

The twenty bunioneers entered New Mexico from the south as they followed the northwest upstream course of the Rio Grande on a forty-four-mile run to Las Cruces, named for the scattered crosses that marked those killed in Apache raids before the town was settled in 1848. In 1929, it was a prosperous town that catered to surrounding farms that used water from the Rio Grande to irrigate their fields.[5] Johnny Salo led the race for thirty miles until Gavuzzi and Richman caught him. Then they ran together and finished in a three-way tie for first at an eight-minute-and-ten-second-per-mile pace.[6]

That night Salo's stomach cramps returned. They had plagued him ever since he had beaten Gavuzzi by almost an hour in the nearly sixty-mile race to Fabens, Texas, where he had disregarded their tacit agreement to refrain from racing beyond fifty miles.[7] The usually conservative Gavuzzi planned to take full advantage of Johnny's troubles on the next day's sixty-three-mile run to Deming, New Mexico. He ran over rolling desert terrain at a seven-minute-fifty-one-second pace per mile to shatter the New Jersey policeman's hold on first place and take a twenty-one-minute lead.[8] It remained to be seen what damage Pete might have done to his body by racing over what Newton called extended distances and whether Salo could recover quickly to challenge him the next day.

The people of Deming seemed particularly unimpressed by Gavuzzi's stage win and anything else associated with Pyle's "derby parade." The editor of the local newspaper, the *Deming Headlight,* claimed that most townspeople did not feel "particularly honored because the bunion derby used our village as a control point" and questioned the collective wisdom of the town's business community for paying for the privilege. Most of Deming's citizens agreed; they had little to do with the derby and avoided Pyle's vaudeville show.[9]

Charley's reception in Deming must have brought back unhappy memories of the welcome he had received when the derby crossed New Mexico on Route 66 the year before. After battling cold, wind, and high altitude in the Rocky Mountains, the exhausted bunioneers reached Albuquerque, the only major city on the route. The city's mayor banned the Bunion Derby from the town and accused his bunioneers of being little better than a gang of thieves. An indignant Pyle detoured his tired runners around the city and forced them to spend the night in a freezing, windswept camp several miles east of town. Charley, however, liked his creature comforts and slunk back to Albuquerque to take a room in one of its finest hotels.[10]

Johnny's Noble Gesture

Day 61, 20 Men

After the director general's unfriendly reception in Deming, he hoped to find a more receptive audience in Lordsburg at the end of a sixty-one-mile run. This was Johnny's chance to even the score. Salo, who had recovered from his bout of stomach cramps, pushed his exhausted rival to keep pace with him as they raced in desert heat. For the first thirty-two miles, they gradually gained about seven hundred feet in elevation until they crossed the Continental Divide.[11] The climb had been so slight that the men would have missed the landmark if a sign had not been placed there to mark the spot.[12] In 1928, it had been a far different story when Route 66 took the bunioneers across the Continental Divide near Flagstaff, Arizona, in the howling, freezing winds above seven thousand feet.[13]

Along this gentle grade, Gavuzzi's support truck broke down. This was Johnny's chance to recover all the time he had lost, but to do so would have meant leaving Pete on his own, without access to water. Johnny Salo would not win that way. He slowed down and the two men ran together at about a nine-minute pace, sharing Johnny's food and water and finishing together.[14] The New Jersey policeman showed his competitor's heart that day: he desperately wanted to win but not at the cost of abandoning his friend.

As Gavuzzi learned, any breakdown could be a disaster on these isolated, sweltering roads. With few towns between control points, it might be hours before a mechanic could be found to fix a car. To survive, a runner needed a trainer who was as adept at fixing an engine as he was at keeping the runner on pace. Salo's trainer, Bill Wicklund, fit both needs perfectly. He kept Johnny on track and his old 1921 sedan in working order while other trainers in more expensive and newer model vehicles experienced frequent breakdowns.[15]

The front-runners left the stage victory to fifty-five-year-old Herbert Hedeman, who completed the course in eight and a half hours. With the win, the bearded and haggard Hedeman moved into eighth place with its $1,750 in prize money.[16] The Australian was a talented and able runner, but age and poor coaching were against him. Across the country, he had wasted his chance to stay with the leaders by blazing to the front to win a stage race or two, only to tumble back into obscurity as he fought to recover his strength. He was now locked in eighth place, fifteen hours behind his countryman and traveling companion, Mike McNamara.[17] He had adopted Eddie Gardner's flashy and unproductive 1928 style and was in the position where the Sheik had finished, in eighth place.

Into Arizona

Day 62, 19 Men

On the last day of May, the bunioneers left Lordsburg, running on a loose, gravel road on a slight downhill grade with a stiff wind at their backs.[18] The men would bid a welcome goodbye to New Mexico, a state that had shown them only scorn and ridicule during both their 1928 and 1929 visits. For the next week and a half, the derby would travel across the length of southern Arizona. The men would follow the Gila River for most of the journey as they descended into the heat and dust of the Sonora Desert after making a side trip to the rich copper-mining towns of Superior and Miami to the north. The Gila was a historic river, the lifeline across the desert and the pathway to California for gold seekers and immigrants.[19]

Sammy Richman led the derby on this well-traveled path at about an eight-minute-per-mile pace, having recovered from the stomach trouble that had plagued him the day before. The three front-runners, Gavuzzi, Salo, and Umek, finished in a three-way tie twenty minutes behind him in Duncan, Arizona, a tiny outpost at about thirty-five hundred feet that survived as a shipping and supply center for the surrounding farms and ranches irrigated by the Gila River.[20] The town was too small for Pyle to stage his derby show.

Along the course, the derby lost one of its international runners, Colombo Pandolfi of Italy. He had struggled for days with an injury, a forgotten bunioneer far from the public eye who gamely stayed in the race. He "succumbed," a reporter wrote, "to the torrid sun and sand swept, arid land of the Great Southwest."[21]

On the first full day in Arizona, Johnny Salo felt better than he had in weeks. With his stomach cramps gone, he bolted across the start line with Paul Simpson by his side, both behind Sammy Richman.[22] Johnny was determined to finish the job he had started before Gavuzzi's car had broken down the day before. On the forty-three-mile run to Safford, Salo finished in second behind Richman, fast enough to cut Gavuzzi's lead by fifty-five minutes to just under a minute.[23] From past experience, Salo and Gavuzzi knew that racing beyond fifty miles had the potential for massive short-term gain but also left the body exhausted and slow to recover. After all the exertions by both men, little had changed in the standings.[24]

The close race led a *Los Angeles Times* reporter to write that the two front-runners were on course to provide "the most exciting finish in the history of foot racing."[25] The reporter was right. Nothing like this had happened before. For the previous sixty-three days and 2,753 miles, the two men had set records for pace and endurance. By Arizona, they had pushed the cumulative pace per mile to eight minutes and forty-seven seconds while averaging forty-five miles a day. They had run on average five miles a day farther than the bunioneers ran in 1928 and almost one minute and twenty seconds per mile faster than Andy Payne's winning pace.[26] Salo and Gavuzzi were the undisputed kings of long-distance running in 1929 and arguably in the history of ultramarathoning.

Richman Leads the Derby to Safford

Day 63, 19 Men

While the front-runners made headlines in the sports section of the *Los Angeles Times*, Sammy Richman led the derby to the finish at the Ramona Theater in Safford. His victory gave him a ten-hour lead over Simpson, effectively locking him into fourth place with its $3,500 in prize money.[27] After the race, he did not wait to celebrate with his brother, Morris. Over the last few weeks, the two had drifted apart. Morris had become an inseparable friend of the grizzled Polish runner George Jusnick, who was in his forties and almost twice his age. Jusnick ran to see America, stopping at every town along the course to get to know the local people, and he often finished with trinkets and presents given to him by his new American friends.[28] If Morris finished first, he would find a room for the two of them, and they would spend most of their free time together. A reporter believed it was a "case of 'misery loves company,'" with both men being days behind the front-runners and out of contention for any prize money.[29] Whatever the nature of the relationship, it left Sammy alone and further strained his meager finances.

For Charley Pyle, the stop in Safford meant a brief return to the glory days he had known in Texas as townspeople and farmers packed the Ramona Theater to watch his follies.[30] This infusion of cash helped cover some of his outstanding bills, but as the *Los Angeles Times* wrote, "Fate never intended to make the derby a monetary success."[31] Pyle no longer claimed that he had made seventy-five-thousand dollars from the race, as he had in Missouri and Oklahoma.[32] In Arizona, he adopted a more philosophical tone: "I am not concerned with making money," he said, adding that "if the race is brought to a successful conclusion then I will believe I have succeeded," but he still clung to his mantra that "the runners will all be paid . . . regardless of how much I lose—or make."[33] He had saved nothing and had no outside sources of funds, and yet he still assured his weary men that a pot of gold awaited them at the end of the long transcontinental rainbow in Los Angeles.

Close to Heaven

Day 64, 19 Men

The next day, the men would follow the Gila River on a thirty-seven-mile course to Bylas, a tiny town on the San Carlos Apache Indian Reservation.[34]

Sam Richman and Guisto Umek led the way, running at just over a seven-minute-per-mile pace to win the stage in four hours and twenty-two minutes. This was breathtakingly fast—the equivalent of running a marathon in about a three-hour pace on a dusty gravel road and in sweltering heat.[35] The two had written their own one-line rulebook for transcontinental racing: run fast in every stage race regardless of conditions or distance. They were reckless and flashy, risking all they had gained in their passion for stage-race glory.

Johnny finished just three minutes behind them, beating Gavuzzi by seventeen minutes and recapturing the lead.[36] After his victory, he soaked in the tranquil waters of the Gila River along with most of the other bunioneers.[37] This was Sunday, a day of rest in the reservation town of Bylas, "with," Newton wrote, "a tiny hotel, a large store, and a large number of Apaches."[38] Floating in the Gila in the warm afternoon sun, surrounded by green trees and irrigated fields, was as close to heaven as the bunioneers would ever get.[39] They were at peace, trying to forget that Pyle would send them on a brutal sixty-two-mile run the next morning. The derby was heading north to the rich copper-mining towns of Superior and Miami, where Charley hoped his follies would find a receptive audience among the lonely miners and mill workers before continuing west.

Dueling in the Mountains

Days 65 and 66, 19 Men

The nineteen surviving bunioneers left Bylas at six o'clock on a poorly surfaced road, headed for Miami at the base of the Pinal Mountains. Richman lead the way, but Gavuzzi was close behind. The Englishman maintained a terrific pace to finish in second place, beating Salo by a half hour and recapturing the lead.[40] The two front-runners had entered a dangerous world. At this late stage in the race, neither man could afford to let the other build up too great an advantage. Like the Cold War arms race, each escalation was answered by an equally dangerous response, which could result in a race-ending injury.

The bunioneers found Miami to be an ugly place with coal-black slag heaps and tailings stretching for miles around the city and with its miners and mill workers cramped into flimsily built and grimy houses.[41] In this isolated place, few reporters filed stories about the Bunion Derby and no record was left about how the follies fared in this rough town. One could imagine it received a warm reception among the lonely but cash-rich miners and mill workers. A good portion of these men probably welcomed the chance to listen to the all-girl band and gaze at the dancing debutantes as they pranced across the stage. In just two years, all but a handful of these men would be on the unemployment line as the Great Depression forced the closure of most of the mines.[42]

The bunioneers would spend one more day in mining country on a deceptively short twenty-one-mile course to Superior.[43] After leaving Miami at about thirty-four hundred feet, the men followed a winding, torturous road that incorporated a two-thousand-foot climb as the road spiraled upward before it plunged through a wild mountain gorge. The road was chiseled out of sheer canyon walls and bordered with marvelous and strange-looking spires and balanced rocks.[44] It was also a blood-soaked place. In the 1870s, the U.S. Army fought pitched battles with Apache warriors along this road. As the course neared Superior at 2,750 feet, it passed Apache Leap, a high, red-streaked cliff visible from the road, where cavalry soldiers had pursued seventy-five Apaches to the top of the cliff. The Apaches had jumped to their deaths rather than surrender.[45] On this strange and haunted road, Johnny Salo set reason aside and raced over its brutal grades in a tit-for-tat response to Gavuzzi's fast run to Miami. He tied for first-place honors with Sammy Richman and regained the lead by thirteen minutes.[46]

The men had reached Superior, another isolated mining town where Pyle's follies probably packed its theater to overflowing. Charley, however, was not there to see it. He had left for Los Angeles to make arrangements for his bunioneers to end their cross-country odyssey.[47] The end of the derby was now just two weeks away, but the men still faced the hellish heat of the Sonora Desert before they reached the palm-lined streets of Los Angeles.

22. Johnny and Amelia Salo, Superior, Arizona, 1929. Source: Guy Gavuzzi, private collection.

23. Close-up of Johnny Salo's muscular legs,
Superior, Arizona, 1929. Source: John Stone,
private collection.

The Right Karma in Mesa

Day 67, 19 Men

The bunioneers would experience their first true desert running this day
as they dropped out of the mountains at Superior. They would run fifty-
one miles to Mesa at 1,161 feet, losing almost 1,600 feet as the road reached
arid desert land—a barren place dotted with giant cacti, saguaro, and

ocotillo.[48] Fourteen miles east of Mesa, the course entered the Salt River Valley, whose cultivated, irrigated fields contrasted sharply with the surrounding desert.[49] As the men neared the city, several thousand spectators drove out to meet them and hundreds more lined Main Street in Mesa to the control point at the Mezona Theater.[50]

The first man they saw was the incredible flying cop from Passaic, who cruised across the finish line in the ninety-five-degree heat after six hours and thirty-five minutes of running—averaging seven minutes and forty-four seconds per mile.[51] He arrived so far ahead of the predicted arrival time for the first runner that city officials had no chance to prepare their welcoming ceremony.[52] Johnny extended his lead to one hour and thirteen minutes. He was "in great fettle today," a reporter wrote, "and his running over arid wastelands was a treat to behold."[53] At the finish, Salo told reporters that he had never felt better and wished the lap was longer.[54] There would be no more tacit agreements between the front-runners. Salo had adopted Richman's and Umek's guide to transcontinental racing: run fast all the time. The New Jersey policeman had put all his proverbial chips on the table. He had decided to win the race now, before Gavuzzi reached the flat roads between San Diego and Los Angeles, where the latter's form and speed would give him the edge. Salo's run to Mesa put him well on the way to reaching that goal.

Behind Salo came Paul Simpson, paced by a caravan of cars and a group of small boys.[55] With his win, he made up some of the time he had lost against Richman in the last few days, but he still trailed the New Yorker by ten hours. Fifty-five-year-old Herbert Hedeman finished next, strengthening his hold on eighth place.[56] After checking in, he quickly found a drugstore with a soda fountain and celebrated by drinking seven malted-milk drinks in a row.[57]

The right karma seemed to fill the air that day. The crowds were happy and excited. Some encircled Pyle's referee and All-American football star, Steve Owen, and last year's winner, Andy Payne. Most had souvenir programs that the two men were happy to sign. Other fans milled about the timekeeper's table, hoping for an autograph from one of the front-runners.[58] A local reporter was amazed at the recuperative powers of the bunioneers. After crossing the finish line, the men were "talking easily and breathing as naturally as if they had walked a block down the street," their skins tanned to a dark brown with most wearing just running shorts and a cap or a handkerchief around their heads.[59]

The fans would get a second chance to see the men as they emerged from their hotel rooms after they had showered and changed. Two hours after the race, that same reporter was shocked to find that most of the runners were out on the streets wearing ordinary clothes, "and except for their bronzed skins and the beards several of them were wearing, [they] could not have been distinguished from the ordinary residents of the valley."[60]

The *Mesa Journal-Tribune* noted that the city's business community was "well pleased" with the four-hundred-dollar contribution it had made to bring the derby to town. The derby brought Mesa "priceless advertising" by putting it in the national spotlight with more than three thousand daily newspapers featuring stories about the race. It had also brought people into town to fill its hotel rooms and restaurants.[61] Many of these visitors jammed the Mezona recreation hall to see Pyle's follies. The *Arizona Republican* called it "one of the finest vaudeville shows ever to visit the valley."[62] And Charley added to the goodwill by hosting fifty of the newspaper's paperboys at the show.[63] If only things had worked out like this across the country, the director general might have been in position to pay his ironmen their well-earned prize money, but like Umek's drive to overtake the front-runners, it was too little, too late.

Pyle had hoped to stop in Phoenix, thirteen miles farther west. It was the state capital and Arizona's largest city, with a population of about fifty thousand, so Pyle probably asked for a much higher contribution to bring his derby there. Charley held conference after conference with members of its business community, but they could not come to terms, and he sent the derby to Mesa instead.[64]

Superman

Day 68, 19 Men

The bunioneers left the city at six o'clock for a brutal fifty-four-mile run to Buckeye, another supply town for the surrounding farms irrigated by the

Gila River.[65] The run would test them with another day of desert running as the temperature approached one hundred degrees. With waves of heat radiating off the desert floor, the *Los Angeles Times* reported that Johnny Salo "continued his mad drive" as he raced over the dusty desert road at "a terrific pace" to capture his third straight victory and increase his lead to one hour and thirty-four minutes.[66] He completed the distance in just under seven hours while averaging seven minutes and forty-four seconds per mile.[67] Gavuzzi, who finished twenty-one minutes behind him, was in awe of Johnny's performance. "What a man," Pete declared as he checked into the control. "He is either not human or super-human."[68] "Johnny is all keyed up," wrote Arthur McMahon, and "he looks like the winner from this writer's angle."[69] With just a week and half to go, the flying cop from Passaic seemed like an unstoppable juggernaut. Salo had, however, proved himself to be all too human after similar feats of speed in the past. It remained to be seen whether stomach cramps would bring him back to earth.

The residents of Phoenix seemed totally oblivious of Johnny Salo's performance. Spurned by C. C. Pyle, who detoured the race around the city, the *Phoenix Evening Gazette* called the bunioneers the most "destitute . . . band of runners [that] could possibly be" and branded the Bunion Derby "a national joke."[70] The race was far from a national joke. The Bunion Derby dramatically changed the public's perception of human endurance and potential. When 199 naïve runners left Los Angeles in March 1928, few sportswriters thought any of them would reach New York City on their own two feet. And if they did, the writers feared that the strain of daily ultramarathons would stress their hearts and shorten their lives by years.[71] When fifty-five did finish and a team of doctors found no ill effects from the race, people had to reevaluate long-held notions about the potential of human beings to run extremely long distances safely.[72] In the 1929 edition of the Bunion Derby, transcontinental racing evolved from a test of survival to a true sport with two superstars, Salo and Gavuzzi, battling for first-place honors. And nothing the *Phoenix Evening Gazette* wrote would alter the fact or take away from the beauty and brilliance of their duel.

Into the Heart of the Sonora

Days 69 and 70, 19 Men

From Buckeye at 960 feet, the men headed into the heart of the Sonora Desert. For the next four days, the men would gradually lose elevation as they followed the Gila River to Yuma on the eastern bank of the Colorado River. Today the bunioneers raced to Gila Bend, another irrigated oasis at 777 feet.[73] Pete powered out of the start line, determined to prevent his rival from adding to his lead. Newton wrote that the two battled for the first twenty miles with the lead switching back and forth until the exhausted men quieted down and jogged along together.[74] A reporter worried about the ability of both men to sustain such effort for much longer: "Three or four more days of such running under similar conditions and either Salo and Gavuzzi, or perhaps both, will fall by the wayside."[75]

The men had picked a good point to halt their duel. At about mile twenty, desert mountains block the river's westward flow and force it south in the Great Bend for about twenty-five miles before it resumes its westerly course to the Colorado River. Along its banks, mesquite thickets, palo verde trees, ironwoods, and cacti filled the air with scent, and the sounds of birds and insects can be heard.[76] Along the way, the duo crossed a river bridge, once a dangerous river crossing where stagecoaches and wagon trains risked Indian attacks and floodwaters.[77] At the end of the bend is the town of Gila Bend, where farmers, with federal help, had built the Gillespie Dam to turn once-arid desert land into fields of cotton.[78]

On the seventieth stage race, with nine days left in the contest, the men plunged deeper into the desert inferno as temperatures pushed well above one hundred degrees. The forty-four-mile course dropped three hundred feet more into the tiny desert outpost of Aztec.[79] At about mile twenty-four, the bunioneers passed Sentinel Peak, an important landmark for travelers heading to California on the old stagecoach route to Yuma.[80] The first runner to see the site was Pete Gavuzzi, running at a "heart breaking pace" over the rough gravel road. His rival, Johnny Salo, was far behind, suffering from his old nemesis, stomach cramps.[81] The flying cop from

Passaic had tempted fate on his magnificent all-or-nothing runs over the previous three days, and now he was in agony as cramps wrenched his body on a dusty road in the scorching fire pit of the Sonora. His trainer, Bill Wicklund, could do little but shepherd him to the finish line and hope that Amelia Salo could, once again, bring him back to racing form.

At Aztec, Guisto Umek pushed past Gavuzzi in another of his flashy stage wins, although just a handful of grizzled townspeople witnessed the deed. Pete finished in second and cut seventeen minutes off Johnny's lead.[82] Derby officials reduced it by eight minutes more as a penalty for an unintended shortcut Salo took while leading the derby around Phoenix the day before.[83]

Running in Hell

Day 71, 19 Men

Johnny's troubles had reenergized his English rival. Pete knew that, at best, it would take Salo several days to return to racing form. With just eight days of racing left, he was on the verge of losing his hold on first place. Running in one-hundred-degree heat with his stomach in knots, he jogged along with Paul Simpson in fifth place.[84] The New Jersey policeman, however, had luck on his side on the forty-three-mile race to Wellton. In the brutal heat and dust, Gavuzzi could not run fast enough to capitalize on Salo's troubles. Any passing car kicked up clouds of dust that coated the men in dust and grit, turning them into sweat-stained ghosts while the sun beat down on the desert road.[85] With each passing mile, they lost altitude and descended deeper into the fire-hot desert as they passed isolated outposts like Mohawk, which had once been a rest station for the overland stagecoach line, and tiny Tacna, named for a Greek priest, Tachnapolis, who had ministered to the local Indians when the Spanish ruled the land.[86]

In similar desert conditions, runners in the 1992 trans-America footrace found that aid stations set up every two and a half miles were barely adequate when they crossed the Mojave Desert to the north. As temperatures reached one hundred degrees, sweat evaporated before it could cool the runners, energy bars turned to mush, and water and fluids left by the roadside became superheated. The bunioneers, like the 1992 runners, were in a death zone, with the skill of their trainers as their only lifeline.[87] Pete Gavuzzi emerged first from the desert heat, reaching Wellton in just over six hours, but he only managed to reduce Salo's lead to forty-nine minutes.[88] After Johnny stumbled across the finish line, Arthur McMahon gave his hometown friend little if any chance to hold first place. "With one grand gesture," he wrote, the Englishman "made the outlook for Salo appear dreary."[89] With just a week of racing left, Gavuzzi seemed well on his way to winning the Bunion Derby.

The men spent the night in tiny Wellton, named for several nearby deep wells that were sunk at the time of railroad construction in the late 1800s. A gravel road known as the Smugglers' Trail that ran south from town was reportedly used to bring liquor and narcotics from Mexico.[90] That night the follies performed, most likely in the open air under a cool desert sky.[91] Perhaps some of the smugglers attended the show along with an assorted cast of prospectors, farmers, ranch hands, and local Indians. While the show went on, Amelia Salo and Bill Wicklund worked desperately to keep Johnny in the race.

Charley Pyle was not with the derby that night. He was back in Los Angeles, finalizing his plan for the conclusion of his Bunion Derby. In a twist of fate, the Los Angeles Times was sponsoring the inaugural Los Angeles Marathon the following Saturday, with its star entry being Clarence DeMar, a six-time Boston Marathon winner and three-time member of the U.S. Olympic Team.[92] His entry had generated great interest in the race because he was the best-known marathon runner in the United States.[93] The Times hoped the marathon would help develop a cadre of talented West Coast runners to compete in the 1932 Los Angeles Olympic Games. "The Pacific Coast has never done much at longer distances in the Olympic Games," wrote a Los Angeles Times reporter, "and local track and field officials think it was about time something was done about it."[94]

Pyle wanted to give the city a weekend of marathon excitement by holding his race finale on Sunday with a 26.2-mile marathon race around a track in Wrigley Park, the home of the minor league Los Angeles Angels baseball team.[95] To do so, Charley needed his men to reach Los Angeles on Saturday night, which would force them to cover 322 miles in five days after they had completed the run to Yuma. After that, the bunioneers would need to run a gut-busting sixty-four miles a day for five days, a distance that would push them beyond the bearable into injury and exhaustion. Pyle knew what he was asking them to do and coldly predicted that only twelve of the nineteen would reach Los Angeles. Charley pointed out that for more than a week, nineteen men had held doggedly to the race, but he believed that they faced some of the hardest going yet in the race's final days.[96]

C. C. Pyle was hoping for a miracle. He planned to pack Wrigley Park to the top of its bleachers with paying fans and pull himself from the brink of bankruptcy. In Los Angeles, a reporter found him "terribly handicapped," with his upper body still encased in plaster, but his old enthusiasm was back. Charley told the reporter that he would "be all right financially if the fans turn out Sunday night to see the big wind-up at Wrigley Field."[97] The director general had regained his evangelical fervor for the Bunion Derby, but in the end he was just indulging in wishful thinking. Even if he filled all the park's ten thousand seats, he would never come close to covering the sixty thousand dollars he had pledged to pay out. He was asking his men to do the impossible, perhaps pushing some to the brink of death, as he clung to his last hope for redemption.

Charley played his part to the last as he tried to build up interest in the finale. He told the press that the fast times of the front-runners were due to a great international rivalry, with the foreigners—Gavuzzi, Umek, and Granville—banded together to beat the Americans—Salo and Richman.[98] When asked whether Johnny or Pete was the better runner, he would say only that he had spoken with each man privately, asking each who would win. Both replied "that they would beat the [other] guy if it was the last act of their respective lives."[99]

Across the Colorado River

Day 72, 19 Men

With a week left in the race, the men would run forty-four miles, which would take them through Yuma and across the Colorado River into

California, where they would make camp on the American side of the border across from Algodones, Mexico.[100] Pyle had planned to finish in Yuma, but he had failed to come to terms with local business leaders about making a contribution. After negotiations fell through, the Bunion Derby pushed on to the California side of the river. As he did in El Paso, Pyle held his follies on the Mexican side of the border, at the Oasis Café in Algodones.[101]

As the men ran, the day became mind-numbingly hot, with the temperature pushing past one hundred degrees. To survive, front-runner Pete Gavuzzi consumed three gallons of liquid a day, taking great gulps of orange juice every mile to counteract fluid loss.[102] In spite of the appalling conditions, he ran at an eight-minute, fourteen-second pace to win the stage. It was more than enough to assume the lead. He beat the ailing Johnny Salo by an hour and a half.[103] Pete was now the undisputed leader of the Bunion Derby and the odds-on favorite to collect the twenty-five-thousand-dollar first prize.

Arthur McMahon engaged in a bit of wishful thinking when he wrote that Salo had been "practicing a bit of psychology" to make Pete "run himself weary" in the past two days.[104] Johnny was not playing psychological games with his English rival. He had raced at the extended distances when conditions were at their worst. He had pushed himself too hard and was in danger of dropping out of the contest. If he had any hope of recovery, it lay with Amelia Salo and Bill Wicklund. Both were road-tested experts on attending to his needs. With those two by his side, Johnny had a fighting chance to stay in the race and hold onto second place.

That night in Algodones, Mexican beer and hard liquor probably flowed freely as the debutantes danced and the all-girl orchestra played while Mexicans and leather-tanned farmers from Yuma sat sipping their drinks at the café's bar. Some of the bunioneers were probably scattered in the audience as they nursed their beers and tried to forget what was coming: five days of hellish racing before they reached Los Angeles. They would average sixty-four miles a day, twenty more than they had averaged since the race had begun seventy-two days before. The men were about to cross the Rubicon as they pushed themselves beyond the known limits of human endurance.

10

"Overcoming the Killing Distances"— The Last Five Days to Los Angeles

Yuma, Arizona, to Los Angeles, June 11–June 15, 1929

AFTER SEVENTY-TWO DAYS of trial and error, the front-runners had a fairly clear idea about how far they could race without pushing themselves to the point of exhaustion. In other words, they had found that vague frontier, the line where sustainable racing was no longer possible if they pushed much beyond it. As both Pete Gavuzzi and Johnny Salo learned in New Mexico and Arizona, it was somewhere beyond fifty miles. When one of the front-runners crossed this line, he often gained an hour or more of time over his opponent, only to lose that or even more after his exhausted body rebelled against racing for the next several days.

The remaining five days of racing would all take place well beyond fifty miles, transforming the Bunion Derby from a footrace into a struggle for survival, a dead-man's march to Los Angeles. Arthur Newton wrote, "A man has only one anxiety now, and that is to be sure of overcoming the killing distances."[1] The prudent approach for the nineteen surviving men would have been to simply walk or jog to Los Angeles, saving any racing for the marathon finale on Sunday. That way, they would protect their prize money and avoid an injury that might put them out of the race.

Such advice, however, was not what a competitor like Johnny Salo wanted to hear. He was determined to beat his English rival at any cost and would risk the ten-thousand-dollar second-place prize money to do so. Johnny could not wait until Los Angeles to challenge Gavuzzi. He trailed him by forty-nine minutes, giving Pete a comfortable margin that

150

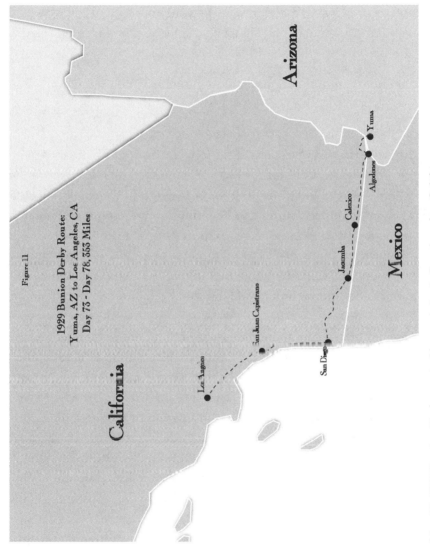

Figure 11

1929 Bunion Derby Route:
Yuma, AZ to Los Angeles, CA
Day 75 - Day 78, 355 Miles

California

Arizona

Mexico

Los Angeles

San Juan Capistrano

San Diego

Jacumba

Calexico

Algodones

Yuma

Map 11. 1929 Bunion Derby route, Yuma, Ariz., to Los Angeles, Calif.

he could use to hold off any charge Salo might make in Wrigley Park.[2] If Salo wanted to win, he had to shake off the stomach cramps and push Gavuzzi across the desert, over the mountains to San Diego, and up the coast to Los Angeles. The New Jersey policeman would have to search for a new level of power and endurance. He would need to push beyond the known frontier of human potential if he wanted to win the Bunion Derby.

Guisto Umek: Fast and Relentless

Day 73, 19 Men

The runners had their first taste of the longer distances on the fifty-nine-mile run to Calexico, California, a town of about six thousand in the fertile Imperial Valley that was made to bloom with irrigated water.[3] They would face another day of desert running on a dusty gravel road with temperatures hovering in the midnineties. Hundreds of automobiles drove out from Calexico to meet them, kicking up clouds of dust and grit as they went. The *Calexico Chronicle* wrote that "a real old fashioned sandstorm" added to the discomfort as it lashed the men.[4]

Guisto Umek led the field as he raced across the desert at a seven-minute-and-forty-second-per-mile pace, fast and relentless, seemingly unfazed by a near miss with an oncoming car on the course.[5] Pete Gavuzzi followed, with Johnny Salo close behind after Amelia had once again brought him back to racing form. The flying cop tried repeatedly to pass Gavuzzi, but the Englishman stubbornly refused to let him do so.[6] As the estimated time for the runners to reach Calexico neared, a city caller asked a local phone operator to place a call to the Bond Corner store on the outskirts of town to see whether the runners were approaching. The operator, however, thought the person said "onion derby," and the effort was lost.[7]

The *Calexico Chronicle* reported that "the sturdy bronzed and hatless Italian" was the first runner to reach the city, arriving at about one in the afternoon after running for seven and a half hours in the desert sun. The first thing the citizens of Calexico saw was his trainer and pace car leading him into town. A few minutes later Guisto appeared, described by the

Chronicle as "a clean shaven man of moderate proportions but compact and well formed."[8] His pace car parked near the finish, and his trainer, "a strapping athletic New Yorker in a red and black jersey," got out and trotted along with his charge carrying a bottle of orange juice from which Umek "took one generous swallow as he pounded the pavement toward [the finish at] the chamber of commerce office" with a big grin on his face.[9] He had won again, an enigma, a man in love with racing and willing to risk all he had earned for the thrill of stage-race glory.

Forty-six minutes later, Gavuzzi, Salo, and Richman crossed the line. Johnny had given Pete a hard fight, but he had to settle for a three-way tie that left the Englishman's forty-nine-minute lead intact.[10] Arthur McMahon reported that Salo remained upbeat and determined to "dethrone the fleet-footed Pete."[11] He spent the afternoon across the border in Mexicali, Calexico's neighboring town, "recovering his strength," probably by sipping a beer or two in a quiet Mexican bar. His English rival, still lacking a visa to cross the border, had to settle for "near beer" in Calexico.[12] The rest of the bunioneers continued to trickle into town throughout the afternoon, wearing what the *Chronicle* described as "abbreviated track suits and their bare arms and legs burned to a dark brown," with none showing any distress.[13] The reporter's perception would be tested the next day as the men left the desert and began to ascend California's coastal mountains, the last barrier between the runners and San Diego.

Fifty-eight Miles and 2,800 Feet to Jacumba

Day 74, 19 Men

On their second day in California, the bunioneers left the searing desert heat and began climbing: fifty-eight miles of spirit-crushing effort that started with the by-now-familiar desert running and ended with a murderous, leg-busting ascent up arid mountainsides. From Calexico, the course would take the men to El Centro, a city of eight thousand, fifty-two feet below sea level, and then west across desert country as they passed a scattering of desert hamlets like Seeley—at twenty-six feet above sea level, once an old stopping place for stagecoaches on the way to San

Diego—before reaching Superstition Mountain, rising out of the desert floor.[14] At about mile twenty-nine, the men climbed out of the Imperial Valley, gaining almost eight hundred feet by the thirty-second mile, and then climbed two thousand feet over the next eleven miles before they reached the control point at Jacumba, at twenty-eight hundred feet.[15]

This brutal course offered Salo his best chance to make up time against his English rival. Across America, the flying cop from Passaic had thrived in conditions that Gavuzzi abhorred—ankle-deep mud, thunder-storms, desert heat, and mountain climbs. Salo had blasted through the worst Mother Nature had thrown at him with his intense, forward-look-ing stare. It remained to be seen whether Johnny had any strength left to use the fifty-eight-mile run to his advantage.[16]

As Salo waited for Steve Owen's command to start the race at six o'clock, he seemed, to Arthur McMahon, "quiet and reserved, his attitude generally when he intends to run hard." Umek took the early lead, but Gavuzzi and Salo passed him near Seeley as the rising desert sun beat down on them and sent the temperature soaring into the nineties. When the two reached the mountain grades, Johnny took the long steep hills at a fast gait while Gavuzzi walked up most of them.[17] The climb was agony for those men nursing injured feet, like Philip Granville, who winced noticeably when he happened to step too heavily to one side on his still-healing foot. The tough Canadian just had to run through the pain as he made his ascent to Jacumba.[18] The youngest member left in the race, the nineteen-year-old New Yorker Joe Spangler, struggled up the grades with his fallen arches. He had entered the derby seeking adventure and mate-rial for a book he planned to write.[19] Arthur Newton was there to pace the aspiring author to the finish and keep his spirits up. Newton, wrote the *Calexico Chronicle*, "is a fine gentleman and loved by every man in the race. He coaches them all and pals with them."[20]

Johnny Salo was the first to reach the control point in just over nine hours, at a nine-and-a-half-minute-per-mile pace. Umek finished ten min-utes behind him. The pace, by derby standards, was slow, but given the harrowing climbs, it was more than enough to cut twenty-nine minutes off Gavuzzi's lead. The New Jersey policeman was now just twenty minutes behind the Englishman, with three days of tough running to go before the marathon finale in Los Angeles.[21] Johnny seemed poised once again to wrench the twenty-five-thousand-dollar first prize from Gavuzzi's grasp. His Passaic fans concurred and began making preparations for a victory celebration when he returned.[22]

Jacumba was a perfect place for the men to rest after their ordeal. It was a resort town perched on the hills, just two hundred yards from the Mexican border. The cool air and its mineral baths had made it a favorite getaway for farmers and townspeople from the Imperial Valley, whose summer homes dotted the mountain slopes.[23] That afternoon, most of the runners soaked in the mineral baths and tried to forget about the next day's seventy-eight-mile run—a race that would take them over the mountains to San Diego.[24]

A Heaven of Green

Day 75, 19 Men

From Jacumba, at twenty-eight-hundred feet, the men began what the *Los Angeles Times* called "the most grueling lap of the entire journey."[25] They climbed rapidly into the Cleveland National Forest on weary legs, most walking or jogging slowly up the steep grades and putting the heat and dust of the Sonora Desert behind them as they reached four thousand feet at Laguna Junction, twenty-six miles into the race. They then entered a heaven of green as they ran through a mixed forest of pine, oak, chaparral, cedar, willow, and alder, which filled the air with the scent of growing things in the cool mountain air. From there, they began a brutal descent as they passed through Alpine at 1,860 feet, where they peered down on the coastal fog belt that enveloped the Pacific. The last miles took them through farms and orchards in the El Cajon Valley until reaching San Diego and the sea.[26]

Salo and Gavuzzi did not challenge each other that day. The *Los Angeles Times* wrote that the two "are plainly saving themselves—if you call running seventy-eight miles a saving occupation—for the final spurt at Wrigley Park."[27] They jogged along together at a ten-minute pace, walking the steepest of the hills, and left the stage victory to Guisto Umek, who seemed to revel in the act of the leading the derby parade to San Diego.[28]

In 1929, San Diego was the third-largest city in California with a population of about 148,000. Blessed with a natural harbor that served as a base for the United States Navy and fleets of fishing boats, it still retained an easygoing spirit from its Spanish colonial days.[29] The citizens of San Diego welcomed the derby's arrival as a happy distraction from the daily routine of unsolved murders and the never-ending run-ins between government agents and alcohol smugglers.[30]

The Italian raced down Broadway Hill in San Diego "like," the *Los Angeles Times* wrote, "the proverbial prairie fire," until one of his shoes wore out at Twentieth and Broadway. After a quick change of footwear, he finished an hour before Salo and Gavuzzi, at around five o'clock. He was given a tremendous cheer by the immense throng that jammed the streets around the control point at the Waldorf Hotel owned by Francis Patrick Shanley, who agreed to put up Pyle's "whole troupe" for the night.[31] For Shanley, wrote the *San Diego Union*, "likes nothing better than a crowd, even a crowd of tired, unshaven foot tourists."[32] Umek was quick to take up Shanley on his offer of free room and board. He was fed and in bed before Gavuzzi and Salo reached the finish line.[33]

Johnny was happy to have put the desert behind him and loved the mountain views. "The scenery was beautiful," he shouted to reporters as he crossed the finish line.[34] Elmer Cowley, from Clifton, New Jersey, was thinking far more about his aching knee than the scenery as he limped into town late that night. Sammy Richman's brother Morris brought up the rear, crossing the finish line around ten that night after almost seventeen hours on the road.[35]

With just two days before the marathon finale, speculation was rampant in the press about who was the favorite to win the race. Arthur McMahon, who knew both men well, made the most insightful comments. He thought Salo needed to erase Gavuzzi's twenty-minute lead and build up one of his own before the marathon race. "Johnny," he wrote, "must open things up to gain a safety margin to hold off Pete in the marathon run," believing that "the diminutive" Gavuzzi is too speedy on a one-day run to let Salo deprive him of the first-prize money.[36] *Los Angeles*

Times sportswriter Braven Dyer believed the race would come down to a battle between finesse and raw power. The power was with the 145-pound Passaic policeman—"powerfully built, having legs like a football tackle and shoulders that you generally find on an All-American halfback." The finesse was with the 118-pound bewhiskered Englishman—"twenty pounds lighter than Salo and appears to be a more polished runner."[37]

Up the Coast on 101

Day 76, 19 Men

The men left San Diego to begin another "killing distance," a sixty-five-mile race to San Juan Capistrano, famed for its ruined mission that was once the glory of Spanish California. Its seven domes and tall belfry could be seen from ten miles away until an earthquake leveled most of the mission in 1812.[38]

Over the preceding two days, the nineteen bunioneers had been pushed to the breaking point, their legs numb with pain. Salo and Gavuzzi walked most of the way, like two zombies, one refusing to let the other out of his sight.[39] They marched and stumbled on, passing many seaside towns as they trudged north on Highway 101, the great coastal road linking the Pacific Coast states of California, Oregon, and Washington. Sixteen miles into the course, they climbed the steep bluffs to Torrey Pines Mesa and nine miles later passed through Encinitas, noted for its bulbs and flowers. On and on they walked until the town of San Clemente came into view, fifty-eight miles into the race.[40] "Here," wrote Arthur McMahon, "as darkness settled, the monotonous rumble of the ocean broke the silence. The flying cop braced himself" and began to run.[41] His startled opponent tried to give chase, but he no longer had the leg strength and could not keep pace as he watched Johnny disappear into the growing darkness in what Arthur McMahon called "probably the most bitterly fought duel in modern foot racing."[42] Newton would later claim that Gavuzzi ruptured the Achilles tendon in his left leg as he fought savagely to catch up, though years later, in an interview with Harry Berry, "Gavuzzi sportily refused to use it as an alibi and declined to confirm it."[43]

Johnny Salo did what he had to do. He needed to cut the twenty-minute gap between them or he had little or no chance of winning the marathon race on Sunday. Using his last bit of strength, he pushed his exhausted body to run the last seven miles and cut an additional ten minutes off Gavuzzi's lead. He covered the sixty-five miles in thirteen hours and twenty minutes and averaged just a twelve-and-a-half-minute pace per mile, his slowest pace of the entire derby, but he still pushed the stage race to the sublime after his seven-mile run from San Clemente.[44]

Johnny showed no outward signs of distress as he finished, but his rival did. "Gavuzzi," McMahon wrote, "his face lined from exhaustion" as he crossed the line, smiled wearily, reached for a cigarette, and then wandered off to get a rubdown before dinner. The reporter was awed by the "beautiful battle" that had taken place, believing that "tomorrow these boys are likely to establish history with their duel."[45]

Both men ate quickly and then went to bed, lulled to sleep by the mission bell announcing each new hour. The dawn would come soon, and they would have to run sixty-two miles more before reaching the palm-lined streets of Los Angeles.[46]

Homecoming

Day 77, 19 Men

The leg to Los Angeles was the last of the massive, extended distances. Guisto Umek, the gifted Italian runner who never seemed to tire of winning stage races, blazed through the sixty-two miles in an eight-and-one-half-minute pace that still left him mired in third, twelve hours behind Johnny Salo.[47] The two front-runners finished an hour later in just under ten hours. Herbert Hedeman, who had lost three hours to Harry Abramowitz the day before, finished in fourth place with the New Yorker finishing far to the rear, ending any hope he had of catching the Australian and recapturing eighth place.[48]

Salo and Gavuzzi would walk and jog the entire sixty-two-mile course together in a nine-and-one-half-minute-per-mile pace, content to let the lead stand at nine minutes, fifty-six seconds, all that separated

Johnny Salo from Pete Gavuzzi after 522 hours of running over seventy-seven days.[49]

A photo in the *San Francisco Chronicle* shows the two walking together toward the finish line in Los Angeles, a police motorcycle escort on either side of them, a flotilla of cars behind them, and a man with a megaphone riding the hood of the lead car describing the action to the crowds. Johnny Salo is on the right, his face and body tanned leather brown, a cap on his head, bandanna tied around his neck, and his loose-fitting tank top revealing the powerful muscularity of his upper body. He wears number 107 pinned to his shirt, with a police badge sewn to his white shorts above his well-muscled legs. He looks determined and confident that he will win the Bunion Derby at the next day's finale at Wrigley Park. Gavuzzi to his left is much thinner and a bit shorter, his dark hair and beard nicely trimmed, in sharp contrast to the whiteness of his face that must have come from wearing a hat during most of his desert runs, for his exposed arms and legs are burnt just as dark as Salo's face. He seems to be enjoying the stage. He looks like a movie star, dashingly handsome with a bandanna tied around his neck, white T-shirt and shorts with number 103 pinned to his chest, his exposed legs much thinner, almost elegant, when compared with his rival's.[50]

The *San Diego Union* wrote the closing epitaph for the next-to-last day of the Bunion Derby: "The survivors of the transcontinental bunion derby today trailed into this Los Angeles suburb [of Huntington Park]—the winner still in doubt."[51] The *San Francisco Examiner* was certain that Charley Pyle would pay the derby winner for his labor. "That is quite certain," it proclaimed, adding that "he paid off last year when nine out of ten suspicioned [sic] that he couldn't."[52] Salo and Gavuzzi certainly hoped so.

The men would spend the night before the finale in Huntington Park, a residential community just four miles away from Wrigley Park, where Salo and Gavuzzi would end their duel the next night. They had reached Los Angeles, a massive, sprawling city of 1.2 million that had doubled in population during the decade to become "a City of Dreams," the new mecca of the West. Los Angeles was many things: the center of the movie industry, the nation's fifth-largest manufacturing center, an oil town, a farm town, a banking and trade center, and a busy seaport. Los Angeles was a city in the making, the growing, vibrant heart of California in the waning days of the Jazz Age.[53]

The Bunion Derby had come home. Pyle had begun his odyssey with trans-America running more than a year before, when 199 naïve and hopeful men had left the city for the first race to New York. Most of the men who arrived in Los Angeles in 1929 were veterans of both races, steely-tough and confident bunioneers after having pushed their bodies through test after test of courage during two trans-America races. The last Bunion Derby would end on the morrow—and with it, most of their hopes and dreams.

11

The End of the Rainbow

Los Angeles, June 16, 1929

Day 78, 19 Men

The bunioneers had reached the end of the long transcontinental rainbow in Los Angeles as they rested for the night in Huntington Park. They had been chasing Pyle's "pot of gold" for the last seventy-seven days. All that remained was the seventy-eighth and last stage race, the 26.2 mile marathon finale at Wrigley Park—131 laps around an outdoor track.[1]

The front-runner, Pete Gavuzzi, held a hairbreadth lead over Johnny Salo, just nine minutes and fifty-six seconds after 552 hours and 3,523.4 miles of running, but that tiny margin made the Englishman the odds-on favorite to win the twenty-five thousand-dollar prize.[2] If Gavuzzi had not ruptured his Achilles tendon as Newton claimed, and if he had had the leg strength to race, his stylish, almost effortless form should have allowed him to hold off any charge Salo might make in a marathon foot-race. Sportswriter Braven Dyer of the *Los Angeles Times* concurred, writing that if the Englishman "doesn't win tonight's wind-up over the marathon distance and thus become the 1929 distance champion we'll be very much surprised."[3]

At about 7:40 P.M., the men received the starting command and began the four-mile run to Wrigley Park. At that moment, the clarity of events ended and a shroud of bitterness descended upon the 1929 Bunion Derby that remains to this day.

The standard view of what happened next comes from three sources: Newton's 1940 autobiography, *Running in Three Continents*; interviews given by Gavuzzi, in Bruce Tulloh's book, *Four Million Footsteps: Los Angeles to New York—The Famous Runner's Account of His Record Breaking Marathon*, published in 1970; and Harry Berry's 1990 self-published history of the 1928 and 1929 races, *From L.A. to New York, from New York to L.A.* Johnny Salo and Charley Pyle might have collaborated on their story or given their own version of events, but both died in the 1930s and did not leave any written account of the race.

In Newton's and Gavuzzi's renditions, the referee called the roll at 7:30 P.M. at Huntington Park and reiterated that the four-mile run would determine only the starting position for the marathon run and would not count toward the cumulative time total. Once all nineteen men had arrived at the park, the men would line up in their order of finish in the four-mile race and then begin the 131-lap race.[4]

Once the referee gave the starting command, Johnny Salo bolted across the start line in company with Abramowitz and Richman.[5] The latter two might have been motivated to race by Pyle's purported offer of additional prize money to the top finishers in the last leg of the race.[6] Three mounted motorcycle officers, with sirens blaring, cleared a path through the mass of traffic for the three lead runners—a pocket of speed as the traffic closed in behind them.[7] "Once started off," wrote Newton, "Salo moved at . . . a tremendous rate actually well over ten miles an hour."[8]

With almost a ten-minute lead, Gavuzzi started out slowly, not wanting to waste energy racing for the sake of the few seconds' advantage he might gain from a good starting position at Wrigley Park. He jogged in the center of a four-man box of bunioneers—Granville, Umek, Simpson, and Hedeman—who ran to protect him from a race-ending accident on the traffic-jammed street.[9] In an interview with Bruce Tulloh, Pete said, "They told us the race would start when we got down there, so I didn't hurry meself."[10] Without the police escort, Gavuzzi and his four companions had to fight through traffic and then were stopped for several minutes while a freight train crossed the road.[11]

In the meantime, the three Americans, Salo, Richman, and Abramowitz, reached the stadium and were surprised, wrote Berry, to see an official waving them onto the track to begin the marathon race.[12] Abramowitz reached the stadium first, with Richman close behind and Salo just behind Richman in thirty-two minutes, forty-five seconds, running at about an eight-minute-per-mile pace.[13]

When Pete entered the park, he was horrified to see Salo racing around the track "like a man demented."[14] As the Englishman began his laps, he shouted above the roar of the crowd to an official for some idea of what remained of his time advantage. Newton dashed down to the track and told him to forget about the mix-up and concentrate on catching Salo.[15] By then, Johnny had reduced Pete's lead by half; by the sixth mile, he had almost drawn even; and by the twelfth, he was four minutes ahead. At about the half-marathon point, Salo began to tire, and his pace slackened.[16] Gavuzzi sensed it and made his move, but Johnny fought back, sweat stained, grimacing in pain, trying desperately to hold off the Englishman's charge.[17] It took Pete four miles to cut Johnny's lead to about three minutes in front of a crowd of ten thousand, all on their feet and screaming in raw excitement.[18] "The din was almost continuous," wrote the *San Diego Union*, "and the crowd refused to subside."[19]

During the final miles, the New Jersey policeman somehow found new reserves of strength and picked up the pace until it was obvious, wrote Berry, to "everyone that Salo could not be beaten."[20] Gavuzzi sprinted occasionally, but his morale was broken. He ran with his head down, eyes on the ground, his fingers clenched nervously, still trying valiantly to catch his American opponent, but in the words of Arthur McMahon, "It was the Flying Cop's night and he gave Los Angeles sports fans the most marvelous exhibition of powerful running it has been their pleasure to behold."[21]

With ten thousand fans cheering, Johnny crossed the finish line to win the Bunion Derby by what the *Los Angeles Times* called "a decidedly scant advantage" of two minutes, forty-seven seconds.[22] Salo had accomplished what most sportswriters thought he could never do: erase Gavuzzi's ten-minute lead to win the twenty-five-thousand-dollar first prize. Johnny ran the 30.2 miles (the four miles from Huntington Park plus the 26.2-mile marathon race) at a seven minutes-thirty-five-seconds-per-mile pace, finishing in three hours, forty-eight minutes, incredibly fast after what the bunioneers had just been through in California.[23] Sammy Richman finished in second just sixteen seconds later, with Gavuzzi in third at four hours, one minute, and twenty seconds.[24]

Amelia Salo and Bill Wicklund met the champion at the finish: Amelia was weeping and Wicklund's eyes were filled with tears. Johnny kissed his wife, his face wreathed in smiles.[25] Under floodlights and with flash cameras popping, the crowd surged out on the field to hail the newly crowned king. With one arm over Wicklund's shoulder and the other around his wife, Johnny credited Amelia with his victory.[26] Wicklund later recalled that "we went nearly crazy that night Johnny passed Gavuzzi in the last lap in Los Angeles. What a heart that man has—and what stamina."[27] When the official result was announced, a tremendous ovation erupted from the crowd. Johnny was full of praise for his opponent: "I am not better than Gavuzzi. It simply happened that I was in better shape on the last lap. Any other night he might have beaten me."[28]

News of his victory spread quickly to Passaic. A switchboard operator stayed on duty for an extra two hours to handle the surge in calls, which was three thousand above the normal level.[29] Salo's boss, Passaic Superintendent of Public Safety John Turner, stayed up until four in the morning waiting to hear whether Johnny had won. Once he heard the good news, he fired off a congratulatory telegram: "Good boy, Johnny, Congratulations! I knew you would do it."[30]

Gavuzzi was crushed by the result. Accordingly to Tulloh, he would tell reporters only that he wished to see a race official to seek an explanation for why Pyle had allowed Salo, Richman, and Abramowitz to begin the marathon before the rest of the runners had assembled at the park. An hour later, still seeking an official to explain the change, he conceded defeat and returned to his hotel room.[31] Newton told him, "You were robbed Peter. That stretch to the stadium should not have been included."[32] Gavuzzi wanted to make an official protest, but Newton counseled him, "It's no good Peter. The Americans will say you are a bad sportsman. You'll be letting your country and the Empire down."[33] Gavuzzi kept quiet and let Salo have his victory. In 1931, Newton would say only that Pete "suffered amazingly bad luck—he was stopped by a traffic jam actually in Los Angeles on the last day of the race when he had only minutes to spare and was beaten at the finish by two minutes only."[34] It was not until years later, with both Pyle and Salo dead, that Newton and Gavuzzi made their claims about the disputed four miles to the stadium.

This much is clear about Gavuzzi's and Newton's accounts of events: they are not supported by first-hand accounts of the race. In articles about the finale by Braven Dyer in the *Los Angeles Times* and by Arthur McMahon in Passaic's *Daily News*—both men who were at Wrigley Park—neither mentioned the disputed finish.[35] Further, in surviving newspapers from the runners' hometowns, none mention the controversy in their accounts of the finish or in subsequent interviews with the runners when they returned home.[36] These newspapers included Passaic's *Daily News* and *Daily Herald* for Salo; the *Burlington Daily Times* for Paul Simpson; the *Santa Rosa Free Democrat Press* for the top rookie finisher, Edwin Harbine; and the *Daily Herald* for Clifton, New Jersey, runner Elmer Cowley. Newspaper reporters in general took a dim view of Charley Pyle as an exploiter of athletes for "the almighty buck." Any runner, especially Simpson, who was part of Gavuzzi's protective box would have found a sympathetic ear with a reporter had he complained about an unfair finish. The two men who might have shed some light on the matter, Salo and Pyle, left no written account of the last day's events. All that survived are Newton's and Gavuzzi's accounts and newspaper stories written at the time of the race.

Also, it made no sense for Johnny to race to the stadium unless he believed the four miles to Wrigley Park would count in the cumulative total. After five days of brutally long runs in California, he was exhausted, having pushed himself far beyond what even he thought it possible to endure. Salo knew that he would need every bit of strength he had left to have any hope of beating Gavuzzi at the park. Why would he run fast for four miles if his only payoff would be to save several seconds by lining up ahead of his rival? He would have been far better off had he jogged along with Pete and arrived together with him, warmed up and ready to race.

In addition, Gavuzzi's and Newton's accounts cast Salo in a very unflattering light by implying that he knowingly cheated Pete out of the twenty-five-thousand-dollar first prize. This characterization is sharply at odds with Johnny's past actions. Salo was widely admired by his fellow bunioneers for his honesty and sense of fair play.[37] Johnny proved it in New Mexico when Gavuzzi's trainer's vehicle broke down. Up to that point in the race, the Englishman had been struggling to stay up with him, and Johnny seemed poised to leave him behind. Pete's misfortune gave Salo his chance to build a significant lead, but he would not leave his rival stranded without water. He stopped racing immediately and they jogged together, sharing the food and water from his trainer's car. Johnny did the same thing on the race to Fabens, Texas, when he was far ahead of Gavuzzi and racing in company with Guisto Umek. When Umek's trainer's car broke down, Johnny slowed down and paced Umek to the finish but still managed to beat Gavuzzi by a wide margin. If Johnny had kept racing, he might have lowered his cumulative time enough to make discussions over the disputed finish a moot point.

Finally, one would expect Newton and Gavuzzi to avoid Salo if they believed he had cheated Pete out of his prize money, which they had promised to share before they entered the derby. The contrary happened. In September, the two Englishmen were guests at Johnny's home in Passaic for several weeks and both had nothing but kind words to say about him in the press.[38] Johnny was a fierce competitor, but he was also a fair man who would not cheat a friend out of his prize money.

Contemporary accounts and all the evidence available suggest that Johnny Salo believed the last stage race started in Huntington Park and that he went to his grave believing that he had won the 1929 Bunion Derby fairly. Gavuzzi may have thought it was a warm-up run, but Salo did not. Johnny, in company with Sammy Richman and Harry Abramowitz, ran hard the entire four miles to the park with three mounted motorcycle policemen blazing a trail through the traffic. Gavuzzi, in his box, started out slowly and was trapped in traffic. He lost almost half his lead in the run to the stadium. He lost the rest of it and the championship during the 131-lap, marathon-distance race in Wrigley Park.[39] Salo beat Gavuzzi by less than three minutes to end what was perhaps the greatest footrace of the twentieth century.[40] Up until Salo's untimely death in 1931, there was never any controversy about the finish in newspapers or from Gavuzzi or Newton. They made their charges public only after Johnny was dead and gone.

Why Johnny thought one thing and Pete another is open to endless speculation. Charley Pyle was a shifty and wily character. He may have given Gavuzzi one set of instructions and Salo another during a quiet chat with each man. Perhaps Charley tried to give the American contingent (Salo, Richman, and Abramowitz) an advantage by telling them the race started at Huntington Park to help ensure that the Americans arrived first at Wrigley Park to the delight of the wildly partisan crowd. A more likely case is that Pyle simply failed to clearly communicate the rules to his men. The director general was a notoriously poor manager. In many cases, his inattention to detail—from failing to get the proper permits, to buying rickety chairs, to leaving bills unpaid—turned what might have been profitable events into financial disasters. Despite what Gavuzzi and Newton claimed, the same thing probably happened at Huntington Park, with Pyle or his referee, Steve Owen, giving confusing instructions or none at all and leaving each man to make his own judgment about what to do.

Gavuzzi also made another, more damning charge to Tulloh, namely that Charley told him to "ease up" in the last days of the race in order to assure "a good gate in Los Angeles."[41] In other words, Pyle ostensibly told Gavuzzi that if he wanted to collect his twenty-five-thousand-dollars, he needed to keep his lead over Salo small enough to build excitement among potential ticket buyers before the marathon finale. Pete, in effect, implied that he did Salo the favor of not beating him too badly before they reached Wrigley Park.

Johnny did not need Pete's help. When he entered California, Salo knew full well that he had to slash Gavuzzi's forty-nine-minute lead to have any chance of beating him on the last day. The Englishman was not toying with him. Johnny was a fierce competitor who was every bit the equal of Pete Gavuzzi. And he proved it when he halved the Englishman's lead after racing up twenty-eight hundred feet from the desert floor to Jacumba and when he halved it again on the run to San Juan Capistrano, where he used the last of his strength to sprint the final six miles and where Pete allegedly ruptured his Achilles tendon trying to catch him.

Both of Gavuzzi's charges are impossible to prove or disprove, and they sadly tarnished the second Bunion Derby. It gave Tulloh license to call the finish a "black comedy" and claim that Pete was cheated out of his victory.[42] His charges, combined with Pyle's mismanagement of the derby, made it easy to dismiss the race as a farce, when in reality it was the culmination of two years of transcontinental racing by courageous and road-hardened men.

The 1929 race changed ultramarathoning from the test of survival it had been in 1928 to a footrace on a continental scale the next year. With the experience of 1928 behind them, the forty-three veterans arrived at the starting line in New York City prepared for the challenge ahead of them. They dominated the race: 35 percent (fifteen) finished, and they won all fifteen prize-money spots except for twelfth place, which went to rookie Edwin Harbine of California.[43] Of the thirty-four rookies, only four finished, just 12 percent.[44] The 1928 veterans had learned hard-won lessons of pace, diet, and training, and they put them to good use the next year. Among this group, three brilliant runners, Salo, Gavuzzi, and Gardner, emerged to battle for the twenty-five-thousand-dollar first prize.

Eddie Gardner discarded his flashy but erratic style from 1928 and became a fast and patient runner who finished among the front-runners day after day. Gardner, however, could not change the color of his skin. In spite of his front-runner status, he was relegated to basement hotel boiler rooms while his white competitors slept soundly in their hotel beds. When he crossed the Mississippi River, he did so with his nation's flag sewn on his shirt, a poignant gesture of defiance against the brutal Jim Crow segregation that kept blacks second-class citizens in the South. His leg injury ended his dazzling run in Oklahoma.

With Gardner gone, the duel between the two remaining front-runners intensified as each man pushed the other to go faster as the lead switched back and forth between them. Along the way, they kept searching for the limit to sustainable daily racing. And they found it somewhere beyond fifty miles, an ill-defined no-man's-land. Both men flirted with it and raced beyond it, only to fall back in exhaustion—a process of trial and error that continued to the end of the race. Each man brought his own style to the race: Salo, power and fire; Gavuzzi, speed and grace. And each brought his own well-trained team to support him. Johnny had Bill Wicklund, the jack-of-all-trades mechanic and road chief, and his wife, Amelia, as cook, nurse, and no-nonsense helpmate—one of the first female trainers in the world to tend to an elite athlete. This combination of Wicklund on the road and Amelia before and after the race helped Johnny survive bouts of stomach cramps that would have forced less-organized men out of the race. Pete was just as well served with Newton as his senior advisor and George Barren as his trainer and cook. These uniquely matched men battled over the dusty roads of Texas, New Mexico, Arizona, and California, pushing transcontinental racing to the sublime.

The finale was what Pyle had always hoped it would be, a wildly exciting spectacle with ten thousand cheering fans on their feet. For a shining moment, just months before the great stock market crash, transcontinental racing had become a true spectator sport and Pyle, to his credit, opened it to men of all races and creeds. He had brought the sport back to its working-class, multiracial roots after a thirty-year hiatus. He had shown the country that long-distance racing was no longer the bastion of university and amateur athletic club athletes. He had opened distance running to anyone with a dream, a sport where a workingman with some talent and guts could earn enough prize money to make a better life for his family. And in towns and cities along the 3,554-mile course to Los Angeles, he opened the eyes of everyday working Americans to the godlike potential for greatness that rested within reach of them. All this has been lost because of Gavuzzi's anger over the disputed finish and Pyle's bumbling direction of the race.

Below is a brief synopsis of each of the top-ten prizewinners (there were fifteen winners in all); a list of the nineteen finishers with each man's time, place, and pace per mile; a comparable chart of the top-ten finishers in 1928; and, finally, a list of those extraordinary individuals who completed two transcontinental crossing in two years, racking up almost seven thousand miles of trans-America running.

The finishers of both derbies and those who were forced out along the way deserve the respect and admiration of all who admire courage and devotion to a dream. Those who made the journey were forever changed men. They had tested the limits of human potential in the most profound way possible. They are the godfathers of modern ultramarathoning, and all those who take up the sport should honor their names and the memory of what they accomplished.

The Top Ten Finishers and Their Prize Money

New York to Los Angeles Footrace (March 31, 1929–June 16, 1929)

•   •   •

Johnny Salo, First Place: $25,000

"The flying cop from Passaic" was the ultimate bunioneer. After his second-place finish in 1928, he was the heir apparent. He lived up to his billing and earned the right to receive the twenty-five-thousand-dollar first prize in 1929. He was the perfect combination of fire and power, tempered by his trainers, Amelia Salo and Bill Wicklund.

•   •   •

Pete Gavuzzi, Second Place: $10,000

Pete was a runner for the ages, agile and fast, a wonder to behold. In 1928, this trilingual ship's steward from Southampton, England, had the twenty-five-thousand-dollar first prize in his grasp before an infected tooth forced him out of the first Bunion Derby in Ohio. He returned to claim it in 1929. Coached by Arthur Newton, he came within a hairbreadth of winning his prize but had to settle for second place. His charges about the disputed finish haunt the memory of the 1929 race to this day.

•   •   •

Guisto Umek, Third Place: $6,000

Umek was potentially the perfect bunioneer, combining Gavuzzi's style with Salo's fury. In his midforties, the Italian auto mechanic from

Clifton, New Jersey, might have beaten both front-runners if he had had a coach to rein in his urge to run for stage-race glory. His young American trainer was not up to the task, and Guisto settled for third.

• • •

Sammy Richman, Fourth Place: $3,000

Sammy was a slightly less formidable version of Umek—highly talented but without a coach until Texas. He wasted his gifts on flashy stage runs as he chased Umek across Texas, New Mexico, and Arizona. Sammy was part of an amazing family of New Yorkers that produced three bunioneers: Sid in 1928, Morris in both races, and Sammy in both as well. Sammy, the young military veteran, was by far the greatest runner of the three.

• • •

Paul Simpson, Fifth Place: $2,500

Paul Simpson, the young physical education teacher from Elon College, North Carolina, lived up to his nickname of Hard Rock. Once he reached Texas, where Charley Hart took him under his wing, he became a much more consistent and patient bunioneer.

• • •

Philip Granville, Sixth Place: $2,250

Philip Granville was the pride of Canada in 1929. He won the hearts of Canadians with his gutsy race, running the last fifteen hundred miles on a broken foot. That he survived to qualify for the $2,250 prize is a testament to his courage. This Hamilton, Ontario, Jamaican-born tailor was the best-funded runner in the race, having the backing of the millionaire sports promoter Ted Oke of Toronto.

• • •

Mike McNamara, Seventh Place: $2,000

Mike McNamara, a powerfully built, thirty-eight-year-old Australian, ran a disciplined race to take seventh place. He and fellow Australian

Herbert Hedeman had refitted a truck and hired a trainer to pace them across America.

• • •

Herbert Hedeman, Eighth Place: $1,750

Herbert Hedeman was the oldest finisher of the Bunion Derby at fifty-five. Despite his age, he was a talented runner, but he squandered it by running for stage-race glory. He paid for his folly by staggering near the back as he took several days to recover from his brief foray into the top ranks of the Bunion Derby. He raced to make a better life for his struggling family.

• • •

Harry Abramowitz, Ninth Place: $1,500

Harry Abramowitz, the Brooklyn race walker turned runner, wore the Star of David on his chest. Harry gave a glimpse of potential in the last days of the race, when he led the field to San Juan Capistrano and paced Salo to the marathon finale at Wrigley Park.

• • •

Mike Joyce, Tenth Place: $1,250

Mike Joyce, the tiny Irish immigrant, rounded out the top ten. He had finished fourth in 1928. This thirty-five-year-old Cleveland factory worker was the town hero when he led the derby through the city in the closing days of the first race, but in 1929 he was forgotten, running the long miles to Los Angeles with barely a mention in the Cleveland press.

• • •

Five other men earned the right to receive prize money ranging from one thousand dollars for eleventh place to seven hundred dollars for fifteenth. These men and the four behind them seldom received a line of print in the national press. They endured, unnoticed, as they ran across America, arriving as a rag-tag bunch of sun-blacked men, a band of brothers, the forgotten masters of the "long trail" to Los Angeles.

Table 1
Finishers, 1929: 3,553.6 Miles in 78 Days

NEW YORK TO LOS ANGELES FOOTRACE (MARCH 31, 1929–JUNE 16, 1929)

Place	Name	Hours	Minutes	Secs	Pace Per Mile
1st	Salo, Johnny	525	56	10	8.53
2nd	Gavuzzi, Pete	525	58	57	8.53
3rd	Umek, Guisto	538	46	52	9.06
4th	Richman, Sam	571	29	29	9.39
5th	Simpson, Paul	586	30	42	9.54
6th	Granville, Philip	618	54	23	10.27
7th	McNamara, M. B.	627	45	28	10.36
8th	Hedeman, Herbert	631	23	48	10.40
9th	Abramowitz, Harry	634	46	20	10.43
10th	Joyce, Mike	689	2	52	11.38
11th	Shields, Guy	696	17	20	11.46
12th	Harbine, Edwin	737	56	16	12.28
13th	Cowley, Elmer	742	0	27	12.32
14th	Harrison, Pat	748	20	51	12.38
15th	Spangler, Joseph	755	50	14	12.46
16th	Rehayn, George	765	0	52	12.55
17th	Eskins, Charles	783	58	48	13.14
18th	Richman, Morris	854	11	11	14.25
19th	Jusnick, George	882	7	34	14.53

Table 2
Top Ten Finishers, 1928: 3,422.3 Miles in 84 Days

LOS ANGELES TO NEW YORK FOOTRACE (MARCH 4, 1928–MAY 26, 1928)

Place	Name	Hours	Minutes	Secs	Pace Per Mile
1st	Payne, Andy	573	40	13	10.04
2nd	Salo, Johnny	588	40	13	10.19
3rd	Granville, Philip	613	42	30	10.46
4th	Joyce, Mike	636	43	8	11.10
5th	Umek, Guisto	641	37	47	11.15
6th	Kerr, William	641	37	47	11.15
7th	Perrella, Louis	658	45	42	11.33
8th	Gardner, Eddie	659	56	47	11.34
9th	Von Flue, Frank	681	41	49	11.57
10th	Cronick, John	681	42	38	11.57

Table 3
List of Runners Who Completed Both

BUNION DERBIES: 6,975.9 MILES

1928	1929	Finishers	City	State/Province	Country
2nd	1st	Salo, Johnny	Passaic	New Jersey	USA
5th	3rd	Umek, Guisto	Trieste		Italy
44th	4th	Richman, Sam	New York City	New York	USA
36th	5th	Simpson, Paul	Burlington	North Carolina	USA
3rd	6th	Granville, Philip	Hamilton	Ontario	Canada
38th	8th	Hedeman, Herbert			Australia
11th	9th	Abramowitz, Harry	New York City	New York	USA
4th	10th	Joyce, Mike	Cleveland	Ohio	USA
40th	11th	Shields, Guy	Baxter Springs	Kansas	USA
49th	14th	Harrison, Pat	Sullivan	Missouri	USA
19th	16th	Rehayn, George			Germany
48th	18th	Richman, Morris	New York City	New York	USA

12

Searching for the Pot of Gold

ON MONDAY, JUNE 17, 1929, the day after the finale at Wrigley Park, Johnny Salo disappeared. He slipped away, to the annoyance of fans and reporters. By late afternoon, they had found him resting with his wife in the secluded home of some Finnish American friends. A reporter asked him if he would ever consider running a third Bunion Derby. He thought for a moment. "I don't know whether I would ever run in such a race again." Then he paused and added, "Of course, you know this running game is somewhat like the fight business: When you finish a tough test you are ready to quit for all time, but after a little rest you are eager to try it all over again."[1]

Salo had time to ponder the future; Charley Pyle did not. He was preoccupied by the immediate concern of trying to pay his bunioneers. After the race, the director general told reporters that "these boys will get their money" on Wednesday.[2] He would, however, need more time than that to solve a math problem of monumental proportions. He had taken in $6,313 in gate receipts from Sunday's finale, an amount that fell far short of the $60,000 he needed to pay out in prize money.[3] In 1928, he had turned to a business associate and the millionaire father of one of the bunioneers to help him cover the debt. This year, as he teetered on the edge of bankruptcy, no one was crazy enough to lend him any cash.

With no outside sources of funds, Charley's day of reckoning was close at hand. On Tuesday, June 18, Passaic's *Daily Herald* reported that Pyle's timetable had changed, that he could not set an exact day for the payoff but that it would probably be at the end of the week.[4] Johnny had planned to return home immediately after the race, but he was now stuck in Los Angeles until Charley paid him the twenty-five-thousand-dollar

175

prize. As he waited, Johnny continued to avoid the limelight, skipping out on a star-studded Hollywood Breakfast Club event with movie stars such as Douglas Fairbanks, Mary Pickford, and Gary Cooper and famed American sprinter Charley Paddock in attendance.[5]

On Friday, Salo was still waiting for his prize money. That night, Johnny, Pete Gavuzzi, and Sammy Richman attended a boxing match at Hollywood's American Legion Stadium. Salo was called to ringside, where a Legion official presented him with a gold wristwatch in appreciation of his victory in the Bunion Derby. Even then, all three men "seemed cheerfully confident that they would be paid," wrote Braven Dyer of the *Los Angeles Times*.[6]

Pyle told the reporter that he would "satisfy the runners on Tuesday" and that the ceremony would be a private affair.[7] In the interim, Gavuzzi and Umek visited San Francisco while Johnny and Amelia went to the mountains for some rest.[8] When they returned to Los Angeles, Charley requested no more delays. Harry Berry claimed that when the prizewinners came to collect their money, Charley was flanked by lawyers and accountants and offered promissory notes instead of cash. For the first time in the race, the director general finally told the truth: "It's no good, Pete. There's no money."[9]

By that time, Charley had been hit by a flurry of lawsuits, formal complaints, and claims from all sides: electricians, race patrolmen, assistants, and even the dancing debutantes.[10] As the outcry grew, Pyle was summoned to the Los Angeles city prosecutor's office and the California Labor Commission to explain why he had not paid his debts.[11] While legal storms whirled around him, Charley apparently had enough money in reserve to make a partial payment to some of his bunioneers. He gave the biggest share to Johnny Salo, probably paying him four-thousand dollars of the twenty-five-thousand-dollar prize money he was due, with a note for the remainder of the debt. Pyle even offered to give Salo his Red G Ranch in Santa Rosa, California, but the runner declined the offer.[12] Pete Gavuzzi fared far worse: he received $750 of the $10,000 prize money, with most of other prizewinners receiving smaller amounts.[13]

The disappointed men then began the long trip home. In early July, fifth-place winner Paul Simpson arrived in Burlington, North Carolina, with one hundred dollars and a promissory note for the remainder. He was "sun-baked, a little thin, broke but smiling," wrote the *Burlington Daily Times*. Asked which hip pocket contained the $2,500 for winning fifth place, he turned around to show that both pockets were empty.[14] The only rookie to qualify for prize money, twelfth-place holder Edwin Harbine of Santa Rosa, California, apparently received no cash, but he had the consolation of having the shortest trip home. "His face," wrote a reporter from the *Santa Rosa Free Democrat*, was "bronzed by sun, wind, and rain, but [Harbine felt] just as good as the day [he] started." Edwin was already planning for the 1930 race, claiming that "next year, I am going out to finish well up among the leaders."[15]

The cause of the prizewinners was not forgotten. A Los Angeles businessman formed a committee of civic leaders and hired an attorney to ensure that "justice [is] done for the fifteen 'prizewinners.'"[16] In late August, Charley apparently surrendered to Los Angeles city police after he was made a defendant in two labor suits and booked into Municipal Court for arraignment, with criminal prosecution and jail time the likely outcome of the court action. He pleaded not guilty and was freed on five-hundred-dollar bond with a trial date set for September 25.[17] He seems to have settled the charges out of court, but the strain of events destroyed his health. The next year, he suffered a massive stroke that paralyzed most of his right side and left him unable to speak, walk, or use his right arm. It would take Pyle three years of rehabilitation before he could work again.[18]

Johnny Salo and his wife seemed to have developed a liking for California and took their time about coming home. "Passaic," wrote Arthur McMahon, "will have to wait indefinitely before it can release its enthusiasm in a triumphant welcome to Johnny Salo."[19] The Salos became tourists, taking in the sights of San Francisco and Long Beach. After two weeks of vacationing, Johnny had regained the sixteen pounds lost during the race and felt "entirely recovered from the grind."[20]

The other members of the Passaic contingent began to make their way home. The Passaic reporter, Arthur McMahon, boarded a Pacific steamer in San Francisco and reached New York City as "brown as the proverbial berry" on July 23.[21] Salo's trainer, Bill Wicklund, arrived home in early August. He hated to leave California, claiming "it's everything they say about it." He went on to become a first-rate marathoner in his own right, taking seventh place in the 1936 Boston Marathon in 2:50:23.[22]

Johnny and Amelia finally returned home in early September.[23] In their absence, Salo's boss, Commissioner Turner, had arranged a rematch with Salo's old derby rivals, Andy Payne, Arthur Newton, and Pete Gavuzzi, in a fifteen-mile race around a track at Passaic High School. His three opponents had moved into Johnny's house a week before his return. The race was set for September 21 with two-thousand dollars for first place, one-thousand dollars for second, and five hundred dollars for third.[24] When the four signed the race contract, Andy Payne told the press that Salo had scared him a bit in the final days of the first derby but that on his best day, Payne believed, "I think I can beat him if I am in form." Johnny gently reminded Andy, "You can never tell [how a race will end] until a thing is over."[25]

Andy should have picked his words more carefully. McMahon, the veteran derby reporter, wrote that Payne was overweight and out of shape and "doubled up and ran from the field" with a stitch in his side after just three and one-half miles. Newton proved to be the fittest of the four and won the event, with Gavuzzi in second and Johnny in third. McMahon added that Salo appeared "overweight and listless," but Salo claimed that he would have performed much better had the distance been longer.[26]

Johnny would redeem himself two days later when he went to Philadelphia with Gavuzzi and Newton to race in a two-man team, man-against-horse competition. The event was a variation of the six-day "go as you please" footraces that were wildly popular in the 1870s and 1880s.[27] In "go as you please" racing, participants—known as pedestrians—were free to walk or run around an indoor track for six days. Many pedestrians set up cots inside the track's oval and rested before resuming their laps. These events took place in a smoke-filled arena, where avid fans packed the stands and place bets on the likely winners. In the 1929 man-versus-horse rendition of the race, Salo teamed up with Joie Ray, a former Olympic marathoner and premier middle-distance runner, while Gavuzzi and Newton raced together along with fellow bunioneers Olli Wanttinen and Harry Abramowitz. Johnny and his partner beat horse and man alike, covering 523 miles in six days of running. Gavuzzi and Newton finished second with 521 miles, and the four-footed competitors, Redwing and Fleetwood, took third with 475 miles.[28]

Johnny Salo finally had his homecoming on October 2, 1929, with an official welcome by the mayor at which he received a scroll and a silver trophy of a runner mounted on a bronzed base. He told the crowd: "I wouldn't part with [these gifts] for a million dollars. I want to thank everyone for the support given me during the race." Mrs. Salo, Pete Gavuzzi, Arthur Newton, and Bill Wicklund were all introduced to the crowd and given hearty applause.[29]

The flying cop from Passaic returned to duty on October 12, 1929, after a seven-month leave of absence without pay, just days before the Black Tuesday stock-market crash sent the country spiraling into the Great Depression.[30] Salo became a model officer, described by the *Daily Herald* as "conscientious in the performance of his duty . . . [and] a valuable and beloved member of the city's Police Department."[31]

Two years later, on Sunday, October 4, 1931, Johnny was working crowd control along the left-field line at a local baseball game between the Second Ward Civic Club and the Garfield Bergen Club. In the seventh inning, at about 4:15 P.M., a Bergen batter lined a ball into left field where "Ziggy" Mayo fielded it. The *Herald* wrote that he threw the ball "with terrific speed" down the left-field line toward the third baseman, trying to put out an advancing base runner. As the crowd surged forward, Officer Salo took a step back as he tried to keep the fans off the field, but in doing so, he put himself in the line of the throw. Ziggy's ball struck him in the side of the head. Salo fell to the ground unconscious but was revived after several minutes by members of both teams. Johnny refused to go to the hospital, telling the anxious crowd, "I'm no quitter. I can take it."[32]

The left fielder was shaken by the incident and wanted to leave the game, but Salo assured him that he was unhurt and shook hands with him as a gesture to encourage the teams to continue the game.[33] Johnny remained on duty until the ballgame ended around five o'clock. As the crowds dispersed, a city worker, Herbert Klein, saw Johnny walking unsteadily with his uniform wet with sweat. Klein persuaded Salo to let him drive him to the hospital, where he briefly collapsed on the hospital steps but regained his balance and walked inside. Shortly after being admitted, he lapsed into a coma and never recovered, dying at 9:40 P.M. from a fracture at the base of his skull and a brain hemorrhage with Amelia and his children, Leo and Helen, by his side.[34]

Passaic went into mourning. His body, dressed in his police uniform, lay in a silver casket at his Spring Street home. Floral displays filled the house. Charley Pyle sent a telegram assuring Amelia that he had not forgotten the debt he owed her husband and would pay her as soon as he had the funds to do so. Thousands of mourners lined the funeral route to the First Presbyterian Church as a police band led the six-horse caisson and police pallbearers marched on either side of the flag-draped casket. Behind the band, members of two American Legion Posts, Elmer Cowley from the Bunion Derby, Commissioner Turner, and a cadre of local judges walked in front of the caisson. In a two-block procession on Lexington Avenue, thousands of schoolchildren waited with bare heads until the procession had passed. The church was filled to capacity two hours before the funeral service, forcing thousands to mill around outside the church with hats off and heads bowed during the service. At the service, Mrs. Salo fainted and had to be escorted to a waiting car. Johnny was buried in nearby Cedar Lawn Cemetery in Paterson, New Jersey.[35]

Johnny's name is inscribed in the National Law Enforcement Memorial in Washington, D.C., one of more than nineteen thousand officers killed in the line of duty. The words of one of the survivors of a fallen officer, Vivian Eney Cross, are carved in the memorial wall. She wrote, "It is not how these officers died that made them heroes, it is how they lived."[36] Johnny's life set an example of extraordinary courage, toughness, and grace that inspired the citizens of Passaic and shattered the limits of human potential in his two magnificent runs across America. He was a rare and mighty force in American distance running and an example of the godlike powers and potential that we all have within us.

Arthur Newton and Pete Gavuzzi continued to race in endurance events. In 1930, the duo competed in the two-hundred-mile Usher Green Stripe Marathon in Montreal, with Newton taking second and Gavuzzi fourth. Later that year, they paired together to win the Peter Dawson five-hundred-mile race in Quebec.[37] In 1931, they moved to Hamilton, Ontario, where Phil Granville made his home. On April 3, 1931, Newton promoted and ran in a twenty-four-hour footrace in the Hamilton Arena together with Gavuzzi, Granville, Mike McNamara, and Paul Simpson from the Bunion Derby. Newton shattered the world record, covering 152 miles, but attendance was dismal and he lost eight hundred dollars on the venture. "At no time during the long grind," wrote the *Hamilton Spectator*, "were there enough people in the house to empanel a coroner's jury."[38] He then returned to England, where he bought a home near London in Ruislip. He ran his last race in 1934. In 1935, he published a book on running technique and strategy and five years later his autobiography, *Running in Three Continents*, was published. Newton's home became a mecca for runners from Britain and its empire. Arthur wrote prolifically until his death in 1959 at seventy-six.[39]

Pete Gavuzzi made his final appearance as a competitor in August 1935, where he broke Newton's 100-mile mark in a 105-mile race from

24. Arthur Newton, final competitive run, England, 1934. Source: Rob Hadgraft, private collection.

Buffalo to Toronto, a record that remained unbroken in North America for thirty-six years.[40] Pete stayed in Canada for the next several years, speaking Quebec French with his cockney accent, and "became," a historian of the Boston Marathon wrote, "the spiritual force behind nearly all Canada long distance runners." He believed in training by running long, slow distance and used his approach to coach an unemployed carpenter, Walter Young, to victory in the 1937 Boston Marathon.[41] Gavuzzi went to the Empire Games in Sydney, Australia, in 1938 as an advisor to the Canadian marathon team.[42] He then found work in France but was trapped in the German invasion of 1940 and interned as a foreign national until war's end.[43] He returned to England, moving near his old friend Arthur Newton. He worked as a caterer at an airbase and eventually as a caretaker at a school. He died in 1980 at age seventy-four, keeping Pyle's worthless promissory note as a bitter memento from his days as a bunioneer.[44]

Charley Pyle recovered from his nearly fatal stroke. He managed the Ripley's Believe It or Not Odditorium at the Chicago World's Fair in 1933.[45] In 1934, Charley left his third wife, divorced her in 1936, and married for the fourth time.[46] When he died of another stroke in 1939 at age fifty-seven, Pyle was well on his way to making another fortune by heading the Radio Transcription Company of America.[47]

After Eddie Gardner dropped out of the race in Oklahoma, he returned to Seattle, where he took a job as a handyman at an apartment house during the 1930s. Throughout the decade, he competed in an annual fifty-two-mile walking race around Lake Washington called the Lake Hike. In 1938, he won the event. During the war years, he worked in steel mills, and in the 1950s he worked at the naval shipyard in nearby Bremerton, Washington. He died in 1966, a quiet, humble man who had twice faced the wrath of Jim Crow segregation as a bunioneer.[48]

Andy Payne, the 1928 derby winner, made an ill-fated try at a film career in Hollywood before returning to Oklahoma, where he went to college, married his hometown sweetheart, and entered politics. He was elected clerk of the Supreme Court of Oklahoma and served in that position for thirty-six years. Payne died in 1977.[49]

Jim Thorpe, Pyle's master of ceremonies for the follies, had a much more successful career "in pictures." He acted in *My Pal, the King*, in 1932,

25. Director General Charley Pyle.
Source: *Official 1929 Program*, John
Stone, private collection.

and had small roles in *Klondike Annie* in 1936 and *Northwest Passage* in 1940.
Thorpe remained in California until his death in 1953.[50] Steve Owens,
Pyle's burly race director, went on to become the head football coach of
New York Giants in 1931.[51]

After the nation's plunge into the Great Depression, Pyle's 1928 and
1929 bunion derbies were largely forgotten. If they were remembered at
all, they were seen as an aberration from a decade that celebrated excess,
from marathon dance contests to marathon flagpole sitting. With the running boom in the early 1980s, sportswriters began to take a fresh look at
Pyle's two trans-America races. The 1929 race was largely ignored, tarred
by Pyle's bankruptcy, mismanagement, and allegations of race fixing.

Those who overlooked it missed an epic event. For seventy-eight
days, Johnny Salo and Pete Gavuzzi chased each other across the mostly

unpaved roads of 1929 America at an eight-minute-and-fifty-three-second pace per mile. Their pace was as good as or better than any other trans-America race or multiday ultramarathon event in history. The duo achieved this pace without today's high-tech running shoes, clothing, nutritional supplements, and medical support, and they did so by using hard-won survival lessons learned in the first Bunion Derby. Gavuzzi and Salo were unique men, blessed with courage, talent, and determination, and they used their gifts to push each other to the limits of human endurance and speed. Both men can vie for the title of the greatest long-distance runner of the last century, but the flying cop from Passaic has the edge with his second- and first-place finishes in the two bunion derbies.

In the second decade of this century, men and women are flocking to ultramarathon racing in ever-increasing numbers as they search for an alternative to the often overcrowded and overpriced marathon races of today. Those who attempt the longer distances have found a quieter world of running, a throwback to the early days of the running boom of the 1980s when a few hundred runners would gather for a marathon race. Here, beyond the 26.2 mile marathon distance, they are discovering what the pedestrians of the 1870s and 1880s and the bunioneers of 1928 and 1929 already knew: that human achievement is limited only by the size of your dreams.

Finally, a word should be written about Eddie Gardner and other forgotten African American endurance athletes who have been long denied the recognition and honor they deserve, and about why no women participated in either the 1928 or 1929 races. When Eddie ran across the Free Bridge into Missouri with an American flag sewn on his singlet, it was not the first time that an African American had draped himself in his nation's flag and stood at the pinnacle of the ultramarathoning world. In 1880, the African American pedestrian Frank Hart stood atop the international craze for six-day, "go as you please" distance racing after smashing the world record by covering 565 miles. He finished the race in Madison Square Garden while waving an American flag as a band played "Yankee Doodle Dandy" amid cheering, "that," wrote the *New York Times*, "fairly shook the building." Another African American, William Pegram of Boston, finished second. Hart, like Gardner, suffered his share of racial slurs and threats, but in New York, he was wildly popular with both white and black fans. Eddie had the same experience in Seattle.[52]

African American participation in long-distance running for cash prizes had far more to do with social class than with skin color. Blue-collar workers who were short on money but long on athletic talent were naturally drawn to sports that offered significant economic rewards. When African Americans were given a chance to participate in long-distance racing, they entered. Charley Pyle, to his credit, opened the bunion derbies to runners of color when it would have been far easier and more profitable to bar them from the races. Eddie Gardner and the other black bunioneers (three African Americans finished the 1928 derby) were, like their white counterparts, hoping to win prize money and grab their share of the American Dream, but blacks had the added burden of risking their lives to do so as they raced across the Jim Crow South. And along the way, they gave hope to thousands of their brothers and sisters who saw them run across America in the last years of the Jazz Age. They were early heralds of the Civil Rights Movement in the second half of the century, civil resisters against injustice.

Around the time of the Bunion Derby, African Americans were attempting to break a number of different long-distance records. According to the *New York Age*, Henry "The Cuban Wonder" Shelton, a former pedestrian star, wanted to better his own coast-to-coast walking record that he had set in 1915 from New York City to San Francisco. Just as the 1929 Bunion Derby was racing across Texas, the nearly seventy-year-old Shelton was starting his second cross-country walk.[53] In 1927, twenty-three-year-old William T. Davis of New York City was setting long-distance speed records on his 1926 twin-model Indian motorcycle in his race from New York City to Halifax, Nova Scotia.[54] Around the same time, Nebraska Williams and his new bride were competing in an around-the-world walking race.[55]

Until the second half of the twentieth century, most whites had no idea that African Americans were capable of competing in long-distance events.[56] The truth was buried and ignored beneath a shroud of ignorance perpetuated by long-held stereotypes and by historians and novelists writing about distance running well into the latter half of the last century.[57] It was a deeply held belief that blacks would never make good marathon runners because their limited attention span made it almost impossible for them to concentrate for anything longer than the sprint distances—and this belief permeated novels and books on the subject.

Even Arthur Newton, the revered sage of British ultramarathoning and two-time bunioneer, claimed that blacks made inferior distance runners because they possessed thicker skulls and therefore had smaller brains than their white competitors.[58] He made this claim despite knowing three African American bunioneers—Eddie Gardner, Sammy Robinson, and Toby Joseph Cotton Junior—who finished the 1928 race in far higher numbers on a percentage basis (60 percent, or three out of five starters) than their white counterparts (27 percent, or 52 out of 194 starters).[59]

Only in the new century, some 150 years after the end of slavery in the United States, have our great black legends of ultramarathoning finally begun to receive an inkling of the tribute that they have been so long denied. Names like Eddie "the Sheik" Gardner and Frank "Black Dan" Hart should be known and honored by anyone who takes up the sport of ultramarathoning, and for that matter, by anyone who admires courage and perseverance in the face of impossible odds.

Women have a similarly proud and largely unknown history to tell. Before the decline of professional foot racing around the turn of the last century, a cadre of females was setting long-distance running records and pushing the boundaries of what was socially acceptable behavior for their gender. In the 1870s and 1880s, many women were caught up in the craze for six-day, "go as you please" racing and competed in towns and cities across America and in Europe.

In December 1879, an international field of twenty-five women met in Madison Square Garden to compete for the first world championship in women's six-day racing. The event was dubbed the Grand Ladies' International Tournament for the Championship of the World. Seventeen-year-old Amy Howard of Brooklyn won the title with its one-thousand-dollar cash prize and the championship belt valued at five hundred dollars. Five thousand enthusiastic fans—many of them women—cheered her on as she crossed the finish line after completing 393 miles in six days, averaging sixty-five miles a day. The publicity about the race led New York

City officials to ban further six-day racing by women because the officials believed that such activity was not a respectable pursuit for a lady. Undeterred, the race organizers moved the championship to San Francisco, where in May 1880, Amy defended her title, covering 409 miles and setting a world distance record for six-day racing that stood unbroken for the next 102 years. Sadly, Howard died during childbirth in 1885, but other women carried on her legacy and continued competing until the turn of the century.[60]

Given this rich history, one might ask where the women were in the two bunion derbies? There is no evidence that Pyle purposely excluded females from becoming bunioneers, but he didn't make it easy for them, either, when he failed to offer them separate prize money or advertise that his derbies were open to both sexes.

When event organizers did do these things, women entered their races in droves. For example, in the grueling twenty-three-mile, open ocean swim from Catalina Island to Los Angeles in 1927, women competed openly with men and raced for their own cash prizes.[61] In Seattle's fifty-two-mile walking race around Lake Washington in 1929, women raced for separate prize money and started a half hour before the men, ensuring that the top female and male walkers finished around the same time, which added to the excitement of the event. The race had its female hero, forty-five-year-old Bertha Woodward. This poor laundry woman won the race and used the prize money to buy a house and move her three daughters out of an unpainted shack that, until then, had served as their home.[62]

With no separate prize money and no encouragement from Pyle, women had little incentive to attempt a trans-America effort. They would have to wait until the running boom of the 1980s before significant numbers of women would again enter long-distance running events—and begin to follow in the footsteps of Amy Howard and a host other long-forgotten female pioneers of ultramarathoning.

Appendixes

Notes

Glossary

Bibliography

Index

Appendix A

List of Starters

Starters	City	State	Country
Abramowitz, Harry	New York City	New York	USA
Ahlfors, Antti	Eveleth	Minnesota	USA
Amos, Paul	Pittsburgh	Pennsylvania	USA
Apelquist, Karl			Sweden
Bagley, W. S.	Newport News	Virginia	USA
Baum, Sylvester	Genoa	Ohio	USA
Baze, M. M.	Los Angeles	California	USA
Black, William	Cumberland	Maryland	USA
Block, Richard	Philadelphia	Pennsylvania	USA
Borden, Eddie	Redwood	California	USA
Chavez, Frank			Mexico
Christensen, Pete	Brooklyn	New York	USA
Cleary, Claude	Amarillo	Texas	USA
Cools, Juul			Belgium
Cools, Karl			Belgium
Crowley, Elmer	Clifton	New Jersey	USA
Dalzell, Jesse	Springfield	Missouri	USA
Diorio, C.			Italy
Downing, William A	Bedford	Iowa	USA
Eastman, Owen	Salem	Massachusetts	USA
Ellis, Thomas	Hamilton	Ontario	Canada
Ellsworth, R. V.	Monongahela	Pennsylvania	USA
Eskins, Charles	Elyria	Ohio	USA
Gardner, Eddie	Seattle	Washington	USA

List of Starters

Starters	City	State	Country
Gattis, Leonard	Fresno	California	USA
Gavuzzi, Pete			England
Gober, John	Moberly	Missouri	USA
Gonzales, Seth	Raton	New Mexico	USA
Granville, Philip			Canada
Harbine, Edwin	Ukiah	California	USA
Harrison, Pat	Sullivan	Missouri	USA
Hart, Charles			England
Hedeman, Herbert	New York City	New York	USA
Houfstater, Voight	Manistee	Michigan	USA
Jensen, Clarence	Glendale	California	USA
Johanson, Martin	Rockford	Illinois	USA
Joyce, Mike	Cleveland	Ohio	USA
Jusnick, George			Poland
Kester, Herman	Sawtelle	California	USA
Lewis, Leonard	Muncie	Indiana	USA
McMurty, Roy	Indianapolis	Indiana	USA
McNamara, M. B.			Australia
Marini, Pietro	Voghera		Italy
Meeks, J.	St. Louis	Missouri	USA
Megrddchian, Moosh	Modesto	California	USA
Miller, Harry	Richmond	Indiana	USA
Miller, Tracey	New Orleans	Louisiana	USA
Montalbo, Anthony	Newark	New Jersey	USA
Morady, William	Newark	New Jersey	USA
Moot, Everett	Marchand	Pennsylvania	USA
Mullen, Ken	Philadelphia	Pennsylvania	USA
Newton, Arthur			S. Africa
Nielson, Niels	Chicago	Illinois	USA
Oakes, Robert	Buffalo	New York	USA
Pandolfi, Colombo			Italy
Perrella, Louis J.	Albany	New York	USA

List of Starters

Starters	City	State	Country
Randall, Milton	Chicago	Illinois	USA
Rea, Harry	Long Beach	California	USA
Rehayn, George			Germany
Richman, Morris	New York City	New York	USA
Richman, Sam	New York City	New York	USA
Salo, Johnny	Passaic	New Jersey	USA
Saperstein, Morris	Wheeling	West Virginia	USA
Savalak, A. M.	Cleveland	Ohio	USA
Shields, Guy	Baxt. Springs	Kansas	USA
Simpson, Paul	Burlington	N. Carolina	USA
Smith, Paul	Bend	Oregon	USA
Suominen, Arne	Chicago	Illinois	USA
Sutton, Harold	Cleveland	Ohio	USA
Spangler, Joseph	New York City	New York	USA
Stone, John Jr.	Marion	Indiana	USA
Trapp, Merle	Atchison	Kansas	USA
Trimble, Troy	Bakersfield	California	USA
Umek, Guisto			Italy
Wanttinen, Olli			Finland
White, John	Duluth	Michigan	USA
Wollenschlager, W.	Los Angeles	California	USA

77 starters

Notes: Seventy-seven appears to be the correct number, given that two dropped out in stage 2 and thirteen after stage 3. Sixty-two started stage 4 according to press reports. Seventy-five runners are listed in the *NYT,* April 1, 1929, as starters. Two others, Charles Eskins and George Rehayn, were not listed but finished the race. Two other runners were listed as finishing a stage but not identified in the list of starters: Anthony Wenneger of Boston, stage 10, and Gus Schmidt of Berlin, Germany, in stage 32.

Appendix B

Daily and Cumulative Mileage

Stage	From	To	Date		Stage Miles	Cum M
1	New York City	Elizabeth, N.J.	Sunday	03/31/29	21.00	21.00
2	Elizabeth, N.J.	Trenton, N.J.	Monday	04/01/29	46.40	67.40
3	Trenton, N.J.	Philadelphia, Pa.	Tuesday	04/02/29	29.30	96.70
4	Philadelphia, Pa.	Wilmington, Del.	Wednesday	04/03/29	37.70	134.40
5	Wilmington, Del.	Havre de Grace, Md.	Thursday	04/04/29	37.00	171.40
6	Havre de Grace, Md.	Baltimore, Md.	Friday	04/05/29	44.00	215.40
7	Baltimore, Md.	Frederick, Md.	Saturday	04/06/29	45.60	261.00
8	Frederick, Md.	Hancock, Md.	Sunday	04/07/29	52.00	313.00
9	Hancock, Md.	Cumberland, Md.	Monday	04/08/29	39.00	352.00
10	Cumberland, Md.	Uniontown, Pa.	Tuesday	04/09/29	62.80	414.80
11	Uniontown, Pa.	Waynesburg, Pa.	Wednesday	04/10/29	32.50	447.30
12	Waynesburg, Pa.	Wheeling, W.Va.	Thursday	04/11/29	52.20	499.50
13	Wheeling, W.Va.	Cambridge, Ohio	Friday	04/12/29	50.20	549.70
14	Cambridge, Ohio	Zanesville, Ohio	Saturday	04/13/29	25.20	574.90
15	Zanesville, Ohio	Columbus, Ohio	Sunday	04/14/29	54.80	629.70
16	Columbus, Ohio	Springfield, Ohio	Monday	04/15/29	43.40	673.10
17	Springfield, Ohio	Richmond, Ind.	Tuesday	04/16/29	63.00	736.10
18	Richmond, Ind.	Knightstown, Ind.	Wednesday	04/17/29	34.70	770.80
19	Knightstown, Ind.	Indianapolis, Ind.	Thursday	04/18/29	35.30	806.10
20	Indianapolis, Ind.	Brazil, Ind.	Friday	04/19/29	57.00	863.10
21	Brazil, Ind.	Marshall, Ind.	Saturday	04/20/29	33.00	896.10
22	Marshall, Ind.	Effingham, Ill.	Sunday	04/21/29	52.40	948.50

Daily and Cumulative Mileage

1929 BUNION DERBY

Stage	From	To	Date		Stage Miles	Cum M
23	Effingham, Ill.	Vandalia, Ill.	Monday	04/22/29	31.80	980.30
24	Vandalia, Ill.	Collinsville, Ill.	Tuesday	04/23/29	59.80	1040.10
25	Collinsville, Ill.	Maplewood, Mo.	Wednesday	04/24/29	22.00	1062.10
26	Maplewood, Mo.	Sullivan, Mo.	Thursday	04/25/29	61.00	1123.10
27	Sullivan, Mo.	Rolla, Mo.	Friday	04/26/29	45.00	1168.10
28	Rolla, Mo.	Waynesville, Mo.	Saturday	04/27/29	32.00	1200.10
29	Waynesville, Mo.	Conway, Mo.	Sunday	04/28/29	50.00	1250.10
30	Conway, Mo.	Springfield, Mo.	Monday	04/29/29	41.00	1291.10
31	Springfield, Mo.	Miller, Mo.	Tuesday	04/30/29	33.70	1324.80
32	Miller, Mo.	Joplin, Mo.	Wednesday	05/01/29	47.00	1371.80
33	Joplin, Mo.	Miami, Okla.	Thursday	05/02/29	36.70	1408.50
34	Miami, Okla.	Chelsea, Okla.	Friday	05/03/29	54.70	1463.20
35	Chelsea, Okla.	Muskogee, Okla.	Saturday	05/04/29	73.40	1536.60
36	Muskogee, Okla.	Okmulgee, Okla.	Sunday	05/05/29	44.00	1580.60
37	Okmulgee, Okla.	Holdenville, Okla.	Monday	05/06/29	60.00	1640.60
38	Holdenville, Okla.	Coalgate, Okla.	Tuesday	05/07/29	54.00	1694.60
39	Coalgate, Okla.	Durant, Okla.	Wednesday	05/08/29	50.00	1744.60
40	Durant, Okla.	Sherman, Tex.	Thursday	05/09/29	33.00	1777.60
41	Sherman, Tex.	Dallas, Tex.	Friday	05/10/29	79.90	1857.50
42	Dallas, Tex.	Fort Worth, Tex.	Saturday	05/11/29	32.00	1889.50
43	Fort Worth, Tex.	Mineral Wells, Tex.	Sunday	05/12/29	53.00	1942.50
44	Mineral Wells, Tex.	Breckenridge, Tex.	Monday	05/13/29	54.40	1996.90
45	Breckenridge, Tex.	Albany, Tex.	Tuesday	05/14/29	24.70	2021.60
46	Albany, Tex.	Anson, Tex.	Wednesday	05/15/29	39.40	2061.00
47	Anson, Tex.	Sweetwater, Tex.	Thursday	05/16/29	56.20	2117.20
48	Sweetwater, Tex.	Colorado, Tex.	Friday	05/17/29	28.00	2145.20
49	Colorado, Tex.	Big Spring, Tex.	Saturday	05/18/29	41.00	2186.20
50	Big Spring, Tex.	Midland, Tex.	Sunday	05/19/29	40.00	2226.20
51	Midland, Tex.	Odessa, Tex.	Monday	05/20/29	21.70	2247.90
52	Odessa, Tex.	Monahans, Tex.	Tuesday	05/21/29	38.00	2285.90
53	Monahans, Tex.	Pecos, Tex.	Wednesday	05/22/29	39.00	2324.90

Daily and Cumulative Mileage

1929 BUNION DERBY

Stage	From	To	Date		Stage Miles	Cum M
54	Pecos, Tex.	Kent, Tex.	Thursday	05/23/29	56.00	2380.90
55	Kent, Tex.	Van Horn, Tex.	Friday	05/24/29	39.50	2420.40
56	Van Horn, Tex.	Sierra Blanca, Tex.	Saturday	05/25/29	34.40	2454.80
57	Sierra Blanca, Tex.	Fabens, Tex.	Sunday	05/26/29	59.40	2514.20
58	Fabens, Tex.	El Paso, Tex.	Monday	05/27/29	30.00	2544.20
59	El Paso, Tex.	Las Cruces, N.M.	Tuesday	05/28/29	44.00	2588.20
60	Las Cruces, N.M.	Deming, N.M.	Wednesday	05/29/29	63.00	2651.20
61	Deming, N.M.	Lordsburg, N.M.	Thursday	05/30/29	64.00	2715.20
62	Lordsburg, N.M.	Duncan, Ariz.	Friday	05/31/29	38.00	2753.20
63	Duncan, Ariz.	Safford, Ariz.	Saturday	06/01/29	43.40	2796.60
64	Safford, Ariz.	Bylas, Ariz.	Sunday	06/02/29	37.00	2833.60
65	Bylas, Ariz.	Miami, Ariz.	Monday	06/03/29	62.00	2895.60
66	Miami, Ariz.	Superior, Ariz.	Tuesday	06/04/29	21.70	2917.30
67	Superior, Ariz.	Mesa, Ariz.	Wednesday	06/05/29	51.00	2968.30
68	Mesa, Ariz.	Buckeye, Ariz.	Thursday	06/06/29	54.20	3022.50
69	Buckeye, Ariz.	Gila Bend, Ariz.	Friday	06/07/29	47.20	3069.70
70	Gila Bend, Ariz.	Aztec, Ariz.	Saturday	06/08/29	44.40	3114.10
71	Aztec, Ariz.	Wellton, Ariz.	Sunday	06/09/29	42.80	3156.90
72	Wellton, Ariz.	Yuma, Ariz.	Monday	06/10/29	44.20	3201.10
73	Yuma, Ariz.	Calexico, Calif.	Tuesday	06/11/29	58.00	3259.90
74	Calexico, Calif.	Jacumba, Calif.	Wednesday	06/12/29	58.00	3317.90
75	Jacumba, Calif.	San Diego, Calif.	Thursday	06/13/29	78.50	3396.40
76	San Diego, Calif.	San Juan Cap., Calif.	Friday	06/14/29	65.00	3461.40
77	San Juan Cap., Calif.	Huntington Beach, Calif.	Saturday	06/15/29	62.00	3523.40
78	Huntington Beach, Calif.	Wrigley Park, Los Angeles	Sunday	06/16/29	30.20	3553.60
Average Miles per Stage					45.56	

Appendix C

Pace by Stage Finishers

STAGE   1

DATE   MARCH 31, 1929

LOCATION   NYC TO ELIZABETH, N.J.

Place	Name	Hours	Minutes	Secs	Miles Run	Pace Per Mile
1st	Gardner, Eddie	1	59	30	21.10	5.40
2nd	Richman, Sam	1	59	45	21.10	5.41
3rd	Cools, Karl	2	4	45	21.10	5.55
4th	Cools, Juul	2	5	0	21.10	5.55
5th	Marini, Pietro	2	8	0	21.10	6.04
6th	Hedeman, Herbert	2	8	15	21.10	6.05
7th	Mullen, Ken	2	10	15	21.10	6.10
8th	Wanttinen, Olli	2	11	41	21.10	6.14
9th	Houfstater, Voight	2	14	30	21.10	6.22
10th	Salo, Johnny	2	16	15	21.10	6.26

STAGE   2

DATE   APRIL 1, 1929

LOCATION   ELIZABETH TO TRENTON, N.J.

Place	Name	Hours	Minutes	Secs	Miles Run	Pace Per Mile
1st	Simpson, Paul	6	10	50	46.40	7.59
2nd	Cools, Juuls	6	24	20	46.40	8.17
3rd	Salo, Johnny	6	32	0	46.40	8.27
4th	Gardner, Eddie	6	37	38	46.40	8.34
5th	Houfstater, Voight	6	39	5	46.40	8.36
6th	Cools, Karl	6	47	10	46.40	8.47

Pace by Stage Finishers

Place	Name	Hours	Minutes	Secs	Miles Run	Pace Per Mile
7th	Hedeman, Herbert	6	47	20	46.40	8.47
8th	Newton, Arthur	6	47	30	46.40	8.47
9th	Richman, Sam	6	54	0	46.40	8.55
10th	Wanttinen, Olli	7	28	50	46.40	9.40

STAGE   3
DATE   APRIL 2, 1929
LOCATION   TRENTON TO PHILADELPHIA, PA.

Place	Name	Hours	Minutes	Secs	Miles Run	Pace Per Mile
1st	Trimble, Tory	3	38	40	29.30	7.28
2nd	Hedeman, Herbert	3	39	0	29.30	7.28
3rd	Umek, Guisto	3	45	20	29.30	7.41
4th	Simpson, Paul	3	50	12	29.30	7.52
5th	Mullen, Ken	3	57	4	29.30	8.05
6th	Salo, Johnny	3	59	43	29.30	8.11
7th	Gardner, Eddie	4	2	2	29.30	8.16
8th	Houfstater, Voight	4	7	10	29.30	8.26
9th		0	0	0	29.30	0.00
10th		0	0	0	29.30	0.00

STAGE   4
DATE   APRIL 3, 1929
LOCATION   WILMINGTON, DEL.

Place	Name	Hours	Minutes	Secs	Miles Run	Pace Per Mile
1st	Salo, Johnny	4	59	35	37.70	7.57
2nd	Gavuzzi, Pete	4	59	35	37.70	7.57
3rd	Wanttinen, Olli	5	3	5	37.70	8.02
4th	Simpson, Paul	5	19	31	37.70	8.29
5th	Gardner, Eddie	5	19	31	37.70	8.29
6th	Hedeman, Herbert	5	29	45	37.70	8.45
7th	Trimble, Troy	5	43	0	37.70	9.06
8th	Houfstater, Voight	5	48	25	37.70	9.14
9th	McNamara, M. B.	5	48	27	37.70	9.14
10th	Newton, Arthur	5	51	4	37.70	9.19

Pace by Stage Finishers

STAGE	5
DATE	APRIL 4, 1929
LOCATION	HAVRE DE GRACE, MD.

Place	Name	Hours	Minutes	Secs	Miles Run	Pace Per Mile
1st	Hedeman, Herbert	4	44	45	37.00	7.42
2nd	Wanttinen, Olli	5	5	52	37.00	8.16
3rd	Salo, Johnny	5	5	52	37.00	8.16

STAGE	6
DATE	APRIL 5, 1929
LOCATION	BALTIMORE, MD.

Place	Name	Hours	Minutes	Secs	Miles Run	Pace Per Mile
1st	Gavuzzi, Pete	5	38	15	44.00	7.41
2nd	Salo, Johnny	5	46	0	44.00	7.52
3rd	Umek, Guisto	5	46	0	44.00	7.52

STAGE	7
DATE	APRIL 6, 1929
LOCATION	FREDERICK, MD.

Place	Name	Hours	Minutes	Secs	Miles Run	Pace Per Mile
1st	Gavuzzi, Pete	6	52	15	45.60	9.02
2nd	Salo, Johnny	7	5	45	45.60	9.20
3rd	Gardner, Eddie	7	5	45	45.60	9.20

STAGE	8
DATE	APRIL 7, 1929
LOCATION	HANCOCK, MD.

Place	Name	Hours	Minutes	Secs	Miles Run	Pace Per Mile
1st	Gardner, Eddie	7	58	1	52.00	9.11
2nd	Salo, Johnny	8	27	45	52.00	9.46

STAGE	9
DATE	APRIL 8, 1929
LOCATION	CUMBERLAND, MD.

Place	Name	Hours	Minutes	Secs	Miles Run	Pace Per Mile
1st	Gardner, Eddie	6	36	45	39.00	10.10

Pace by Stage Finishers

Place	Name	Hours	Minutes	Secs	Miles Run	Pace Per Mile
2nd	Salo, Johnny	7	10	5	39.00	11.02
3rd	Gavuzzi, Pete	7	10	5	39.00	11.02
4th	Umek, Guisto	7	33	1	39.00	11.37

STAGE 10
DATE APRIL 9, 1929
LOCATION UNIONTOWN, PA.

Place	Name	Hours	Minutes	Secs	Miles Run	Pace Per Mile
1st	Umek, Guisto	10	18	15	62.80	9.50
2nd	Granville, Philip	11	16	15	62.80	10.46
3rd	Gavuzzi, Pete	11	16	15	62.80	10.46
4th	Gardner, Eddie	11	36	15	62.80	11.05
5th	Richman, Sam	11	36	30	62.80	11.05

STAGE 11
DATE APRIL 10, 1929
LOCATION WAYNESBURG, PA.

Place	Name	Hours	Minutes	Secs	Miles Run	Pace Per Mile
1st	Simpson, Paul	4	46	10	32.50	8.49
2nd	Trimble, Troy	5	1	45	32.50	9.17
3rd	Gardner, Eddie	5	11	30	32.50	9.35
4th	Gavuzzi, Pete	5	11	30	32.50	9.35
5th	Richman, Sam	5	13	45	32.50	9.39
6th	Jenson, Clarence	5	20	30	32.50	9.52
7th	Umek, Guisto	5	58	45	32.50	11.02
8th	Harbine, Edwin	6	0	15	32.50	11.05
9th	Granville, Philip	6	5	20	32.50	11.14
10th	Newton, Arthur	6	18	0	32.50	11.38

STAGE 12
DATE APRIL 11, 1929
LOCATION WHEELING, W.VA.

Place	Name	Hours	Minutes	Secs	Miles Run	Pace Per Mile
1st	Gavuzzi, Pete	8	2	54	52.20	9.15

Pace by Stage Finishers

Place	Name	Hours	Minutes	Secs	Miles Run	Pace Per Mile
2nd	Simpson, Paul	8	32	15	52.20	9.49
3rd	Gardner, Eddie	9	42	30	52.20	11.10
4th	Trimble, Troy	9	42	30	52.20	11.10
5th	Richman, Sam	10	2	50	52.20	11.33
6th	Umek, Guisto	10	2	50	52.20	11.33
7th	Salo, Johnny	10	44	0	52.20	12.20
8th	McNamara, M. B.	11	12	15	52.20	12.53
9th	Rea, Harry	11	16	0	52.20	12.57

STAGE	13
DATE	APRIL 12, 1929
LOCATION	CAMBRIDGE, OHIO

Place	Name	Hours	Minutes	Secs	Miles Run	Pace Per Mile
1st	Gavuzzi, Pete	7	31	15	50.20	8.59
2nd	Simpson, Paul	0	0	0	50.20	0.00
3rd	Gardner, Eddie	8	35	45	50.20	10.16

STAGE	14
DATE	APRIL 13, 1929
LOCATION	ZANESVILLE, OHIO

Place	Name	Hours	Minutes	Secs	Miles Run	Pace Per Mile
1st	Gavuzzi, Pete	3	0	18	25.20	7.29
2nd	Salo, Johnny	3	21	45	25.20	8.01
3rd	Gardner, Eddie	3	39	30	25.20	8.43

STAGE	15
DATE	APRIL 14, 1929
LOCATION	COLUMBUS, OHIO

Place	Name	Hours	Minutes	Secs	Miles Run	Pace Per Mile
1st	Gavuzzi, Pete	7	53	15	54.80	8.38
2nd	Gardner, Eddie	7	53	15	54.80	8.38
3rd	Salo, Johnny	8	9	45	54.80	8.56
4th	Umek, Guisto	8	35	15	54.80	9.24

Pace by Stage Finishers

STAGE 16
DATE APRIL 15, 1929
LOCATION SPRINGFIELD, OHIO

Place	Name	Hours	Minutes	Secs	Miles Run	Pace Per Mile
1st	Gavuzzi, Pete	6	38	15	43.40	9.11
2nd	Gardner, Eddie	6	58	40	43.40	9.39
3rd	McNamara, M. B.	0	0	0	43.40	0.00
4th	Salo, Johnny	0	0	0	43.40	0.00
5th	Granville, Philip	8	5	5	43.40	11.11
6th	Joyce, Mike	0	0	0	43.40	0.00
7th	Richman, Sam	0	0	0	43.40	0.00

STAGE 17
DATE APRIL 16, 1929
LOCATION RICHMOND, IND.

Place	Name	Hours	Minutes	Secs	Miles Run	Pace Per Mile
1st	Salo, Johnny	8	47	10	63.00	8.22
2nd	Gavuzzi, Pete	9	37	50	63.00	9.10
3rd	Gardner, Eddie	9	56	10	63.00	9.28
4th	Umek, Guisto	0	0	0	63.00	0.00
5th	Joyce, Mike	0	0	0	63.00	0.00
6th	Richman, Sam	0	0	0	63.00	0.00
7th	Granville, Philip	0	0	0	63.00	0.00

STAGE 18
DATE APRIL 17, 1929
LOCATION KNIGHTSBRIDGE, IND.

Place	Name	Hours	Minutes	Secs	Miles Run	Pace Per Mile
1st	Salo, Johnny	4	25	24	34.70	7.39
2nd	Gavuzzi, Pete	5	19	15	34.70	9.12
3rd	Gardner, Eddie	5	19	15	34.70	9.12

Pace by Stage Finishers

STAGE	19
DATE	APRIL 18, 1929
LOCATION	INDIANAPOLIS, IND.

Place	Name	Hours	Minutes	Secs	Miles Run	Pace Per Mile
1st	Salo, Johnny	4	27	15	35.30	7.34
2nd	Gavuzzi, Pete	4	39	20	35.30	7.55
3rd	Gardner, Eddie	4	49	10	35.30	8.11

STAGE	20
DATE	APRIL 19, 1929
LOCATION	BRAZIL, IND.

Place	Name	Hours	Minutes	Secs	Miles Run	Pace Per Mile
1st	Salo, Johnny	7	49	1	57.00	8.14
2nd	Gavuzzi, Pete	7	56	15	57.00	8.22
3rd	Simpson, Paul	0	0	0	57.00	0.00
4th	Granville, Philip	8	5	20	57.00	8.31
5th	McNamara, M. B.	0	0	0	57.00	0.00
6th	Umek, Guisto	0	0	0	57.00	0.00
7th	Newton, Arthur	0	0	0	57.00	0.00
8th	Gardner, Eddie	10	15	20	57.00	10.48

STAGE	21
DATE	APRIL 20, 1929
LOCATION	MARSHALL, IND.

Place	Name	Hours	Minutes	Secs	Miles Run	Pace Per Mile
1st	Simpson, Paul	4	31	45	33.00	8.14
2nd	Gavuzzi, Pete	4	51	10	33.00	8.49
3rd	Gardner, Eddie	4	51	10	33.00	8.49
4th	Salo, Johnny	4	51	10	33.00	8.49

Pace by Stage Finishers

STAGE 22
DATE APRIL 21, 1929
LOCATION EFFINGHAM, ILL.

Place	Name	Hours	Minutes	Secs	Miles Run	Pace Per Mile
1st	Salo, Johnny	7	11	45	52.40	8.14
2nd	Umek, Guisto	7	15	15	52.40	8.19
3rd	Simpson, Paul	0	0	0	52.40	0.00
4th	Granville, Philip	7	34	10	52.40	8.40
5th	Gavuzzi, Pete	7	34	10	52.40	8.40
6th	Gardner, Eddie	0	0	0	52.40	0.00

STAGE 23
DATE APRIL 22, 1929
LOCATION VANDALIA, ILL.

Place	Name	Hours	Minutes	Secs	Miles Run	Pace Per Mile
1st	Gavuzzi, Pete	4	6	5	31.80	7.44
2nd	Gardner, Eddie	4	6	5	31.80	7.44
3rd	Simpson, Paul	4	23	10	31.80	8.17
4th	Salo, Johnny	4	29	10	31.80	8.28
5th	Granville, Philip	4	31	15	31.80	8.32
6th	Umek, Guisto	4	31	15	31.80	8.32

STAGE 24
DATE APRIL 23, 1929
LOCATION COLLINSVILLE, ILL.

Place	Name	Hours	Minutes	Secs	Miles Run	Pace Per Mile
1st	Salo, Johnny	8	12	50	59.80	8.14
2nd	Simpson, Paul	8	18	55	59.80	8.20
3rd	Gardner, Eddie	0	0	0	59.80	0.00
4th	Gavuzzi, Pete	0	0	0	59.80	0.00
5th	Granville, Philip	0	0	0	59.80	0.00
6th	Richman, Sam	0	0	0	59.80	0.00
7th	Harrison, Pat	0	0	0	59.80	0.00

Pace by Stage Finishers

STAGE 25

DATE APRIL 24, 1929

LOCATION MAPLEWOOD, MO.

Place	Name	Hours	Minutes	Secs	Miles Run	Pace Per Mile
1st	Gardner, Eddie	2	28	50	22.00	6.46
2nd	Gavuzzi, Pete	2	52	50	22.00	7.52
3rd	Salo, Johnny	2	55	0	22.00	7.57
4th	Richman, Sam	2	55	0	22.00	7.57
5th	Umek, Guisto	2	58	45	22.00	8.08
6th	Dalzell, Jesse	3	11	50	22.00	8.43
7th	Granville, Philip	3	30	45	22.00	9.35
8th	Abramowitz, Harry	3	35	10	22.00	9.47
9th	Harrison, Pat	3	47	20	22.00	10.20
10th	McNamara, M. B.	3	47	20	22.00	10.20

STAGE 26

DATE APRIL 25, 1929

LOCATION SULLIVAN, MO.

Place	Name	Hours	Minutes	Secs	Miles Run	Pace Per Mile
1st	Salo, Johnny	8	42	10	61.00	8.34
2nd	Simpson, Paul	9	11	15	61.00	9.02
3rd	Umek, Guisto	9	23	10	61.00	9.14
4th	Gavuzzi, Pete	9	39	20	61.00	9.30
5th	Harrison, Pat	0	0	0	61.00	0.00

STAGE 27

DATE APRIL 26, 1929

LOCATION ROLLA, MO.

Place	Name	Hours	Minutes	Secs	Miles Run	Pace Per Mile
1st	Simpson, Paul	6	3	1	45.00	8.04
2nd	Umek, Guisto	6	22	45	45.00	8.31
3rd	Gavuzzi, Pete	6	56	40	45.00	9.16
4th	Salo, Johnny	0	0	0	45.00	0.00

Pace by Stage Finishers

Place	Name	Hours	Minutes	Secs	Miles Run	Pace Per Mile
5th	Gardner, Eddie	0	0	0	45.00	0.00
6th	Richman, Sam	6	59	40	45.00	9.20
7th	Granville, Philip	0	0	0	45.00	0.00

STAGE 28
DATE APRIL 27, 1929
LOCATION WAYNESVILLE, MO.

Place	Name	Hours	Minutes	Secs	Miles Run	Pace Per Mile
1st	Gavuzzi, Pete	4	9	0	32.00	7.47
2nd	Salo, Johnny	4	20	0	32.00	8.08
3rd	Umek, Guisto	4	22	0	32.00	8.11
4th	Simpson, Paul	0	0	0	32.00	0.00
5th	Richman, Sam	0	0	0	32.00	0.00
6th	Granville, Philip	0	0	0	32.00	0.00
7th	Gardner, Eddie	0	0	0	32.00	0.00

STAGE 29
DATE APRIL 28, 1929
LOCATION CONWAY, MO.

Place	Name	Hours	Minutes	Secs	Miles Run	Pace Per Mile
1st	Umek, Guisto	6	57	45	50.00	8.22
2nd	Richman, Sam	7	3	1	50.00	8.28
3rd	Gardner, Eddie	7	51	10	50.00	9.25
4th	Salo, Johnny	8	2	20	50.00	9.39
5th	Granville, Philip	8	2	20	50.00	9.39
6th	Gavuzzi, Pete	8	2	20	50.00	9.39

STAGE 30
DATE APRIL 29, 1929
LOCATION SPRINGFIELD, MO.

Place	Name	Hours	Minutes	Secs	Miles Run	Pace Per Mile
1st	Gavuzzi, Pete	4	51	10	41.00	7.06
2nd	Salo, Johnny	5	11	45	41.00	7.36
3rd	Hedeman, Herbert	5	20	50	41.00	7.50

Pace by Stage Finishers

Place	Name	Hours	Minutes	Secs	Miles Run	Pace Per Mile
4th	Dalzell, Jesse	5	27	10	41.00	7.59
5th	Umek, Guisto	5	28	20	41.00	8.01
6th	Richman, Sam	5	41	30	41.00	8.20
7th	Granville, Philip	5	48	40	41.00	8.30
8th	Abramowitz, Harry	6	15	20	41.00	9.09

STAGE   31
DATE   APRIL 30, 1929
LOCATION   MILLER, MO.

Place	Name	Hours	Minutes	Secs	Miles Run	Pace Per Mile
1st	Gavuzzi, Pete	4	15	10	33.70	7.34
2nd	Richman, Sam	4	25	15	33.70	7.52

STAGE   32
DATE   MAY 1, 1929
LOCATION   JOPLIN, MO.

Place	Name	Hours	Minutes	Secs	Miles Run	Pace Per Mile
1st	Salo, Johnny	5	51	10	47.00	7.28
2nd	Hedeman, Herbert	6	5	0	47.00	7.46
3rd	Gardner, Eddie	6	10	15	47.00	7.53
4th	Simpson, Paul	6	14	20	47.00	7.58
5th	Umek, Guisto	6	22	40	47.00	8.08
6th	Gavuzzi, Pete	6	35	20	47.00	8.25
7th	Richman, Sam	6	35	20	47.00	8.25
8th	Granville, Philip	7	4	40	47.00	9.02
9th	Abramowitz, Harry	7	19	35	47.00	9.21
10th	Joyce, Mike	7	19	35	47.00	9.21

STAGE   33
DATE   MAY 2, 1929
LOCATION   MIAMI, OKLA.

Place	Name	Hours	Minutes	Secs	Miles Run	Pace Per Mile
1st	Salo, Johnny	4	36	50	36.70	7.32
2nd	Richman, Sam	4	36	50	36.70	7.32

Pace by Stage Finishers

Place	Name	Hours	Minutes	Secs	Miles Run	Pace Per Mile
3rd	Gavuzzi, Pete	4	57	10	36.70	8.06

STAGE 34
DATE MAY 3, 1929
LOCATION CHELSEA, OKLA.

Place	Name	Hours	Minutes	Secs	Miles Run	Pace Per Mile
1st	Umek, Guisto	7	3	45	54.70	7.45
2nd	Salo, Johnny	7	41	10	54.70	8.26
3rd	Gavuzzi, Pete	7	47	5	54.70	8.32
4th	Granville, Philip	7	53	50	54.70	8.40
5th	McNamara, MB	8	5	10	54.70	8.53
6th	Simpson, Paul	8	33	15	54.70	9.23
7th	Abramowitz, Harry	8	46	10	54.70	9.37
8th	Richman, Sam	9	9	20	54.70	10.02
9th	Joyce, Mike	9	10	5	54.70	0.00

STAGE 35
DATE MAY 4, 1929
LOCATION MUSKOGEE, OKLA.

Place	Name	Hours	Minutes	Secs	Miles Run	Pace Per Mile
1st	Umek, Guisto	9	42	20	73.40	7.56
2nd	Salo, Johnny	11	1	0	73.40	9.01
3rd	Gavuzzi, Pete	11	1	1	73.40	9.01
4th	Simpson, Paul	11	38	20	73.40	9.31

STAGE 36
DATE MAY 5, 1929
LOCATION OKMULGEE, OKLA.

Place	Name	Hours	Minutes	Secs	Miles Run	Pace Per Mile
1st	Umek, Guisto	5	40	50	44.00	7.45
2nd		0	0	0	44.00	0.00
3rd	Gavuzzi, Pete	6	40	50	44.00	0.00
4th	Salo, Johnny	6	40	50	44.00	0.00
5th	Granville, Philip	7	11	45	44.00	9.49

Pace by Stage Finishers

STAGE   37
DATE   MAY 6, 1929
LOCATION   HOLDENVILLE, OKLA.

Place	Name	Hours	Minutes	Secs	Miles Run	Pace Per Mile
1st	Salo, Johnny	8	6	40	60.00	8.07
2nd	Umek, Guisto	8	38	10	60.00	8.38
3rd	Gavuzzi, Pete	0	0	0	60.00	0.00
4th	Simpson, Paul	0	0	0	60.00	0.00
5th	Richman, Sam	0	0	0	60.00	0.00
6th	Granville, Philip	10	5	0	60.00	10.05

STAGE   38
DATE   MAY 7, 1929
LOCATION   COALGATE, OKLA.

Place	Name	Hours	Minutes	Secs	Miles Run	Pace Per Mile
1st	Gavuzzi, Pete	7	27	30	54.00	8.17
2nd	Salo, Johnny	8	8	5	54.00	9.02
3rd	Granville, Philip	8	27	40	54.00	9.24

STAGE   39
DATE   MAY 8, 1929
LOCATION   DURANT, OKLA.

Place	Name	Hours	Minutes	Secs	Miles Run	Pace Per Mile
1st	Salo, Johnny	6	45	10	50.00	8.06
2nd	Simpson, Paul	7	10	40	50.00	8.37
3rd	Gavuzzi, Pete	7	28	40	50.00	8.58

STAGE   40
DATE   MAY 9, 1929
LOCATION   SHERMAN, TEX.

Place	Name	Hours	Minutes	Secs	Miles Run	Pace Per Mile
1st	Simpson, Paul	4	27	30	33.00	8.07
2nd	Granville, Philip	4	35	20	33.00	8.20
3rd	Gavuzzi, Pete	4	39	10	33.00	8.28
4th	Richman, Sam	0	0	0	33.00	0.00

Pace by Stage Finishers

Place	Name	Hours	Minutes	Secs	Miles Run	Pace Per Mile
5th	Umek, Guisto	0	0	0	33.00	0.00
6th	Salo, Johnny	0	0	0	33.00	0.00

STAGE   41
DATE   MAY 10, 1929
LOCATION   DALLAS, TEX.

Place	Name	Hours	Minutes	Secs	Miles Run	Pace Per Mile
1st	Salo, Johnny	11	22	15	79.90	8.32
2nd	Gavuzzi, Pete	12	14	30	79.90	9.11

STAGE   42
DATE   MAY 12, 1929
LOCATION   FORT WORTH, TEX.

Place	Name	Hours	Minutes	Secs	Miles Run	Pace Per Mile
1st	Hedeman, Herbert	4	20	40	32.00	8.09
2nd	Richman, Sam	4	25	10	32.00	8.17
3rd	Granville, Philip	4	50	10	32.00	9.04

STAGE   43
DATE   MAY 12, 1929
LOCATION   MINERAL WELLS, TEX.

Place	Name	Hours	Minutes	Secs	Miles Run	Pace Per Mile
1st	Umek, Guisto	7	1	20	53.00	7.57
2nd		0	0	0	53.00	0.00
3rd		0	0	0	53.00	0.00
4th	Simpson, Paul	8	6	5	53.00	9.10

STAGE   44
DATE   MAY 13, 1929
LOCATION   BRECKENRIDGE, TEX.

Place	Name	Hours	Minutes	Secs	Miles Run	Pace Per Mile
1st	Hedeman, Herbert	7	25	50	54.40	8.12
2nd	Richman, Sam	0	0	0	54.40	0.00

Pace by Stage Finishers

Place	Name	Hours	Minutes	Secs	Miles Run	Pace Per Mile
3rd	Umek, Guisto	8	7	55	54.40	8.58
4th	McNamara, M. B.	8	44	10	54.40	9.38
5th	Simpson, Paul	0	0	0	54.40	0.00
6th	Gavuzzi, Pete	0	0	0	54.40	9.44
7th	Salo, Johnny	0	0	0	54.40	9.44

STAGE 45
DATE MAY 14, 1929
LOCATION ALBANY, TEX.

Place	Name	Hours	Minutes	Secs	Miles Run	Pace Per Mile
1st	Richman, Sam	2	57	40	24.70	7.11
2nd	Hedeman, Herbert	3	6	5	24.70	7.32
3rd	Salo, Johnny	3	22	1	24.70	8.11
4th	Gavuzzi, Pete	3	22	1	24.70	8.11

STAGE 46
DATE MAY 15, 1929
LOCATION ANSON, TEX.

Place	Name	Hours	Minutes	Secs	Miles Run	Pace Per Mile
1st	Salo, Johnny	5	6	5	39.40	7.46
2nd	Richman, Sam	5	21	10	39.40	8.09
3rd	Hedeman, Herbert	5	21	10	39.40	8.09
4th	Gavuzzi, Pete	5	27	5	39.40	8.18

STAGE 47
DATE MAY 16, 1929
LOCATION SWEETWATER, TEX.

Place	Name	Hours	Minutes	Secs	Miles Run	Pace Per Mile
1st	Salo, Johnny	7	35	40	56.20	8.07
2nd	Gavuzzi, Pete	7	47	10	56.20	8.19
3rd	Richman, Sam	7	47	10	56.20	8.19
4th	Simpson, Paul	7	53	0	56.20	8.25

Pace by Stage Finishers

STAGE	48
DATE	MAY 17, 1929
LOCATION	COLORADO, TEX.

Place	Name	Hours	Minutes	Secs	Miles Run	Pace Per Mile
1st	Richman, Sam	4	5	15	28.00	8.46
2nd	Salo, Johnny	4	29	10	28.00	9.37

STAGE	49
DATE	MAY 18, 1929
LOCATION	BIG SPRING, TEX.

Place	Name	Hours	Minutes	Secs	Miles Run	Pace Per Mile
1st	Salo, Johnny	6	9	40	41.00	9.01
2nd	Umek, Guisto	6	9	40	41.00	0.00
3rd	Gavuzzi, Pete	6	39	30	41.00	9.44

STAGE	50
DATE	MAY 19, 1929
LOCATION	MIDLAND, TEX.

Place	Name	Hours	Minutes	Secs	Miles Run	Pace Per Mile
1st	Salo, Johnny	5	9	5	40.00	7.44
2nd	Richman, Sam	0	0	0	40.00	0.00
3rd	Gavuzzi, Pete	5	26	5	40.00	8.09

STAGE	51
DATE	MAY 20, 1929
LOCATION	ODESSA, TEX.

Place	Name	Hours	Minutes	Secs	Miles Run	Pace Per Mile
1st	Richman, Sam	2	24	40	21.70	6.40
2nd	Umek, Guisto	0	0	0	21.70	0.00
3rd	Hedeman, Herbert	2	30	30	21.70	6.56
4th	Salo, Johnny	2	40	1	21.70	7.22
5th	Gavuzzi, Pete	2	40	1	21.70	7.22

Pace by Stage Finishers

STAGE	52
DATE	MAY 21, 1929
LOCATION	MONAHANS, TEX.

Place	Name	Hours	Minutes	Secs	Miles Run	Pace Per Mile
1st	Richman, Sam	4	17	5	38.00	6.49
2nd	Umek, Guisto	4	17	5	38.00	6.46
3rd	Salo, Johnny	4	52	10	38.00	7.41
4th	Gavuzzi, Pete	4	52	10	38.00	7.41
5th	Simpson, Paul	5	12	5	38.00	8.13
6th	McNamara, M. B.	5	12	5	38.00	8.13

STAGE	53
DATE	MAY 22, 1929
LOCATION	PECOS, TEX.

Place	Name	Hours	Minutes	Secs	Miles Run	Pace Per Mile
1st	Richman, Sam	4	39	40	39.00	7.10
2nd	Umek, Guisto	4	56	5	39.00	7.35
3rd	Salo, Johnny	5	1	4	39.00	7.43
3rd	Gavuzzi, Pete	5	1	4	39.00	7.43

STAGE	54
DATE	MAY 23, 1929
LOCATION	KENT TEX

Place	Name	Hours	Minutes	Secs	Miles Run	Pace Per Mile
1st	Richman, Sam	7	2	2	56.00	7.32
2nd	Umek, Guisto	7	13	50	56.00	7.45

STAGE	55
DATE	MAY 24, 1929
LOCATION	VAN HORN, TEX.

Place	Name	Hours	Minutes	Secs	Miles Run	Pace Per Mile
1st	Umek, Guisto	5	6	20	39.50	7.46
2nd	Richman, Sam	5	15	30	39.50	7.53

Pace by Stage Finishers

STAGE   56
DATE   MAY 25, 1929
LOCATION   SIERRA BLANCA, TEX.

Place	Name	Hours	Minutes	Secs	Miles Run	Pace Per Mile
1st	Umek, Guisto	4	47	2	34.40	8.20
1st	Granville, Philip	4	47	2	34.40	8.20
3rd	Hedeman, Herbert	4	58	10	34.40	8.40
3rd	McNamara, M. B.	4	58	10	34.40	8.40

STAGE   57
DATE   MAY 26, 1929
LOCATION   FABENS, TEX.

Place	Name	Hours	Minutes	Secs	Miles Run	Pace Per Mile
1st	Salo, Johnny	8	11	10	59.40	8.16
2nd	Umek, Guisto	0	0	0	59.40	0.00
3rd	Hedeman, Herbert	8	43	5	59.40	8.49
4th	Gavuzzi, Pete	9	6	30	59.40	9.12
4th	Richman, Sam	9	6	30	59.40	9.12

STAGE   58
DATE   MAY 27, 1929
LOCATION   EL PASO, TEX.

Place	Name	Hours	Minutes	Secs	Miles Run	Pace Per Mile
1st	Gavuzzi, Pete	3	23	40	30.00	6.47
2nd	Hedeman, Herbert	3	51	5	30.00	7.42
2nd	Richman, Sam	3	51	5	30.00	7.42
4th	Umek, Guisto	3	56	0	30.00	7.52
5th	Salo, Johnny	3	58	0	30.00	7.56
6th	Simpson, Paul	4	9	25	30.00	8.19
7th	McNamara, M. B.	4	32	5	30.00	9.04

STAGE   59
DATE   MAY 28, 1929
LOCATION   LAS CRUCES, N.M.

Place	Name	Hours	Minutes	Secs	Miles Run	Pace Per Mile
1st	Salo, Johnny	5	59	10	44.00	8.10

Pace by Stage Finishers

Place	Name	Hours	Minutes	Secs	Miles Run	Pace Per Mile
1st	Gavuzzi, Pete	0	0	0	44.00	8.10
1st	Richman, Sam	0	0	0	44.00	8.10

STAGE	60					
DATE	MAY 29, 1929					
LOCATION	DEMING, N.M.					

Place	Name	Hours	Minutes	Secs	Miles Run	Pace Per Mile
1st	Gavuzzi, Pete	8	14	30	63.00	7.51
2nd	Umek, Guisto	8	43	20	63.00	8.19
3rd	Salo, Johnny	9	18	10	63.00	8.52

STAGE	61					
DATE	MAY 30, 1929					
LOCATION	LORDSBURG, N.M.					

Place	Name	Hours	Minutes	Secs	Miles Run	Pace Per Mile
1st	Hedeman, Herbert	8	27	40	64.00	7.56
2nd	Salo, Johnny	9	36	15	64.00	9.00
3rd	Gavuzzi, Pete	0	0	0	64.00	9.00

STAGE	62					
DATE	MAY 29, 1929					
LOCATION	DUNCAN, ARIZ.					

Place	Name	Hours	Minutes	Secs	Miles Run	Pace Per Mile
1st	Richman, Sam	4	57	50	38.00	7.50
2nd	Umek, Guisto	5	12	10	38.00	8.13
2nd	Gavuzzi, Pete	5	12	10	38.00	8.13
2nd	Salo, Johnny	5	12	10	38.00	8.13

STAGE	63					
DATE	JUNE 1, 1929					
LOCATION	SAFFORD, ARIZ.					

Place	Name	Hours	Minutes	Secs	Miles Run	Pace Per Mile
1st	Richman, Sam	5	18	10	43.40	7.20
2nd	Salo, Johnny	5	37	5	43.40	7.46
2nd	Simpson, Paul	5	37	5	43.40	7.46

Pace by Stage Finishers

Place	Name	Hours	Minutes	Secs	Miles Run	Pace Per Mile
4th	Gavuzzi, Pete	5	57	28	43.40	8.14
5th	Umek, Guisto	6	5	10	43.40	8.25
6th	Harrison, Pat	7	11	30	43.40	9.56
7th	Hedeman, Herbert	7	21	5	43.40	10.10

STAGE 64
DATE JUNE 2, 1929
LOCATION BYLAS, ARIZ.

Place	Name	Hours	Minutes	Secs	Miles Run	Pace Per Mile
1st	Richman, Sam	4	22	30	37.00	7.05
1st	Umek, Guisto	4	22	30	37.00	7.05
3rd	Salo, Johnny	4	25	20	37.00	7.10
4th		0	0	0	37.00	0.00
5th	Gavuzzi, Pete	4	43	0	37.00	7.39

STAGE 65
DATE JUNE 3, 1929
LOCATION MIAMI, ARIZ.

Place	Name	Hours	Minutes	Secs	Miles Run	Pace Per Mile
1st	Richman, Sam	8	45	58	62.00	8.29
2nd	Gavuzzi, Pete	9	4	55	62.00	8.47
3rd	Umek, Guisto	9	30	50	62.00	9.13
4th	Salo, Johnny	9	38	22	62.00	9.20

STAGE 66
DATE JUNE 4, 1929
LOCATION SUPERIOR, ARIZ.

Place	Name	Hours	Minutes	Secs	Miles Run	Pace Per Mile
1st	Salo, Johnny	2	38	0	21.70	7.17
1st	Richman, Sam	0	0	0	21.70	7.17
3rd	Umek, Guisto	2	59	40	21.70	8.17
4th	Simpson, Paul	0	0	0	21.70	0.00
5th	Gavuzzi, Pete	3	7	54	21.70	8.40

Pace by Stage Finishers

STAGE	67
DATE	JUNE 5, 1929
LOCATION	MESA, ARIZ.

Place	Name	Hours	Minutes	Secs	Miles Run	Pace Per Mile
1st	Salo, Johnny	6	34	55	51.00	7.44
2nd	Simpson, Paul	7	13	18	51.00	8.30
3rd	Umek, Guisto	7	28	30	51.00	8.47
4th	Gavuzzi, Pete	7	34	48	51.00	8.55

STAGE	68
DATE	JUNE 6, 1929
LOCATION	BUCKEYE, ARIZ.

Place	Name	Hours	Minutes	Secs	Miles Run	Pace Per Mile
1st	Salo, Johnny	6	58	45	54.20	7.44
2nd	Gavuzzi, Pete	7	19	55	54.20	8.07
3rd	Umek, Guisto	7	47	40	54.20	8.38

No information is available for stage 69.

STAGE	70
DATE	JUNE 8, 1929
LOCATION	AZTEC, ARIZ.

Place	Name	Hours	Minutes	Secs	Miles Run	Pace Per Mile
1st	Umek, Guisto	6	13	0	44.40	8.24
2nd	Gavuzzi, Pete	6	23	5	44.40	8.38
3rd	Salo, Johnny	6	40	10	44.40	9.01

STAGE	71
DATE	JUNE 9, 1929
LOCATION	WELLTON, ARIZ.

Place	Name	Hours	Minutes	Secs	Miles Run	Pace Per Mile
1st	Umek, Guisto	6	5	0	42.80	8.32
2nd	Gavuzzi, Pete	6	21	5	42.80	8.54
3rd	Richman, Sam	6	39	10	42.80	9.20
4th	Eskins, Charles	6	47	5	42.80	9.31
5th	Salo, Johnny	6	50	59	42.80	9.36

Pace by Stage Finishers

STAGE 72
DATE JUNE 10, 1929
LOCATION YUMA, ARIZ.

Place	Name	Hours	Minutes	Secs	Miles Run	Pace Per Mile
1st	Harrison, Pat	5	55	50	44.20	8.03
2nd	Gavuzzi, Pete	6	3	45	44.20	8.14
3rd	Umek, Guisto	6	38	50	44.20	9.01
4th	Richman, Sam	6	57	5	44.20	9.26
5th	McNamara, M. B.	7	30	10	44.20	10.11
6th		0	0	0	44.20	0.00
7th	Salo, Johnny	7	39	0	44.20	10.23

STAGE 73
DATE JUNE 11, 1929
LOCATION CALEXICO, CALIF.

Place	Name	Hours	Minutes	Secs	Miles Run	Pace Per Mile
1st	Umek, Guisto	7	30	10	58.80	7.40
2nd	Gavuzzi, Pete	8	16	5	58.80	8.26
2nd	Salo, Johnny	8	16	5	58.80	8.26
2nd	Richman, Sam	8	16	5	58.80	8.26
5th	McNamara, M. B.	9	3	50	58.80	9.15
5th	Hedeman, Herbert	9	3	50	58.80	9.15
5th	Cowley, Elmer	9	3	50	58.80	9.15
8th	Abramowitz, Harry	9	24	15	58.80	9.36

STAGE 74
DATE JUNE 12, 1929
LOCATION JACUMBA, CALIF.

Place	Name	Hours	Minutes	Secs	Miles Run	Pace Per Mile
1st	Salo, Johnny	9	9	5	58.00	9.28
2nd	Umek, Guisto	9	22	50	58.00	9.42
3rd	Gavuzzi, Pete	9	44	55	58.00	10.05
4th	Harrison, Pat	11	4	20	58.00	11.27
5th	Granville, Philip	11	41	20	58.00	12.05

Pace by Stage Finishers

Place	Name	Hours	Minutes	Secs	Miles Run	Pace Per Mile
5th	Hedeman, Herbert	0	0	0	58.00	12.05
5th	McNamara M. B.	0	0	0	58.00	12.05
5th	Simpson, Paul	0	0	0	58.00	12.05

STAGE 75
DATE JUNE 13, 1929
LOCATION SAN DIEGO, CALIF.

Place	Name	Hours	Minutes	Secs	Miles Run	Pace Per Mile
1st	Umek, Guisto	12	0	5	78.50	9.10
2nd	Salo, Johnny	13	3	2	78.50	9.58
2nd	Gavuzzi, Pete	13	3	2	78.50	9.58

STAGE 76
DATE JUNE 14, 1929
LOCATION SAN JUAN CAPISTRANO, CALIF.

Place	Name	Hours	Minutes	Secs	Miles Run	Pace Per Mile
1st	Abramowitz, Harry	10	18	20	65.00	9.31
2nd	Salo, Johnny	13	29	0	65.00	12.27
2nd	Umek, Guisto	13	29	0	65.00	12.27
4th	Gavuzzi, Pete	13	39	0	65.00	12.36

STAGE 77
DATE JUNE 15, 1929
LOCATION HUNTINGTON BEACH, CALIF.

Place	Name	Hours	Minutes	Secs	Miles Run	Pace Per Mile
1st	Umek, Guisto	8	45	50	62.00	8.29
2nd	Gavuzzi, Pete	9	54	10	62.00	9.35
2nd	Salo, Johnny	9	54	10	62.00	9.35
4th	Hedeman, Herbert	9	57	0	62.00	9.38
4th	Abramowitz, Harry	9	57	0	62.00	9.38
6th	Simpson, Paul	10	16	5	62.00	9.56
7th	McNamara, M. B.	11	2	10	62.00	10.41

Pace by Stage Finishers

STAGE	78
DATE	JUNE 16, 1929
LOCATION	WRIGLEY PARK, CALIF.

Place	Name	Hours	Minutes	Secs	Miles Run	Pace Per Mile
1st	Salo, Johnny	3	48	00	30.20	7.35
2nd	Richman, Sam	3	49	2	30.20	7.35
3rd	Gavuzzi, Pete	4	1	0	30.20	7.59

Note: Pace-per-mile data by stage race is calculated from finishing times listed in newspapers that covered the event. In one stage race, stage 69 to Gila Bend, Arizona, surviving newspapers did not provide sufficient data to calculate pace per mile.

Appendix D

Cumulative Pace by Stage Finishers

STAGE 3
DATE APRIL 2, 1929
LOCATION TRENTON TO PHILADELPHIA, PA.

Place	Name	Hours	Minutes	Secs	Miles Run	Pace Per Mile
1st	Simpson, Paul	12	20	17	96.70	7.28
2nd	Hedeman, Herbert	12	34	43	96.70	7.48
3rd	Gardner, Eddie	12	39	20	96.70	7.51
4th	Salo, Johnny	12	47	58	96.70	7.56
5th	Houfstater, Voight	13	1	30	96.70	8.05
6th	Richman, Sam	13	25	50	96.70	8.20
7th	Gardner, Eddie	13	25	50	96.70	8.20
8th	Mullen, Ken	13	40	39	96.70	8.29
9th	Trimble, Troy	13	55	51	96.70	8.38
10th	Umek, Guisto	14	1	51	96.70	8.43

STAGE 4
DATE APRIL 3, 1929
LOCATION WILMINGTON, DEL.

Place	Name	Hours	Minutes	Secs	Miles Run	Pace Per Mile
1st	Simpson, Paul	17	41	48	134.40	7.54
2nd	Salo, Johnny	17	47	33	134.40	7.56
3rd	Gardner, Eddie	17	58	51	134.40	8.02
4th	Hedeman, Herbert	18	4	28	134.40	8.04
5th	Houfstater, Voight	18	40	55	134.40	8.20
6th	Newton, Arthur	19	16	34	134.40	8.37

223

Cumulative Pace by Stage Finishers

Place	Name	Hours	Minutes	Secs	Miles Run	Pace Per Mile
7th	Trimble, Troy	19	39	52	134.40	8.47
8th	Richman, Sam	19	44	58	134.40	8.49
9th	Gavuzzi, Pete	19	46	35	134.40	8.50
10th	McNamara, M. B.	19	52	47	134.40	8.52

STAGE   5
DATE   APRIL 4, 1929
LOCATION   HAVRE DE GRACE, MD.

Place	Name	Hours	Minutes	Secs	Miles Run	Pace Per Mile
1st	Hedeman, Herbert	22	49	43	171.40	7.59
2nd	Salo, Johnny	22	55	23	171.40	8.01
3rd	Gardner, Eddie	23	9	35	171.40	8.07
4th	Simpson, Paul	24	5	50	171.40	8.26
5th	Houfstater, Voight	24	27	23	171.40	8.34
6th	Newton, Arthur	24	41	0	171.40	8.38
7th	Gavuzzi, Pete	25	1	47	171.40	8.46
8th	Trimble, Troy	25	16	42	171.40	8.51
9th	McNamara, M. B.	25	22	17	171.40	8.53
10th	Umek, Guisto	25	28	14	171.40	8.55

STAGE   6
DATE   APRIL 5, 1929
LOCATION   BALTIMORE, MD.

Place	Name	Hours	Minutes	Secs	Miles Run	Pace Per Mile
1st	Salo, Johnny	28	51	42	215.40	8.02
2nd	Gardner, Eddie	29	42	30	215.40	8.17
3rd	Hedeman, Herbert	30	3	5	215.40	8.22
4th	Simpson, Paul	30	12	13	215.40	8.25
5th	Gavuzzi, Pete	30	40	2	215.40	8.32
6th	Newton, Arthur	30	56	22	215.40	8.37
7th	Wanttinen, Olli	31	21	15	215.40	8.44
8th	Trimble, Troy	31	23	55	215.40	8.45

Cumulative Pace by Stage Finishers

Place	Name	Hours	Minutes	Secs	Miles Run	Pace Per Mile
9th	Houfstater, Voight	31	24	25	215.40	8.45
10th	Umek, Guisto	31	24	31	215.40	8.45

STAGE   7
DATE   APRIL 6, 1929
LOCATION   FREDERICK, MD.

Place	Name	Hours	Minutes	Secs	Miles Run	Pace Per Mile
1st	Salo, Johnny	35	57	27	261.00	8.16
2nd	Gardner, Eddie	36	48	13	261.00	8.28
3rd	Gavuzzi, Pete	37	32	17	261.00	8.38
4th	Hedeman, Herbert	38	41	28	261.00	8.53
5th	Newton, Arthur	38	44	34	261.00	8.55
6th	Wanttinen, Olli	39	1	3	261.00	8.58
7th	Simpson, Paul	39	28	58	261.00	9.05
8th	Houfstater, Voight	39	29	55	261.00	9.05
9th	Umek, Guisto	39	37	51	261.00	9.07
10th	Richman, Sam	40	0	55	261.00	9.12

STAGE   8
DATE   APRIL 7, 1929
LOCATION   HANCOCK, MD.

Place	Name	Hours	Minutes	Secs	Miles Run	Pace Per Mile
1st	Salo, Johnny	44	25	17	313.00	8.31
2nd	Gardner, Eddie	44	46	25	313.00	8.35
3rd	Gavuzzi, Pete	46	50	2	313.00	8.59
4th	Newton, Arthur	47	43	24	313.00	9.09
5th	Houfstater, Voight	48	45	10	313.00	9.21
6th	Umek, Guisto	49	11	56	313.00	9.26
7th	Hedeman, Herbert	49	18	38	313.00	9.27
8th	Richman, Sam	49	18	40	313.00	9.27
9th	Simpson, Paul	49	23	8	313.00	9.28
10th	Wanttinen, Olli	51	2	2	313.00	9.47

Cumulative Pace by Stage Finishers

STAGE 9
DATE APRIL 8, 1929
LOCATION CUMBERLAND, MD.

Place	Name	Hours	Minutes	Secs	Miles Run	Pace Per Mile
1st	Gardner, Eddie	51	21	10	352.00	8.45
2nd	Salo, Johnny	51	57	12	352.00	8.52
3rd	Gavuzzi, Pete	54	57	12	352.00	9.22
4th	Newton, Arthur	54	58	29	352.00	9.22
5th	Umek, Guisto	56	35	6	352.00	9.39

STAGE 10
DATE APRIL 9, 1929
LOCATION UNIONTOWN, PA.

Place	Name	Hours	Minutes	Secs	Miles Run	Pace Per Mile
1st	Gardner, Eddie	62	59	40	414.80	9.07
2nd	Salo, Johnny	64	12	57	414.80	9.17
3rd	Gavuzzi, Pete	65	46	7	414.80	9.31
4th	Umek, Guisto	66	53	21	414.80	9.41
5th	Richman, Sam	68	15	55	414.80	9.52
6th	Newton, Arthur	70	14	44	414.80	10.10
7th	Granville, Philip	70	17	52	414.80	10.10
8th	Houfstater, Voight	71	0	40	414.80	10.16
9th	Simpson, Paul	71	19	3	414.80	10.19
10th	Hedeman, Herbert	71	25	3	414.80	10.20

STAGE 11
DATE APRIL 10, 1929
LOCATION WAYNESBURG, PA.

Place	Name	Hours	Minutes	Secs	Miles Run	Pace Per Mile
1st	Gardner, Eddie	68	11	11	447.30	9.09
2nd	Salo, Johnny	70	53	42	447.30	9.31
3rd	Gavuzzi, Pete	70	57	37	447.30	9.31
4th	Umek, Guisto	72	57	37	447.30	9.47
5th	Richman, Sam	73	29	40	447.30	9.52

Cumulative Pace by Stage Finishers

Place	Name	Hours	Minutes	Secs	Miles Run	Pace Per Mile
6th	Simpson, Paul	76	5	18	447.30	10.13
7th	Granville, Philip	76	23	12	447.30	10.15
8th	Newton, Arthur	76	32	14	447.30	10.16
9th	Houfstater, Voight	79	9	25	447.30	10.37
10th	Hedeman, Herbert	79	19	13	447.30	10.38

STAGE   12
DATE   APRIL 11, 1929
LOCATION   WHEELING, W.VA.

Place	Name	Hours	Minutes	Secs	Miles Run	Pace Per Mile
1st	Gardner, Eddie	77	53	40	499.50	9.22
2nd	Gavuzzi, Pete	79	0	22	499.50	9.29
3rd	Salo, Johnny	81	38	27	499.50	9.49
4th	Richman, Sam	83	32	30	499.50	10.02
5th	Umek, Guisto	03	36	51	499.50	10.02
6th	Simpson, Paul	84	37	33	499.50	10.10
7th	Granville, Philip	88	19	57	499.50	10.37
8th	Newton, Arthur	88	42	54	499.50	10.40
9th	Houfstater, Voight	91	10	38	499.50	10.57
10th	Hedeman, Herbert	92	20	33	499.50	11.05

STAGE   13
DATE   APRIL 12, 1929
LOCATION   CAMBRIDGE, OHIO

Place	Name	Hours	Minutes	Secs	Miles Run	Pace Per Mile
1st	Gardner, Eddie	86	29	25	549.70	9.26
2nd	Gavuzzi, Pete	86	31	27	549.70	9.26
3rd	Salo, Johnny	91	23	7	549.70	9.58
4th	Umek, Guisto	92	17	21	549.70	10.04
5th	Simpson, Paul	92	32	18	549.70	10.06
6th	Richman, Sam	93	2	20	549.70	10.10
7th	Granville, Philip	98	29	57	549.70	10.45

Cumulative Pace by Stage Finishers

Place	Name	Hours	Minutes	Secs	Miles Run	Pace Per Mile
8th	Newton, Arthur	103	9	14	549.70	11.16
9th	Hedeman, Herbert	103	9	14	549.70	11.16
10th	Houfstater, Voight	104	3	53	549.70	11.22

STAGE 14
DATE APRIL 13, 1929
LOCATION ZANESVILLE, OHIO

Place	Name	Hours	Minutes	Secs	Miles Run	Pace Per Mile
1st	Gavuzzi, Pete	89	39	52	574.90	9.22
2nd	Gardner, Eddie	90	8	55	574.90	9.25
3rd	Salo, Johnny	94	44	52	574.90	9.53
4th	Umek, Guisto	96	4	31	574.90	10.02
5th	Richman, Sam	97	8	0	574.90	10.08
6th	Simpson, Paul	97	13	33	574.90	10.09
7th	Granville, Philip	102	17	7	574.90	10.41
8th	Newton, Arthur	107	53	59	574.90	11.16
9th	Hedeman, Herbert	109	20	53	574.90	11.25
10th	McNamara, M. B.	111	36	22	574.90	11.39

STAGE 15
DATE APRIL 14, 1929
LOCATION COLUMBUS, OHIO

Place	Name	Hours	Minutes	Secs	Miles Run	Pace Per Mile
1st	Gavuzzi, Pete	97	33	7	629.70	9.18
2nd	Gardner, Eddie	98	2	10	629.70	9.20
3rd	Salo, Johnny	102	54	37	629.70	9.49
4th	Umek, Guisto	105	6	11	629.70	10.01
5th	Richman, Sam	106	34	40	629.70	10.10
6th	Simpson, Paul	109	11	43	629.70	10.24
7th	Granville, Philip	113	2	17	629.70	10.46
8th	Hedeman, Herbert	118	58	3	629.70	11.20
9th	Gonzales, Seth	120	41	14	629.70	11.30
10th	Newton, Arthur	120	54	44	629.70	11.31

Cumulative Pace by Stage Finishers

STAGE   16
DATE   APRIL 15, 1929
LOCATION   SPRINGFIELD, OHIO

Place	Name	Hours	Minutes	Secs	Miles Run	Pace Per Mile
1st	Gavuzzi, Pete	104	1	22	673.10	9.16
2nd	Gardner, Eddie	105	0	50	673.10	9.22
3rd	Salo, Johnny	110	0	5	673.10	9.49
4th	Umek, Guisto	113	37	21	673.10	10.80
5th	Richman, Sam	114	49	30	673.10	10.14
6th	Simpson, Paul	119	31	58	673.10	10.40
7th	Granville, Philip	121	9	7	673.10	10.48
8th	McNamara M. B.	128	12	42	673.10	11.26
9th	Hedeman, Herbert	130	17	43	673.10	11.37
10th	Newton, Arthur	132	34	44	673.10	11.49

STAGE   17
DATE   APRIL 16, 1929
LOCATION   RICHMOND, IND.

Place	Name	Hours	Minutes	Secs	Miles Run	Pace Per Mile
1st	Gavuzzi, Pete	113	13	12	736.10	9.14
2nd	Gardner, Eddie	114	57	0	736.10	9.22
3rd	Salo, Johnny	119	2	7	736.10	9.42
4th	Umek, Guisto	124	30	51	736.10	10.09
5th	Richman, Sam	127	4	45	736.10	10.22
6th	Granville, Philip	133	24	22	736.10	10.52
7th	Simpson, Paul	133	54	28	736.10	10.55
8th	McNamara M. B.	140	33	57	736.10	11.28
9th	Hedeman, Herbert	144	43	28	736.10	11.48
10th	Newton, Arthur	147	27	14	736.10	12.01

STAGE   18
DATE   APRIL 17, 1929
LOCATION   KNIGHTSBRIDGE, IND.

Place	Name	Hours	Minutes	Secs	Miles Run	Pace Per Mile
1st	Gavuzzi, Pete	118	58	27	770.80	9.16
2nd	Gardner, Eddie	120	16	15	770.80	9.22

Cumulative Pace by Stage Finishers

Place	Name	Hours	Minutes	Secs	Miles Run	Pace Per Mile
3rd	Salo, Johnny	123	28	12	770.80	9.37
4th	Umek, Guisto	130	51	51	770.80	10.11
5th	Richman, Sam	132	32	30	770.80	10.19
6th	Granville, Philip	139	43	7	770.80	10.53
7th	Simpson, Paul	140	58	28	770.80	10.58
8th	McNamara, Mike	146	3	12	770.80	11.22
9th	Hedeman, Herbert	152	11	28	770.80	11.51
10th	Newton, Arthur	154	32	14	770.80	12.02

STAGE 19
DATE APRIL 18, 1929
LOCATION INDIANAPOLIS, IND.

Place	Name	Hours	Minutes	Secs	Miles Run	Pace Per Mile
1st	Gavuzzi, Pete	123	37	47	806.10	9.12
2nd	Gardner, Eddie	125	55	27	806.10	9.22
3rd	Salo, Johnny	127	55	27	806.10	9.31
4th	Umek, Guisto	135	57	31	806.10	10.07
5th	Richman, Sam	138	8	5	806.10	10.17
6th	Simpson, Paul	145	23	18	806.10	10.49
7th	Granville, Philip	146	17	57	806.10	10.53
8th	McNamara, M. B.	151	49	22	806.10	11.18
9th	Hedeman, Herbert	160	39	4	806.10	11.58
10th	Newton, Arthur	160	39	4	806.10	11.58

STAGE 20
DATE APRIL 19, 1929
LOCATION BRAZIL, IND.

Place	Name	Hours	Minutes	Secs	Miles Run	Pace Per Mile
1st	Gavuzzi, Pete	131	34	2	863.10	9.09
2nd	Gardner, Eddie	135	20	45	863.10	9.25
3rd	Salo, Johnny	135	44	37	863.10	9.26
4th	Umek, Guisto	145	6	51	863.10	10.05
5th	Richman, Sam	148	48	35	863.10	10.20

Cumulative Pace by Stage Finishers

Place	Name	Hours	Minutes	Secs	Miles Run	Pace Per Mile
6th	Simpson, Paul	153	55	28	863.10	10.42
7th	Granville, Philip	155	13	17	863.10	10.47
8th	McNamara, M. B.	160	59	2	863.10	11.11
9th	Newton, Arthur	170	10	19	863.10	11.50
10th	Hedeman, Herbert	170	10	19	863.10	11.50

STAGE   21
DATE   APRIL 20, 1929
LOCATION   MARSHALL, IND.

Place	Name	Hours	Minutes	Secs	Miles Run	Pace Per Mile
1st	Gavuzzi, Pete	136	25	12	896.10	9.08
2nd	Gardner, Eddie	140	11	55	896.10	9.23
3rd	Salo, Johnny	140	35	47	896.10	9.25
4th	Umek, Guisto	152	16	21	896.10	10.12
5th	Richman, Sam	154	28	20	896.10	10.20
6th	Simpson, Paul	158	27	13	896.10	10.37
7th	Granville, Philip	160	56	27	896.10	10.47
8th	McNamara M. B.	166	30	42	896.10	11.09
9th	Hedeman, Herbert	177	28	28	896.10	11.53
10th	Abramowitz, Harry	182	22	42	896.10	12.13

STAGE   22
DATE   APRIL 21, 1929
LOCATION   EFFINGHAM, ILL.

Place	Name	Hours	Minutes	Secs	Miles Run	Pace Per Mile
1st	Gavuzzi, Pete	143	59	22	948.50	9.07
2nd	Salo, Johnny	147	47	32	948.50	9.21
3rd	Gardner, Eddie	148	34	5	948.50	9.24
4th	Umek, Guisto	159	31	36	948.50	10.05
5th	Richman, Sam	164	47	10	948.50	10.25
6th	Simpson, Paul	166	54	23	948.50	10.34
7th	Granville, Philip	168	30	37	948.50	10.40
8th	McNamara, M. B.	174	38	2	948.50	11.03

Cumulative Pace by Stage Finishers

STAGE 23

DATE APRIL 22, 1929

LOCATION VANDALIA, ILL.

Place	Name	Hours	Minutes	Secs	Miles Run	Pace Per Mile
1st	Gavuzzi, Pete	148	6	12	980.30	9.04
2nd	Salo, Johnny	152	40	55	980.30	9.21
3rd	Gardner, Eddie	152	40	55	980.30	9.21
4th	Umek, Guisto	164	2	51	980.30	10.02
5th	Richman, Sam	169	54	15	980.30	10.24
6th	Simpson, Paul	171	17	33	980.30	10.29
7th	Granville, Philip	173	1	32	980.30	10.35
8th	McNamara, M. B.	179	41	17	980.30	11.00
9th	Hedeman, Herbert	196	12	53	980.30	12.01
10th	Abramowitz, Harry	197	17	12	980.30	12.05

STAGE 24

DATE APRIL 23, 1929

LOCATION COLLINSVILLE, ILL.

Place	Name	Hours	Minutes	Secs	Miles Run	Pace Per Mile
1st	Gavuzzi, Pete	157	2	57	1040.10	9.04
2nd	Salo, Johnny	160	39	32	1040.10	9.16
3rd	Gardner, Eddie	161	44	5	1040.10	9.20
4th	Umek, Guisto	175	5	1	1040.10	10.06
5th	Simpson, Paul	179	36	28	1040.10	10.22
6th	Richman, Sam	180	15	0	1040.10	10.24
7th	Granville, Philip	182	45	37	1040.10	10.32
8th	McNamara, M. B.	187	1	22	1040.10	10.47
9th	Abramowitz, Harry	207	45	22	1040.10	11.59
10th	Hedeman, Herbert	208	27	0	1040.10	12.01

STAGE 25

DATE APRIL 24, 1929

LOCATION MAPLEWOOD, MO.

Place	Name	Hours	Minutes	Secs	Miles Run	Pace Per Mile
1st	Gavuzzi, Pete	159	55	47	1062.10	9.02

Cumulative Pace by Stage Finishers

Place	Name	Hours	Minutes	Secs	Miles Run	Pace Per Mile
2nd	Salo, Johnny	163	34	22	1062.10	9.14
3rd	Gardner, Eddie	164	22	55	1062.10	9.17
4th	Umek, Guisto	178	3	46	1062.10	10.04
5th	Simpson, Paul	182	33	38	1062.10	10.19
6th	Richman, Sam	183	10	0	1062.10	10.21
7th	Granville, Philip	186	16	22	1062.10	10.31

STAGE 26

DATE APRIL 25, 1929

LOCATION SULLIVAN, MO.

Place	Name	Hours	Minutes	Secs	Miles Run	Pace Per Mile
1st	Gavuzzi, Pete	169	35	7	1123.10	9.04
2nd	Salo, Johnny	172	16	32	1123.10	9.12
3rd	Gardner, Eddie	175	30	5	1123.10	9.23
4th	Umek, Guisto	187	26	56	1123.10	10.01
5th	Simpson, Paul	191	44	53	1123.10	10.14
6th	Richman, Sam	194	17	10	1123.10	10.23
7th	Granville, Philip	197	40	30	1123.10	10.34

STAGE 27

DATE APRIL 26, 1929

LOCATION ROLLA, MO

Place	Name	Hours	Minutes	Secs	Miles Run	Pace Per Mile
1st	Gavuzzi, Pete	176	22	34	1168.10	9.04
2nd	Salo, Johnny	179	16	12	1168.10	9.13
3rd	Gardner, Eddie	182	29	45	1168.10	9.22
4th	Umek, Guisto	197	48	3	1168.10	10.10
5th	Simpson, Paul	198	49	41	1168.10	10.13
6th	Richman, Sam	201	16	50	1168.10	10.20
7th	Granville, Philip	204	50	10	1168.10	10.31
8th	McNamara, M. B.	219	33	42	1168.10	11.17
9th	Abramowitz, Harry	231	50	52	1168.10	11.55
10th	Hedeman, Herbert	236	42	45	1168.10	12.10

Cumulative Pace by Stage Finishers

STAGE 28
DATE APRIL 27, 1929
LOCATION WAYNESVILLE, MO.

Place	Name	Hours	Minutes	Secs	Miles Run	Pace Per Mile
1st	Gavuzzi, Pete	180	31	47	1200.10	9.02
2nd	Salo, Johnny	183	36	12	1200.10	9.11
3rd	Gardner, Eddie	187	48	5	1200.10	9.23
4th	Umek, Guisto	198	11	41	1200.10	9.55
5th	Simpson, Paul	202	31	3	1200.10	10.07
6th	Richman, Sam	206	4	0	1200.10	10.18
7th	Granville, Philip	209	52	15	1200.10	10.29
8th	McNamara, M. B.	224	6	52	1200.10	11.12
9th	Abramowitz, Harry	237	23	7	1200.10	11.52
10th	Hedeman, Herbert	237	23	7	1200.10	11.52

STAGE 29
DATE APRIL 28, 1929
LOCATION CONWAY, MO.

Place	Name	Hours	Minutes	Secs	Miles Run	Pace Per Mile
1st	Gavuzzi, Pete	188	46	8	1250.10	9.04
2nd	Salo, Johnny	191	38	52	1250.10	9.12
3rd	Gardner, Eddie	195	39	15	1250.10	9.23
4th	Umek, Guisto	205	8	51	1250.10	9.51
5th	Simpson, Paul	210	41	28	1250.10	10.70
6th	Richman, Sam	213	7	20	1250.10	10.14
7th	Granville, Philip	217	54	35	1250.10	10.28
8th	McNamara, M. B.	233	35	2	1250.10	11.13
9th	Abramowitz, Harry	246	20	47	1250.10	11.49
10th	Hedeman, Herbert	251	17	43	1250.10	12.04

STAGE 30
DATE APRIL 29, 1929
LOCATION SPRINGFIELD, MO.

Place	Name	Hours	Minutes	Secs	Miles Run	Pace Per Mile
1st	Gavuzzi, Pete	193	37	17	1291.10	9.00

Cumulative Pace by Stage Finishers

Place	Name	Hours	Minutes	Secs	Miles Run	Pace Per Mile
2nd	Salo, Johnny	196	50	17	1291.10	9.09
3rd	Gardner, Eddie	203	8	5	1291.10	9.26
4th	Umek, Guisto	210	37	11	1291.10	9.47
5th	Simpson, Paul	217	17	38	1291.10	10.06
6th	Richman, Sam	218	49	10	1291.10	10.10
7th	Granville, Philip	223	52	15	1291.10	10.24
8th	McNamara, M. B.	240	22	47	1291.10	11.10
9th	Abramowitz, Harry	252	38	55	1291.10	11.44
10th	Hedeman, Herbert	256	38	35	1291.10	11.56

STAGE   31
DATE   APRIL 30, 1929
LOCATION   MILLER, MO.

Place	Name	Hours	Minutes	Secs	Miles Run	Pace Per Mile
1st	Gavuzzi, Pete	197	12	27	1324.80	8.56
2nd	Salo, Johnny	201	50	22	1324.80	9.08
3rd	Gardner, Eddie	209	8	55	1324.80	9.28
4th	Umek, Guisto	215	14	21	1324.80	9.45
5th	Simpson, Paul	222	17	43	1324.80	10.04
6th	Richman, Sam	223	15	15	1324.80	10.07
7th	Granville, Philip	220	30	30	1324.80	10.11
8th	McNamara, M.B.	246	10	7	1324.80	11.09
9th	Abramowitz, Harry	257	32	7	1324.80	11.40
10th	Hedeman, Herbert	261	11	40	1324.80	11.50

STAGE   32
DATE   MAY 1, 1929
LOCATION   JOPLIN, MO.

Place	Name	Hours	Minutes	Secs	Miles Run	Pace Per Mile
1st	Gavuzzi, Pete	204	27	47	1371.80	8.56
2nd	Salo, Johnny	207	41	32	1371.80	9.05
3rd	Gardner, Eddie	215	19	10	1371.80	9.25
4th	Umek, Guisto	221	37	1	1371.80	9.41

Cumulative Pace by Stage Finishers

Place	Name	Hours	Minutes	Secs	Miles Run	Pace Per Mile
5th	Simpson, Paul	228	43	0	1371.80	10.00
6th	Richman, Sam	229	49	45	1371.80	10.03
7th	Granville, Philip	235	43	0	1371.80	10.19
8th	McNamara, M. B.	253	49	17	1371.80	11.06
9th	Abramowitz, Harry	264	51	42	1371.80	11.35
10th	Hedeman, Herbert	267	16	40	1371.80	11.41

STAGE   33
DATE   MAY 2, 1929
LOCATION   MIAMI, OKLA.

Place	Name	Hours	Minutes	Secs	Miles Run	Pace Per Mile
1st	Gavuzzi, Pete	209	24	57	1408.50	8.55
2nd	Salo, Johnny	212	24	57	1408.50	9.03
3rd	Gardner, Eddie	220	54	20	1408.50	9.25
4th	Umek, Guisto	226	50	46	1408.50	9.40
5th	Simpson, Paul	233	32	8	1408.50	9.57
6th	Richman, Sam	234	26	35	1408.50	9.59
7th	Granville, Philip	250	52	40	1408.50	10.41
8th	McNamara, M, B.	259	5	17	1408.50	11.02
9th	Abramowitz, Harry	270	43	2	1408.50	11.32
10th	Hedeman, Herbert	271	32	40	1408.50	11.34

STAGE   34
DATE   MAY 3, 1929
LOCATION   CHELSEA, OKLA.

Place	Name	Hours	Minutes	Secs	Miles Run	Pace Per Mile
1st	Gavuzzi, Pete	217	12	2	1463.20	8.55
2nd	Salo, Johnny	219	59	32	1463.20	9.01
3rd	Umek, Guisto	233	54	31	1463.20	9.35
4th	Gardner, Eddie	234	54	31	1463.20	9.38
5th	Simpson, Paul	242	5	23	1463.20	9.56
6th	Richman, Sam	243	25	55	1463.20	9.59
7th	Granville, Philip	248	46	30	1463.20	10.12

Cumulative Pace by Stage Finishers

Place	Name	Hours	Minutes	Secs	Miles Run	Pace Per Mile
8th	McNamara, M. B.	267	10	27	1463.20	10.58
9th	Abramowitz, Harry	279	28	12	1463.20	11.28
10th	Hedeman, Herbert	282	56	45	1463.20	11.36

STAGE 35

DATE MAY 4, 1929

LOCATION MUSKOGEE, OKLA.

Place	Name	Hours	Minutes	Secs	Miles Run	Pace Per Mile
1st	Gavuzzi, Pete	228	13	12	1536.60	8.55
2nd	Salo, Johnny	231	0	42	1536.60	9.01
3rd	Umek, Guisto	243	36	51	1536.60	9.31
4th	Gardner, Eddie	0	0	0	1536.60	0.00
5th	Simpson, Paul	253	43	43	1536.60	9.55
6th	Richman, Sam	255	51	5	1536.60	9.59
7th	Granville, Philip	260	27	35	1536.60	10.10
8th	McNamara, M.	279	56	38	1536.60	10.56
9th	Abramowitz, Harry	291	53	22	1536.60	11.24
10th	Hedeman, Herbert	295	21	55	1536.60	11.32

STAGE 36

DATE MAY 5, 1929

LOCATION OKMULGEE, OKLA.

Place	Name	Hours	Minutes	Secs	Miles Run	Pace Per Mile
1st	Gavuzzi, Pete	234	54	2	1580.60	8.55
2nd	Salo, Johnny	237	41	32	1580.60	9.01
3rd	Umek, Guisto	249	17	41	1580.60	9.28
4th	Simpson, Paul	260	11	13	1580.60	9.53
5th	Richman, Sam	263	26	35	1580.60	10.00
6th	Granville, Philip	267	39	20	1580.60	10.10
7th	McNamara M. B.	288	10	27	1580.60	10.56
8th	Abramowitz, Harry	299	28	42	1580.60	11.22
9th	Hedeman, Herbert	306	1	25	1580.60	11.37
10th	Joyce, Mike	331	0	19	1580.60	12.34

Cumulative Pace by Stage Finishers

STAGE	37
DATE	MAY 6, 1929
LOCATION	HOLDENVILLE, OKLA.

Place	Name	Hours	Minutes	Secs	Miles Run	Pace Per Mile
1st	Gavuzzi, Pete	243	52	42	1640.60	8.55
2nd	Salo, Johnny	245	48	12	1640.60	8.59
3rd	Umek, Guisto	257	55	51	1640.60	9.26
4th	Simpson, Paul	269	18	28	1640.60	9.51
5th	Richman, Sam	273	7	45	1640.60	9.59
6th	Granville, Philip	277	40	20	1640.60	10.10
7th	McNamara, M. B.	298	53	32	1640.60	10.56
8th	Abramowitz, Harry	310	24	32	1640.60	11.21

STAGE	38
DATE	MAY 7, 1929
LOCATION	COALGATE, OKLA.

Place	Name	Hours	Minutes	Secs	Miles Run	Pace Per Mile
1st	Gavuzzi, Pete	251	20	12	1694.60	8.54
2nd	Salo, Johnny	253	56	17	1694.60	8.59
3rd	Umek, Guisto	266	58	1	1694.60	9.27
4th	Simpson, Paul	277	46	0	1694.60	9.50
5th	Richman, Sam	282	17	45	1694.60	10.00
6th	Granville, Philip	286	12	0	1694.60	10.08
7th	McNamara, M. B.	307	50	47	1694.60	10.54
8th	Abramowitz, Harry	319	41	37	1694.60	0.00

STAGE	39
DATE	MAY 8, 1929
LOCATION	DURANT, OKLA.

Place	Name	Hours	Minutes	Secs	Miles Run	Pace Per Mile
1st	Gavuzzi, Pete	258	48	12	1744.60	8.54
2nd	Salo, Johnny	260	41	27	1744.60	8.58
3rd	Umek, Guisto	274	34	31	1744.60	9.26
4th	Simpson, Paul	284	56	48	1744.60	9.48

Cumulative Pace by Stage Finishers

Place	Name	Hours	Minutes	Secs	Miles Run	Pace Per Mile
5th	Richman, Sam	290	24	25	1744.60	8.59
6th	Granville, Philip	295	26	45	1744.60	10.10
7th	McNamara, M. B.	316	18	57	1744.60	10.53
8th	Abramowitz, Harry	327	48	17	1744.60	11.16
9th	Hedeman, Herbert	338	57	5	1744.60	11.40
10th	Joyce, Mike	348	11	24	1744.60	11.58

STAGE 40
DATE MAY 9, 1929
LOCATION SHERMAN, TEX.

Place	Name	Hours	Minutes	Secs	Miles Run	Pace Per Mile
1st		263	27	42	1777.60	8.53
2nd	Salo, Johnny	265	49	42	1777.60	8.58
3rd	Umek, Guisto	279	34	41	1777.60	9.26
4th	Simpson, Paul	289	24	18	1777.60	9.46
5th	Richman, Sam	295	24	35	1777.60	9.58
6th	Granville, Philip	300	2	0	1777.60	10.08
7th	McNamara, M. B.	321	16	37	1777.60	10.50
8th	Abramowitz, Harry	333	17	22	1777.60	11.15
9th	Hedeman, Herbert	345	45	15	1777.60	11.40
10th	Joyce, Mike	353	43	20	1777.60	11.56

STAGE 41
DATE MAY 10, 1929
LOCATION DALLAS, TEX.

Place	Name	Hours	Minutes	Secs	Miles Run	Pace Per Mile
1st	Gavuzzi, Pete	275	42	12	1857.50	8.55
2nd	Salo, Johnny	277	11	57	1857.50	8.57
3rd	Umek, Guisto	291	39	25	1857.50	9.25
4th	Simpson, Paul	303	51	23	1857.50	9.49
5th	Richman, Sam	308	51	23	1857.50	9.59
6th	Granville, Philip	312	37	20	1857.50	10.06
7th	McNamara, M. B.	334	54	57	1857.50	10.49

Cumulative Pace by Stage Finishers

Place	Name	Hours	Minutes	Secs	Miles Run	Pace Per Mile
8th	Abramowitz, Harry	347	27	2	1857.50	11.13
9th	Hedeman, Herbert	358	20	30	1857.50	11.34

STAGE 42
DATE MAY 12, 1929
LOCATION FORT WORTH, TEX.

Place	Name	Hours	Minutes	Secs	Miles Run	Pace Per Mile
1st	Gavuzzi, Pete	280	35	22	1889.50	8.55
2nd	Salo, Johnny	282	5	7	1889.50	8.58
3rd	Umek, Guisto	296	34	31	1889.50	9.25
4th	Simpson, Paul	308	43	13	1889.50	9.48
5th	Richman, Sam	313	13	5	1889.50	9.57
6th	Granville, Philip	317	27	25	1889.50	10.05
7th	McNamara, M. B.	340	46	17	1889.50	10.49
8th	Abramowitz Harry	352	51	12	1889.50	11.12
9th	Hedeman, Herbert	362	41	10	1889.50	11.31
10th	Joyce, Mike	376	120	29	1889.50	12.00

STAGE 43
DATE MAY 12, 1929
LOCATION MINERAL WELLS, TEX.

Place	Name	Hours	Minutes	Secs	Miles Run	Pace Per Mile
1st	Gavuzzi, Pete	288	41	27	1942.50	8.55
2nd	Salo, Johnny	290	11	12	1942.50	8.58
3rd	Umek, Guisto	303	35	51	1942.50	9.23
4th	Simpson, Paul	316	42	23	1942.50	9.47
5th	Richman, Sam	321	13	15	1942.50	9.55

STAGE 44
DATE MAY 13, 1929
LOCATION BRECKENRIDGE, TEX.

Place	Name	Hours	Minutes	Secs	Miles Run	Pace Per Mile
1st	Gavuzzi, Pete	297	30	22	1996.90	8.56

Cumulative Pace by Stage Finishers

Place	Name	Hours	Minutes	Secs	Miles Run	Pace Per Mile
2nd	Salo, Johnny	299	0	17	1996.90	8.59
3rd	Umek, Guisto	311	43	31	1996.90	9.22
4th	Simpson, Paul	325	26	33	1996.90	9.47
5th	Richman, Sam	328	38	5	1996.90	9.52
6th	Granville, Philip	334	49	25	1996.90	10.04
7th	McNamara, M. B.	358	6	37	1996.90	10.46
8th	Abramowitz, Harry	370	53	27	1996.90	11.08
9th	Hedeman, Herbert	378	13	5	1996.90	11.22
10th	Joyce, Mike	396	35	39	1996.90	11.55

STAGE   45
DATE   MAY 15, 1929
LOCATION   ALBANY, TEX.

Place	Name	Hours	Minutes	Secs	Miles Run	Pace Per Mile
1st	Gavuzzi, Pete	300	52	40	2021.60	8.56
2nd	Salo, Johnny	302	22	28	2021.60	8.58

STAGE   46
DATE   MAY 15, 1929
LOCATION   ANSON, TEX.

Place	Name	Hours	Minutes	Secs	Miles Run	Pace Per Mile
1st	Gavuzzi, Pete	306	19	47	2061.00	8.56
2nd	Salo, Johnny	307	30	32	2061.00	8.57
3rd	Umek, Guisto	321	35	16	2061.00	9.22
4th	Simpson, Paul	334	53	53	2061.00	8.45
5th	Richman, Sam	336	56	55	2061.00	9.49
6th	Granville, Philip	345	5	15	2061.00	10.03
7th	McNamara, M. B.	368	24	27	2061.00	10.44
8th	Abramowitz, Harry	381	39	2	2061.00	11.07
9th	Hedeman, Herbert	386	40	20	2061.00	11.16
10th	Joyce, Mike	408	36	14	2061.00	11.54

Cumulative Pace by Stage Finishers

STAGE 47
DATE MAY 16, 1929
LOCATION SWEETWATER, TEX.

Place	Name	Hours	Minutes	Secs	Miles Run	Pace Per Mile
1st	Gavuzzi, Pete	314	5	57	2117.20	8.54
2nd	Salo, Johnny	315	6	12	2117.20	8.56
3rd	Umek, Guisto	329	28	18	2117.20	9.20
4th	Simpson, Paul	344	15	13	2117.20	9.46
5th	Richman, Sam	344	44	5	2117.20	9.46
6th	Granville, Philip	353	59	20	2117.20	10.02
7th	McNamara, M. B.	377	16	22	2117.20	10.41
8th	Abramowitz, Harry	390	32	55	2117.20	11.04
9th	Hedeman, Herbert	395	32	55	2117.20	11.13
10th	Joyce, Mike	419	35	4	2117.20	11.53

STAGE 48
DATE MAY 17, 1929
LOCATION COLORADO, TEX.

Place	Name	Hours	Minutes	Secs	Miles Run	Pace Per Mile
1st	Gavuzzi, Pete	318	51	2	2145.20	8.55
2nd	Salo, Johnny	319	26	22	2145.20	8.56
3rd	Umek, Guisto	335	56	6	2145.20	9.24
4th	Richman, Sam	348	49	20	2145.20	9.46
5th	Simpson, Paul	349	11	13	2145.20	9.46
6th	Granville, Philip	359	43	30	2145.20	10.04
7th	McNamara, M. B.	382	59	42	2145.20	10.43
8th	Abramowitz, Harry	396	21	52	2145.20	11.05
9th	Hedeman, Herbert	401	29	5	2145.20	11.14
10th	Joyce, Mike	424	46	9	2145.20	11.53

STAGE 49
DATE MAY 18, 1929
LOCATION BIG SPRING, TEX.

Place	Name	Hours	Minutes	Secs	Miles Run	Pace Per Mile
1st	Salo, Johnny	325	36	9	2186.20	8.56

Cumulative Pace by Stage Finishers

Place	Name	Hours	Minutes	Secs	Miles Run	Pace Per Mile
2nd	Gavuzzi, Pete	325	40	32	2186.20	8.56
3rd	Umek, Guisto	342	5	46	2186.20	9.23
4th	Richman, Sam	356	9	2	2186.20	9.46
5th	Simpson, Paul	358	9	2	2186.20	9.50

STAGE   50
DATE   MAY 19, 1929
LOCATION   MIDLAND, TEX.

Place	Name	Hours	Minutes	Secs	Miles Run	Pace Per Mile
1st	Salo, Johnny	330	45	7	2226.20	8.55
2nd	Gavuzzi, Pete	331	6	37	2226.20	8.55
3rd	Umek, Guisto	347	54	26	2226.20	9.23
4th	Richman, Sam	361	18	25	2226.20	9.44
5th	Simpson, Paul	362	53	33	2226.20	9.47
6th	Granville, Philip	375	52	50	2226.20	10.08
7th	McNamara, M. B.	396	39	52	2226.20	10.41
8th	Abramowitz, Harry	411	6	31	2226.20	11.05

STAGE   51
DATE   MAY 20, 1929
LOCATION   ODESSA, TEX.

Place	Name	Hours	Minutes	Secs	Miles Run	Pace Per Mile
1st	Salo, Johnny	333	25	27	2247.90	8.54
2nd	Gavuzzi, Pete	333	46	47	2247.90	8.55
3rd	Umek, Guisto	350	22	16	2247.90	9.21
4th	Richman, Sam	363	43	5	2247.90	9.43
5th	Simpson, Paul	365	48	38	2247.90	9.46
6th	Granville, Philip	378	37	50	2247.90	10.07
7th	McNamara, M. B.	399	43	23	2247.90	10.40
8th	Abramowitz, Harry	414	18	42	2247.90	11.04
9th	Hedeman, Herbert	417	15	45	2247.90	11.08
10th	Joyce, Mike	442	47	4	2247.90	11.49

Cumulative Pace by Stage Finishers

STAGE   52
DATE   MAY 21, 1929
LOCATION   MONAHANS, TEX.

Place	Name	Hours	Minutes	Secs	Miles Run	Pace Per Mile
1st	Salo, Johnny	338	17	27	2285.90	8.53
1st	Gavuzzi, Pete	338	38	57	2285.90	8.53
3rd	Umek, Guisto	354	39	21	2285.90	9.19
4th	Richman, Sam	368	0	10	2285.90	9.40
5th	Simpson, Paul	371	0	43	2285.90	9.44
6th	Granville, Phil	384	2	0	2285.90	10.05

STAGE   53
DATE   MAY 22, 1929
LOCATION   PECOS, TEX.

Place	Name	Hours	Minutes	Secs	Miles Run	Pace Per Mile
1st	Salo, Johnny	343	19	7	2324.90	8.52
2nd	Gavuzzi, Pete	343	40	37	2324.90	8.52
3rd	Umek, Guisto	359	35	26	2324.90	9.17
4th	Richman, Sam	372	40	0	2324.90	9.37
5th	Simpson, Paul	376	18	3	2324.90	9.43
6th	Granville, Philip	392	6	5	2324.90	10.07
7th	McNamara, M. B.	410	23	42	2324.90	10.35

No information is available for Stage 54.

STAGE   55
DATE   MAY 24, 1929
LOCATION   VAN HORN, TEX.

Place	Name	Hours	Minutes	Secs	Miles Run	Pace Per Mile
1st	Salo, Johnny	357	27	22	2420.40	8.52
2nd	Gavuzzi, Pete	357	48	52	2420.40	8.52
3rd	Umek, Guisto	371	55	26	2420.40	9.13
4th	Richman, Sam	384	57	32	2420.40	9.32
5th	Simpson, Paul	389	40	3	2420.40	9.40
6th	Granville, Philip	410	18	50	2420.40	10.10

Cumulative Pace by Stage Finishers

Place	Name	Hours	Minutes	Secs	Miles Run	Pace Per Mile
7th	McNamara, M. B.	420	21	47	2420.40	10.25
8th	Abramowitz, Harry	441	19	32	2420.40	10.56
9th	Hedeman, Herbert	446	33	10	2420.40	11.04
10th	Joyce, Mike	470	41	9	2420.40	11.67

STAGE 56
DATE MAY 25, 1929
LOCATION SIERRA BLANCA, TEX.

Place	Name	Hours	Minutes	Secs	Miles Run	Pace Per Mile
1st	Salo, Johnny	362	30	2	2454.80	8.52
2nd	Gavuzzi, Pete	362	51	32	2454.80	8.52
3rd	Umek, Guisto	376	42	38	2454.80	9.13
4th	Richman, Sam	390	18	12	2454.80	9.32
5th	Simpson, Paul	394	44	48	2454.80	9.39
6th	Granville, Philip	415	5	52	2454.80	10.09
7th	McNamara, M. B.	431	39	37	2454.80	10.33

STAGE 57
DATE MAY 26, 1929
LOCATION FABENS, TEX.

Place	Name	Hours	Minutes	Secs	Miles Run	Pace Per Mile
1st	Salo, Johnny	370	41	12	2514.20	8.51
2nd	Gavuzzi, Pete	371	58	2	2514.20	8.53
3rd	Umek, Guisto	384	53	48	2514.20	9.11
4th	Richman, Sam	399	24	42	2514.20	9.32
5th	Simpson, Paul	404	14	48	2514.20	9.39

STAGE 58
DATE MAY 27, 1929
LOCATION EL PASO, TEX.

Place	Name	Hours	Minutes	Secs	Miles Run	Pace Per Mile
1st	Salo, Johnny	374	39	12	2544.20	8.50
2nd	Gavuzzi, Pete	375	21	42	2544.20	8.51

Cumulative Pace by Stage Finishers

Place	Name	Hours	Minutes	Secs	Miles Run	Pace Per Mile
3rd	Umek, Guisto	388	49	48	2544.20	9.10
4th	Richman, Sam	403	14	37	2544.20	9.31
5th	Simpson, Paul	408	25	13	2544.20	9.38
6th	Granville, Philip	430	57	57	2544.20	10.10
7th	McNamara, M. B.	446	18	32	2544.20	10.32
8th	Abramowitz, Harry	461	41	2	2544.20	10.53
9th	Hedeman, Herbert	464	5	30	2544.20	10.56
10th	Joyce, Mike	492	15	49	2544.20	11.37

No information is available for Stage 59.

STAGE   60
DATE   MAY 29, 1929
LOCATION   DEMING, N.M.

Place	Name	Hours	Minutes	Secs	Miles Run	Pace Per Mile
1st	Gavuzzi, Pete	389	35	22	2651.20	8.49
2nd	Salo, Johnny	389	56	32	2651.20	8.49
3rd	Umek, Guisto	403	53	28	2651.20	9.08
4th	Richman, Sam	419	42	27	2651.20	9.30

No information is available for Stage 61.

STAGE   62
DATE   MAY 29, 1929
LOCATION   DUNCAN, ARIZ.

Place	Name	Hours	Minutes	Secs	Miles Run	Pace Per Mile
1st	Gavuzzi, Pete	404	23	47	2753.20	8.49
2nd	Salo, Johnny	404	44	57	2753.20	8.49
3rd	Umek, Guisto	418	48	58	2753.20	9.08
4th	Richman, Sam	440	2	22	2753.20	9.35
5th	Simpson, Paul	447	10	43	2753.20	9.45
6th	Granville, Philip	468	26	47	2753.20	10.13
7th	McNamara, M. B.	484	35	37	2753.20	10.34
8th	Hedeman, Herbert	494	49	28	2753.20	10.47
9th	Abramowitz, Harry	496	51	2	2753.20	10.50

Cumulative Pace by Stage Finishers

Place	Name	Hours	Minutes	Secs	Miles Run	Pace Per Mile
10th	Joyce, Mike	529	53	39	2753.20	11.33

No information is available for Stage 63.

STAGE   64
DATE   JUNE 2, 1929
LOCATION   BYLAS, ARIZ.

Place	Name	Hours	Minutes	Secs	Miles Run	Pace Per Mile
1st	Salo, Johnny	414	48	22	2833.60	8.47
2nd	Gavuzzi, Pete	415	5	11	2833.60	8.47
3rd	Umek, Guisto	429	16	38	2833.60	9.05
4th	Richman, Sam	449	43	2	2833.60	9.31
5th	Simpson, Paul	457	15	40	2833.60	9.41
6th	Granville, Philip	481	45	0	2833.60	10.12
7th	McNamara, M. B.	497	20	25	2833.60	10.32
8th	Hedeman, Herbert	507	25	13	2833.60	10.44
9th	Abramowitz Harry	510	1	47	2833.60	10.48
10th	Joyce, Mike	544	20	9	2833.60	11.32

STAGE   65
DATE   JUNE 3, 1929
LOCATION   MIAMI, ARIZ.

Place	Name	Hours	Minutes	Secs	Miles Run	Pace Per Mile
1st	Gavuzzi, Pete	424	10	6	2895.60	8.47
2nd	Salo, Johnny	424	26	14	2895.60	8.47
3rd	Umek, Guisto	438	47	8	2895.60	9.05
4th	Richman, Sam	458	38	0	2895.60	9.30
5th	Simpson, Paul	467	45	12	2895.60	9.41

STAGE   66
DATE   JUNE 4, 1929
LOCATION   SUPERIOR, ARIZ.

Place	Name	Hours	Minutes	Secs	Miles Run	Pace Per Mile
1st	Salo, Johnny	427	4	44	2917.30	8.47

Cumulative Pace by Stage Finishers

Place	Name	Hours	Minutes	Secs	Miles Run	Pace Per Mile
2nd	Gavuzzi, Pete	427	18	0	2917.30	8.47
3rd	Umek, Guisto	441	46	48	2917.30	9.05
4th	Richman, Sam	461	18	0	2917.30	9.29

STAGE 67
DATE JUNE 5, 1929
LOCATION MESA, ARIZ.

Place	Name	Hours	Minutes	Secs	Miles Run	Pace Per Mile
1st	Salo, Johnny	433	30	39	2968.30	8.46
2nd	Gavuzzi, Pete	434	52	48	2968.30	8.47
3rd	Umek, Guisto	449	15	18	2968.30	9.05
4th	Richman, Sam	468	50	48	2968.30	9.29
5th	Simpson, Paul	478	4	16	2968.30	9.40
6th	Granville, Philip	507	52	0	2968.30	10.16
7th	McNamara M. B.	520	47	22	2968.30	10.32
8th	Hedeman, Herbert	522	53	48	2968.30	10.34
9th	Abramowitz, Harry	533	51	41	2968.30	10.47
10th	Joyce, Mike	569	32	39	2968.30	11.31

STAGE 68
DATE JUNE 6, 1929
LOCATION BUCKEYE, ARIZ.

Place	Name	Hours	Minutes	Secs	Miles Run	Pace Per Mile
1st	Salo, Johnny	440	38	24	3022.50	8.45
2nd	Gavuzzi, Pete	442	12	43	3022.50	8.47
3rd	Umek, Guisto	457	2	58	3022.50	9.04

STAGE 69
DATE JUNE 7, 1929
LOCATION GILA BEND, ARIZ.

Place	Name	Hours	Minutes	Secs	Miles Run	Pace Per Mile
1st	Salo, Johnny	447	15	17	3069.70	8.44
2nd	Gavuzzi, Pete	448	41	22	3069.70	8.46
3rd	Umek, Guisto	463	21	33	3069.70	9.04

Cumulative Pace by Stage Finishers

Place	Name	Hours	Minutes	Secs	Miles Run	Pace Per Mile
4th	Richman, Sam	485	31	0	3069.70	9.29
5th	Simpson, Paul	498	43	36	3069.70	9.45
6th	Granville, Philip	523	45	0	3069.70	10.14

STAGE   70
DATE   JUNE 8, 1929
LOCATION   AZTEC, ARIZ.

Place	Name	Hours	Minutes	Secs	Miles Run	Pace Per Mile
1st	Salo, Johnny	453	55	24	3114.10	8.45
2nd	Gavuzzi, Pete	455	4	38	3114.10	8.46
3rd	Umek, Guisto	469	34	38	3114.10	9.03
4th	Richman, Sam	492	52	38	3114.10	9.30
5th	Simpson, Paul	505	56	26	3114.10	9.45
6th	Granville, Philip	532	7	20	3114.10	10.15
7th	McNamara, M. B.	546	14	14	3114.10	10.32

STAGE   71
DATE   JUNE 9, 1929
LOCATION   WELLTON, ARIZ.

Place	Name	Hours	Minutes	Secs	Miles Run	Pace Per Mile
1st	Salo, Johnny	460	46	14	3156.90	8.46
2nd	Gavuzzi, Pete	461	25	43	3156.90	8.46
3rd	Umek, Guisto	475	39	38	3156.90	9.02
4th	Richman, Sam	499	31	48	3156.90	9.29
5th	Simpson, Paul	512	47	16	3156.90	9.45
6th	Granville, Philip	540	0	2	3156.90	10.16

STAGE   72
DATE   JUNE 10, 1929
LOCATION   YUMA, ARIZ.

Place	Name	Hours	Minutes	Secs	Miles Run	Pace Per Mile
1st	Gavuzzi, Pete	467	29	28	3201.10	8.46
2nd	Salo, Johnny	468	18	3	3201.10	8.47
3rd	Umek, Guisto	482	18	3	3201.10	9.02

Cumulative Pace by Stage Finishers

Place	Name	Hours	Minutes	Secs	Miles Run	Pace Per Mile
4th	Richman, Sam	506	28	53	3201.10	9.29
5th	Simpson, Paul	521	49	36	3201.10	9.47

STAGE 73
DATE JUNE 11, 1929
LOCATION CALEXICO, CALIF.

Place	Name	Hours	Minutes	Secs	Miles Run	Pace Per Mile
1st	Gavuzzi, Pete	475	45	33	3259.90	8.46
2nd	Salo, Johnny	476	41	19	3259.90	8.46

STAGE 74
DATE JUNE 12, 1929
LOCATION JACUMBA, CALIF.

Place	Name	Hours	Minutes	Secs	Miles Run	Pace Per Mile
1st	Gavuzzi, Pete	485	30	28	3317.90	8.47
2nd	Salo, Johnny	485	50	24	3317.90	8.47
3rd	Umek, Guisto	500	10	8	3317.90	9.02

No information is available for Stage 75.

STAGE 76
DATE JUNE 14, 1929
LOCATION SAN JUAN CAP, CALIF.

Place	Name	Hours	Minutes	Secs	Miles Run	Pace Per Mile
1st	Gavuzzi, Pete	512	4	28	3461.40	8.53
2nd	Salo, Johnny	512	14	24	3461.40	8.53
3rd	Umek, Guisto	525	31	38	3461.40	9.07
4th	Richman, Sam	555	24	53	3461.40	9.38
5th	Simpson, Paul	571	30	36	3461.40	9.55
6th	Granville, Philip	601	34	5	3461.40	10.26
7th	McNamara, M. B.	612	0	9	3461.40	10.37
8th	Hedeman, Herbert	616	53	40	3461.40	10.41
9th	Abramowitz, Harry	620	24	11	3461.40	10.45
10th	Joyce, Mike	670	27	6	3461.40	11.37

Cumulative Pace by Stage Finishers

STAGE 77
DATE JUNE 15, 1929
LOCATION HUNTINGTON BEACH, CALIF.

Place	Name	Hours	Minutes	Secs	Miles Run	Pace Per Mile
1st	Gavuzzi, Pete	521	58	38	3523.40	8.53
2nd	Salo, Johnny	522	8	34	3523.40	8.53
3rd	Umek, Guisto	534	17	28	3523.40	9.06
4th	Richman, Sam	567	16	58	3523.40	9.40
5th	Simpson, Paul	582	6	41	3523.40	9.55
6th	Granville, Philip	614	21	15	3523.40	10.28
7th	McNamara, M. B.	628	11	19	3523.40	10.42

STAGE 78
DATE JUNE 16, 1929
LOCATION WRIGLEY PARK, CALIF.

Place	Name	Hours	Minutes	Secs	Miles Run	Pace Per Mile
1st	Salo, Johnny	525	56	10	3553.60	8.53
2nd	Gavuzzi, Pete	525	58	57	3553.60	8.53
3rd	Umek, Guisto	538	46	52	3553.60	9.06
4th	Richman, Sam	571	29	29	3553.60	9.39
5th	Simpson, Paul	586	30	42	3553.60	9.54
6th	Granville, Philip	618	54	23	3553.60	10.27
7th	McNamara, M. B.	627	45	28	3553.60	10.36
8th	Hedeman, Herbert	631	23	48	3553.60	10.40
9th	Abramowitz, Harry	634	46	20	3553.60	10.43
10th	Joyce, Mike	689	2	52	3553.60	11.38
11th	Shields, Guy	696	17	20	3553.60	11.46
12th	Harbine, Edwin	737	56	16	3553.60	12.28
13th	Cowley, Elmer	742	0	27	3553.60	12.32
14th	Harrison, Pat	748	20	51	3553.60	12.38
15th	Spangler, Joseph	755	50	14	3553.60	12.46
16th	Rehayn, George	765	0	52	3553.60	12.55
17th	Eskins, Charles	783	58	48	3553.60	13.14

Cumulative Pace by Stage Finishers

Place	Name	Hours	Minutes	Secs	Miles Run	Pace Per Mile
18th	Richman, Morris	854	11	11	3553.60	14.25
19th	Jusnick, George	882	7	34	3553.60	14.53

Note: Cumulative pace-per-mile data is calculated from finishing times listed in newspapers that covered the event. In five Stage races—Stage 54 to Kent, Texas; Stage 59 to Las Cruces, New Mexico; Stage 61 to Lordsburg, New Mexico; Stage 63 to Safford, Arizona; and Stage 75 to San Diego, California— surviving newspapers did not provide sufficient data to calculate pace per mile.

Appendix E

Marathon Pace by Mile

Time	Pace
2:50:00	6:29
3:00:00	6:52
3:10:00	7:15
3:15:00	7:26
3:20:00	7:38
3:30:00	8:01
3:40:00	8:23
3:45:00	8:35
3:50:00	8:46
3:55:00	8:58
4:00:00	9:09
4:10:00	9:32
4:20:00	9:55
4:30:00	10:18
4:40:00	10:41
4:50:00	11:04
5:00:00	11:27
5:15:00	12:01
5:30:00	12:35

Notes

Introduction

1. "Returns Home with News of 'Johnny Salo,'" *Daily Herald* (Passaic, N.J.), Aug. 7, 1929; Appendix C, "Pace by Stage Finishers," Stage 68; "Another Big Gain by Salo," *Daily Herald* (Passaic, N.J.), June 6, 1929.

2. William K. Klingaman, *1929: The Year of the Great Crash* (New York: Harper and Row, 1990), 11; *Official Program: C. C. Pyle's Second Annual International-Trans-Continental Foot Race, 1929* (New York: Longacre Press, ca. 1929).

3. Braven Dyer, "Gavuzzi Holds Lead in Derby," *Los Angeles Times*, June 14, 1929; "The Home Stretch of the Bunion Derby," *San Francisco Chronicle*, June 16, 1929.

4. "Salo Nears Gavuzzi in Pyle's Race," *Daily Herald* (Passaic, N.J.), May 17, 1929; Ed A. Fetting, "Salo's Seriousness and Grit Make Him a Winner," *Daily Herald* (Passaic, N.J.), Apr. 29, 1929; Edward J. Rearson, "Patrolman Dies in St. Mary's of Fractured Skull," *Daily Herald* (Passaic, N.J.), Oct. 5, 1931.

5. Charles B. Kastner, *Bunion Derby: The 1928 Footrace across America* (Albuquerque: Univ. of New Mexico Press, 2007), 137–39, 174.

6. "Peter Gavuzzi to Seek Record for Forty Mile Mark," *Hamilton Spectator* (Ontario, Canada), Sept. 30, 1931; Braven Dyer, "Pyle to Pay Off Tuesday," *Los Angeles Times*, June 23, 1929.

7. Rob Hadgraft, *Tea with Mr. Newton: 100,000 Miles: The Longest Protest March in History* (Essex, UK: Desert Island Books, 2009), 159–60; Harry Berry, *From L.A. to New York, from New York to L.A.* (Self-published, 1990), 85.

8. Robert W. Peterson, *Pigskin: The Early Years of Professional Football* (New York: Oxford Univ. Press, 1997), 88–89, 99; Jim Reisler, *Cash and Carry: The Spectacular Rise and Fall of C. C. Pyle, America's First Sports Agent* (Jefferson, N.C.: McFarland, 2009), 118–19, 183.

9. Robert W. Safford, "Pyle and Racers Plugging Away to Collinsville," *St. Louis Post Dispatch*, Apr. 23, 1929; *Official 1929 Program*; "2,200 Witness Pyle Show," *Miami News Record* (Okla.), May 3, 1929.

10. *Official 1929 Program*.

255

1. Race Day

1. David E. Kyvig, *Daily Life in the United States, 1920–1949* (Chicago: Ivan R. Dee, 2004), 3–4.

2. Michael E. Parrish, *Anxious Decades: America in Prosperity and Depression, 1920–1941* (New York: W. W. Norton, 1992), 31.

3. Maury Klein, *Rainbow's End: The Crash of 1929* (New York: Oxford Univ. Press, 2001), xvii; Kyvig, *Daily Life,* 27.

4. Klingaman, *1929,* 11–12.

5. Ibid.

6. Appendix A, "List of Starters"; *The WPA Guide to New York City: The Federal Writers Project Guide to 1930s New York with an Introduction by William H. Whyte* (1939; repr., New York: New Press, 1992), 180; Westbrook Pegler, "Joyce Jogs Along in Easter Parade," *Cleveland Plain Dealer,* Apr. 1 1929.

7. "Gardner Leads as 2nd Edition of Pyle Race Starts; Vets Bunch," *Philadelphia Inquirer,* Apr. 1, 1929; Arthur J. Daley, "76 Start Long Run, 500,000 Line Course," *New York Times,* Apr. 1, 1929.

8. *Bunion Derby,* Tape Master 5404, Catalog 56943 (Orland Park, IL: WPA Film Library, 1929).

9. "Gardner Leads," *Philadelphia Inquirer,* Apr. 1, 1929.

10. Pegler, "Joyce Jogs," *Cleveland Plain Dealer,* Apr. 1, 1929; Daley, "76 Start," *New York Times,* Apr. 1, 1929.

11. Daley, "76 Start," *New York Times,* Apr. 1, 1929.

12. Pegler, "Joyce Jogs," *Cleveland Plain Dealer,* Apr. 1, 1929.

13. Daley, "76 Start," *New York Times,* Apr. 1, 1929.

14. Ibid.

15. Arthur F. H. Newton, *Running in Three Continents* (London: H. F. and G. Witherby, 1940), 67; "Gardner Leads," *Philadelphia Inquirer,* Apr 1, 1929.

16. Daley, "76 Start," *New York Times,* Apr. 1, 1929.

17. Appendix C, "Pace by Stage Finishers," Stage 1; Kastner, *Bunion Derby,* 164–65.

18. Daley, "76 Start," *New York Times,* Apr. 1, 1929.

19. "Salo Running Strong Despite Bad Stomach," *Daily Herald* (Passaic, N.J.), Apr. 2, 1929.

20. Bill Gibson, "Gardner, Granville, Both Confident of $25,000 Plum," *Afro-American* (Baltimore), Apr. 13, 1929.

21. Kastner, *Bunion Derby,* 156–58; Wendell Merrill, "Given Another Great Ovation Last Night at School Stadium," *Daily News* (Passaic, N.J.), May 26, 1928.

22. Kastner, *Bunion Derby,* 159.

23. Ibid.

24. "Salo Running Strong," *Daily News* (Passaic, N.J.), Apr. 2, 1929.

25. Daley, "76 Start," *New York Times,* Apr. 1 1929.

26. Ibid.

27. "Pyle Bunion Derby Hopes for Better Days," *Wilmington Evening Journal* (Del.), Apr. 4, 1929.

28. Kastner, *Bunion Derby*, 29, 54.

29. Westbrook Pegler, "Bunioneers in Toils of Law," *Los Angeles Times*, Apr. 2, 1929.

30. "Off the Nut," *Elizabeth Daily Journal* (N.J.), Mar. 30, 1929.

31. Fred J. Betz, "Pyle Runners Depart," *Elizabeth Daily Journal* (N.J.), Apr. 1, 1929.

32. Ibid.

33. Pegler, "Bunioneers in Toils," *Los Angeles Times*, Apr. 2, 1929.

34. Pegler, "Joyce Jogs," *Cleveland Plain Dealer*, Apr. 1, 1929.

35. Ibid.; Arthur G. McMahon, "500,000 Watch Start of Pyle's Marathon in New York and Jersey," *Daily News* (Passaic, N.J.), Apr. 1, 1929.

36. Daley, "76 Start," *New York Times*, Apr. 1, 1929.

37. Gibson, "Gardner, Granville," *Afro American*, Apr. 13, 1929.

38. "Salo Running Strong," *Daily News* (Passaic, N.J.), Apr. 2, 1929.

39. "Ken Mullen Is 12th as Bunion Runners Cash in at Trenton," *Philadelphia Inquirer*, Apr. 2, 1929.

40. Ibid.

41. *Official 1929 Program.*

2. Down the Eastern Seaboard

1. Newton, *Running in Three Continents*, 68.

2. "Peter Gavuzzi to Seek Record for the Forty Mile Mark," *Hamilton Spectator* (Ontario, Canada), Mar. 30, 1931.

3. Tom Derderian, *Boston Marathon: The First Century of the World's Premier Running Event* (Champaign, Ill.: Human Kinetics, 1994), 156; Berry, *L.A. to New York*, 9, 21; Bruce Tulloh, *Four Million Footsteps: Los Angeles to New York—The Famous Runner's Account of His Record Breaking Marathon* (London: Mayflower, 1970) 19.

4. Kastner, *Bunion Derby*, 29; Berry, *L.A. to New York*, 9.

5. Kastner, *Bunion Derby*, 49.

6. Ibid., 64.

7. Ibid., 138–39.

8. Ibid., 15.

9. Berry, *L.A. to New York*, 19

10. Tim Noakes, *Lore of Running*, 4th ed. (Champaign, Ill.: Human Kinetics, 2001), 378; Edward Sears, *Running through the Ages* (Jefferson, N.C.: McFarland, 2001), 228.

11. Noakes, *Lore of Running*, 378.

12. Kastner, *Bunion Derby*, 59–60.

13. Hadgraft, *Tea with Mr. Newton*, 156–59; Berry, *L.A. to New York*, 85.

14. Berry, *L.A. to New York*, 85.

15. Newton, *Running in Three Continents*, 67.

16. Pegler, "Bunioneers in Toils," *Los Angeles Times*, Apr. 2, 1929.

17. *New Jersey: A Guide to Its Present and Past Compiled and Written by the Federal Writers' Project of the Works Progress Administration for the State of New Jersey* (1939; repr., New York: Hastings House, 1959), 398–401.

18. Newton, *Running in Three Continents*, 68.

19. Kastner, *Bunion Derby*, 169; Burgess Gordon and John C. Baker, "Observations on the Apparent Adaptability of the Body to Infections, Unusual Hardships, Changing Environment and Prolonged Strenuous Exertion," in *From L.A. to New York, from New York to L.A.*, by Harry Berry, 161–63.

20. Kastner, *Bunion Derby*, 49.

21. Ibid., 68.

22. "Ken Mullen Is 12th," *Philadelphia Inquirer*, Apr. 2, 1929.

23. Kastner, *Bunion Derby*, 123.

24. Ibid., 41, 164–67.

25. Pegler, "Bunioneers in Toils," *Los Angeles Times*, Apr. 2, 1929.

26. "Ken Mullen Is 12th," *Philadelphia Inquirer*, Apr. 2, 1929; Pegler, "Bunioneers in Toils," *Los Angeles Times*, Apr. 2, 1929.

27. Westbrook Pegler, "Sound of Cash Register Music to Pyle's Ears," *Cleveland Plain Dealer*, Apr. 3, 1929.

28. Ibid.

29. "Pyle Given Gate," *Elizabeth Daily Journal* (N.J.), Apr. 2, 1929.

30. Pegler, "Bunioneers in Toils," *Los Angeles Times*, Apr. 2, 1929.

31. "Pyle and Bunioneers Encounter Troubles," *Wilmington Evening Journal* (Del.), Apr. 2, 1929.

32. *Pennsylvania: A Guide to The Keystone State Compiled and Written by Workers of the Writers' Program of the Works Progress Administration in the State of Pennsylvania* (1940; repr., New York: Oxford Univ. Press, 1963), 256.

33. John Webster, "Trimble in First as Pack Reaches Philadelphia," *Philadelphia Inquirer*, Apr. 3, 1929.

34. "Salo Leads Runners to Wilmington," *Daily Herald* (Passaic, N.J.), Apr. 2, 1929.

35. Webster, "Trimble in First," *Philadelphia Inquirer*, Apr. 3, 1929.

36. Appendix C, "Pace by Stage Finishers," Stage 3.

37. "Simpson in Lead of Pyle Caravan," *New York Post*, Apr. 3, 1929.

38. "Bunioneers Here; Simpson Leading Man," *Wilmington Evening Journal* (Del.), Apr. 3, 1929; John Stone Jr., *The Hells of the Bunion Derby: Written to Be Understood* (Self-published, ca. 1928).

39. Newton, *Running in Three Continents*, 68.

40. Webster, "Trimble in First," *Philadelphia Inquirer*, Apr. 3, 1929.

41. "Simpson in Lead," *New York Post*, Apr. 3, 1929.

42. Berry, *L.A. to New York*, 86–87.

43. "Bunioneers Here," *Wilmington Evening Journal* (Del.), Apr. 3, 1929.

44. Webster, "Trimble in First," *Philadelphia Inquirer*, Apr. 3, 1929.

45. "Bunioneers Here," *Wilmington Evening Journal* (Del.), Apr. 3, 1929.

46. Safford, "Pyle and Racers," *St. Louis Post Dispatch*, Apr. 23, 1929.

47. "Bunioneers Here," *Wilmington Evening Journal* (Del.), Apr. 3, 1929.

48. Safford, "Pyle and Racers," *St. Louis Post Dispatch*, Apr. 23, 1929.

49. Webster, "Trimble in First," *Philadelphia Inquirer*, Apr. 3, 1929; "2,200 Witness Pyle's Show," *Miami News Record* (Okla.), May 3, 1929.

50. "Pyle Derby Runners Leave Leader Behind," *Columbus Evening Dispatch* (Ohio), Apr. 15, 1929; J. Alan Gonder, "The Sports Wheel," *Zanesville Signal* (Ohio), Apr. 14, 1929; "Have We Been Honored," *Deming Headlight* (N.Mex.), May 31, 1929; "Derbyists Here Wednesday," *Deming Headlight* (N.Mex.), May 31, 1929.

51. Sears, *Running through the Ages*, 62, 67–68, 80–81.

52. Ibid., 140–43, 146–47; P. S. Marshall, *King of the Peds* (Bloomington, Ind: Author-House, 2008), 261–62; Charles Kastner, "Frank 'Black Dan' Hart (1858–1908)," encyclopedia entry, *BlackPast.org, An Online Reference Guide to African American History*, http://www.blackpast.org/?q=aah/hart-frank-black-dan-1859.

53. Kastner, *Bunion Derby*, 191–92.

54. Parrish, *Anxious Decades*, 179–82.

55. Edward E. Anderson, "C. C. Pyle and Vanguard of Bunion Derby Are in El Paso," *El Paso Times* (Tex.), May 23, 1929.

56. Peterson, *Pigskin*, 85–88.

57. Ibid., 92.

58. Ibid., 98.

59. Ibid., 99.

60. Reisler, *Cash and Carry*, 108.

61. Peterson, *Pigskin*, 102.

62. Kastner, *Bunion Derby*, 7.

63. Ibid., 182.

64. Ibid.; Reisler, *Cash and Carry*, 183.

65. Brian Bell, "Pyle's Bunioneers Start on Big Trek to Gotham," *Cleveland Plain Dealer*, Mar. 31, 1929.

66. "Noted Runners Here Sun. with Bunion Derby," *Effington Daily Record* (Ill.), Apr. 22, 1929.

67. Reisler, *Cash and Carry*, 6; "Bunion Derby," *Elizabeth Daily Journal* (N.J.), Mar. 30, 1929; *Bunion Derby*, WPA Film Library.

68. Earl Arnett, Robert J. Brugger, and Edward C. Papenfuse, *Maryland: A New Guide to the Old Line State*, 2nd ed. (Baltimore: The Johns Hopkins Univ. Press, 1999), 488.

69. Ibid.

70. "Salo Runs Dead Heat, He'll Take It Easier," *Daily News* (Passaic, N.J.), Apr. 4. 1929; Newton, *Running in Three Continents*, 68; Appendix D, "Pace By Stage Finishers," Stage 4.

71. Newton, *Running in Three Continents*, 68.

72. Arthur McMahon, "Salo in Second," *Daily News* (Passaic, N.J.), Apr. 4, 1929.

73. Appendix D, "Cumulative Pace by Stage Finishers," Stage 4.

74. Arthur McMahon, "Salo in Second," *Daily News* (Passaic, N.J.), Apr. 4, 1929.

75. "Returns Home," *Daily Herald* (Passaic, N.J.), Aug. 7, 1929; Fetting, "Salo's Seriousness and Grit," *Daily Herald* (Passaic, N.J.), Apr. 29, 1929.

76. Fetting, "Salo Seriousness and Grit," *Daily Herald*, (Passaic, N.J.), Apr. 29, 1929.

77. Rearson, "Patrolman Dies," *Daily Herald* (Passaic, N.J.), Oct. 5, 1931.

78. Fetting, "Salo's Seriousness and Grit," *Daily Herald* (Passaic, N.J.), Apr. 29, 1929.

79. Rearson, "Patrolman Dies," *Daily Herald* (Passaic, N.J.), Oct. 5, 1931.

80. "Salo Ill, Finishes in Thirteen," *Daily News* (Passaic, N.J.), Apr. 11, 1929; "Gavuzzi Leads Pack, Simpson Finishing Next," *Wheeling Register* (W.Va.), Apr. 12, 1929.

81. "Gavuzzi Leads Pack," *Wheeling Register* (W.Va.), Apr. 12, 1929.

82. *Delaware: A Guide to the First State Compiled and Written by the Federal Writers' Project of the Works Progress Administration for the State of Delaware* (New York: Viking Press, 1938), 3.

83. Ibid.

84. "Pyle's Bunion Derby," *Wilmington Evening Journal* (Del.), Apr. 4, 1929.

85. Ibid.

86. Newton, *Running in Three Continents*, 68.

87. Arnett, Brugger, and Papenfuse, *Maryland: A New Guide*, 488.

88. Ibid.

89. "Hedeman Leading Cross Country Run," *New York Times*, Apr. 5, 1929.

90. Andy Milroy, "Herbert Hedemann—Tough Versatile Veteran," http://www.ultra legends.com/herbert-hedemann-tough-versatile-veteran; Andy Milroy, "Mike McNamara," http://www.aura.asn.au/MikeMcNamara.html; Berry, *L. A. to New York*, 86.

91. "Pyle's Bunion Derby Racers Limp into Havre de Grace," *Baltimore Sun*, Apr. 5, 1929.

92. Berry, *L.A. to New York*, 91.

93. "Pyle Pack Runs to Baltimore in a Biting Drizzle," *Daily Herald* (Passaic, N.J.), Apr. 5, 1929; *The World 1931 Almanac and Book of Facts* (New York: The World, 1932), 180.

94. Newton, *Running in Three Continents*, 68–69; Arthur McMahon, "Favored to Take Honors," *Daily News* (Passaic, N.J.), Apr. 6, 1929.

95. "Gavuzzi Leading Race," *Frederick Post* (Md.), Apr. 6, 1929.

96. "Race Success, Declares Director," *Baltimore Sun*, Apr. 6, 1929; Appendix C, "Pace by Stage Finishers," Stage 6.

97. "Race Success," *Baltimore Sun*, Apr. 6, 1929.

98. Appendix D, "Cumulative Pace by Stage Finishers," Stage 6.

99. "British Entry Wins Cross-Country Race," *New York Times*, Apr. 6, 1929.

100. "Gavuzzi Leading Race," *Frederick Post* (Md.), Apr. 6, 1929.

101. "Race Success," *Baltimore Sun*, Apr. 6, 1929.

102. Ibid.

103. Ibid.

104. Ibid.

3. Six Days of Hell—Crossing the Appalachian Plateau

1. Stone, *Hells of the Bunion Derby*, 9–10.

2. John C. Hudson, *Across This Land: A Regional Geography of the United States and Canada* (Baltimore: The Johns Hopkins Univ. Press, 2002), 93–94.

3. *The WPA Guide to Illinois: The Federal Writers' Project Guide to 1930s Illinois with a New Introduction by Neil Harris and Michael Conzen* (New York: Pantheon Books, 1983), 604.

4. Merritt Ierley, *Traveling the National Road: Across the Centuries on America's First Highway* (Woodstock, N.Y.: Overlook Press, 1990), 73.

5. Hudson, *Across This Land*, 95.

6. Ierley, *Traveling the National Road*, 199.

7. "Weather Today," *Frederick Post* (Md.), Apr. 8, 1929.

8. Newton, *Running in Three Continents*, 69.

9. Ibid.

10. Ibid.

11. "Bunion Derby Runners Due by Noon Today," *Frederick Post* (Md.), Apr. 6, 1929.

12. Arnett, Brugger, and Papenfuse, *Maryland: A New Guide*, 514–15.

13. "Pyle's Distance Sprinters Limp into Hancock," *Frederick Post* (Md.), Apr. 8, 1929.

14. Ibid.

15. Appendix D, "Cumulative Pace by Stage Finishers," Stage 7.

16. Newton, *Running in Three Continents*, 69.

17. "Injury Forces Ellis Out of Pyle Derby," *Globe and Mail* (Toronto), Apr. 8, 1929; "Four More Drop Out of Pyle's Coast to Coast Race," *Frederick Daily News* (Md.), Apr. 8, 1929; Newton, *Running in Three Continents*, 69.

18. "Bunion Derby Runners," *Frederick Post* (Md.), Apr. 6, 1929.

19. Ibid.

20. "Pyle's Distance Sprinters," *Frederick Post* (Md.), Apr. 8 1929.

21. Ibid.

22. Newton, *Running in Three Continents*, 69; "Weather Today," *Frederick Post* (Md.), Apr. 8, 1929; "Pyle's Distance Sprinters," *Frederick Post* (Md.), Apr. 8, 1929.

23. "Pyle's Distance Sprinters," *Frederick Post* (Md.), Apr. 8, 1929.

24. Ibid.

25. Arnett, Brugger, and Papentuse, *Maryland: A New Guide*, 526–28; Karl B. Raitz, ed., *A Guide to the National Road* (Baltimore: The Johns Hopkins Univ. Press, 1996), 49.

26. Arnett, Brugger, and Papenfuse, *Maryland: A New Guide*, 528.

27. Arthur G. McMahon, "Salo Still Leads Pack," *Daily News* (Passaic, N.J.), Apr. 8, 1929; Newton, *Running in Three Continents*, 69.

28. "Gardner Wins Derby Lap," *Los Angeles Times*, Apr. 8, 1929.

29. McMahon, "Salo Still Leads," *Daily News* (Passaic, N.J.), Apr. 8, 1929.

30. Newton, *Running in Three Continents*, 69; Appendix C, "Pace by Stage Finishers," Stage 8.

31. "Pyle's Distance Sprinters," *Frederick Post* (Md.), Apr. 8, 1929.

32. Raitz, ed., *Guide to the National Road*, 58.

33. Ibid., 69.

34. Ibid., 60.

35. "Salo Is Second in Race Now," *Daily News* (Passaic, N.J.), Apr. 9, 1929; Appendix C, "Pace by Stage Finishers," Stage 9.

36. "Salo Is Second," *Daily News* (Passaic, N.J.), Apr. 9, 1929.

37. "Negro Passes John Salo in Elapsed Time," *Cleveland Plain Dealer*, Apr. 9, 1929; Appendix D, "Cumulative Pace by Stage Finishers," *Stage 9*.

38. "Negro Passes John Salo," *Cumberland Daily News* (Md.), Apr. 9, 1929.

39. Ibid.

40. Kastner, *Bunion Derby*, 19–21.

41. Bill Gibson, "Gardner, Granville," *Afro-American* (Baltimore, Md.), Apr. 13, 1929.

42. Kastner, *Bunion Derby*, 166.

43. Gibson, "Gardner, Granville," *Afro-American* (Baltimore, Md.), Apr. 13, 1929.

44. Ibid.

45. Ibid.

46. "Negro Passes John Salo," *Cumberland Daily News* (Md.), Apr. 9, 1929.

47. "Italian Passes Negro, Leads to Somerfield; Finish Here about 4," *Daily News Standard* (Uniontown, Pa.), Apr. 9, 1929.

48. Raitz, *Guide to the National Road*, 94.

49. "Dalzell Gets Warm Send Off in Bunion Hop," *Springfield Leader* (Mo.), Apr. 30, 1929.

50. "Italian Passes Negro" *Daily News Standard* (Uniontown, Pa.), Apr. 9, 1929; Ierley, *Traveling the National Road*, "A National Road Gazetteer

51. Raitz, *Guide to the National Road*, 97; *Pennsylvania: A Guide*, 597–98.

52. Newton, *Running in Three Continents*, 69.

53. "Umek Wins Tenth Lap of Pyle Race," *Cleveland Plain Dealer*, Apr. 10, 1929; Arthur G. McMahon, "Umek Wins Long Grind Over Hills," *Daily News* (Passaic, N.J.), Apr. 10, 1929: Appendix C, "Pace by Stage Finishers," Stage 10.

54. "Pyle's Indoor Circus Announced in Morning," *Daily News Standard* (Uniontown, Pa.), Apr. 8, 1929.

55. Berry, *L.A. to New York*, 91.

56. "Simpson Leads Pack into Greene County Stop," *Daily News Standard* (Uniontown, Pa.), Apr. 10, 1929.

57. Ibid.

58. "Bunion Derby Men Being Surrounded by Money Seekers," *Hamilton Spectator* (Ontario, Canada), June 18, 1929.

59. "Granville Praises Y.M.C.A," *Daily News Standard,* (Uniontown, Pa.), Apr. 10, 1929.

60. Gibson, "Gardner, Granville," *Afro-American* (Baltimore, Md.), Apr. 13, 1929.

61. Walter McMullen, "To Accompany Granville," *Hamilton Spectator* (Ontario, Canada), Mar. 19, 1929; "Bunion Derby Runners," *Frederick Post* (Md.), Apr. 6, 1929.

62. "Simpson Leads Pack," *Daily News Standard* (Uniontown, Pa.), Apr. 10, 1929.

63. Appendix B, "Daily and Cumulative Mileage, 1929 Bunion Derby."

64. "Simpson Leads Pack," *Daily News Standard* (Uniontown, Pa.), Apr. 10, 1929.

65. Raitz, *Guide to the National Road*, 70; *Pennsylvania: A Guide,* 598.

66. Newton, *Running in Three Continents*, 69; "Salo Still Ill," *Daily Herald* (Passaic, N.J.), Apr. 11, 1929.

67. Kastner, *Bunion Derby*, 138.

68. Appendix D, "Cumulative Pace by Stage Finishers," Stage 11.

69. "Paul Simpson Runs 33 Miles in Good Time," *Cumberland Daily News* (Md.), Apr. 11, 1929.

70. "Paul Simpson is First 'Bunioneer' into Waynesburg," *Democrat Messenger* (Waynesburg, Pa.), Apr. 12, 1929.

71. "Large Crowds to Greet Athletes in Waynesburg," *Democrat Messenger* (Waynesburg, Pa.), Apr. 12, 1929.

72. *World 1931 Almanac*, 189; John Alexander Williams, *West Virginia: A Bicentennial History* (New York: W. W Norton, 1976), 49, 79.

73. Newton, *Running in Three Continents*, 70.

74. "Gavuzzi Is Lap Winner by Small Margin," *Wheeling Daily News* (W.Va.), Apr. 11, 1929; Arthur G. McMahon, "Salo Now Third in Pyle Run," *Daily News* (Passaic, N.J.), Apr. 12, 1929.

75. "Paul Simpson is First," *Democrat Messenger* (Waynesburg, Pa.), Apr. 12, 1929.

76. "Gavuzzi Lead," *Wheeling Register* (W.Va.), Apr. 11, 1929.

77. "Pyle Runners Near Wheeling," *Wheeling Daily News* (W.Va.), Apr.11, 1929.

78. Ibid.

79. "Gavuzzi Is Lap Winner," *Wheeling Daily News* (W.Va.), Apr. 11, 1929; Appendix C, "Pace by Stage Finishers," Stage 12.

80. "Gavuzzi Is Lap Winner," *Wheeling Daily News* (W.Va.), Apr. 11, 1929.

81. Appendix C, "Pace by Stage Finishers," Stage 12; McMahon, "Salo Now Third," *Daily News* (Passaic, N.J.), Apr. 12, 1929.

82. "Mud and Rain Handicap to Bunioneers," *Cumberland Daily News* (Md.), Apr. 12, 1929.

83. McMahon, "Salo Now Third," *Daily News* (Passaic, N.J.), Apr. 12, 1929.

84. "Gavuzzi Leads Pack," *Wheeling Register* (W.Va.), Apr. 12, 1929.

85. McMahon, "Salo Now Third," *Daily News* (Passaic, N.J.), Apr. 12, 1929.

86. "Gavuzzi Leads Pack," *Wheeling Register* (W.Va.), Apr. 12, 1929.

4. Fast Times in the Old Northwest

1. Mabel V. Pollock, *Our State, Ohio, 1803–2003: A Bicentennial History* (Newcomer, Ohio: 1st Book Library, 2001), 3–4.

2. "Negro Leads as Derby Boys Leave Wheeling," *Wheeling Daily News* (W.Va.), Apr. 12, 1929.

3. Appendix C, "Pace by Stage Finishers," Stage 13.

4. Newton, *Running in Three Continents*, 70; "Gavuzzi Menaces Lead of Gardner," *Cleveland Plain Dealer*, Apr. 13, 1929; "Gavuzzi Leads Pack" *Wheeling Register* (W.Va.), Apr. 12, 1929.

5. Appendix D, "Cumulative Pace by Stage Finishers," Stage 13.

6. "Salo Is Running in Form," *Daily News* (Passaic, N.J.), Apr. 15, 1929; "Gavuzzi Leads Pack," *Wheeling Register* (W.Va.), Apr. 12, 1929.

7. "Ed Gardner Holds Slender Lead in Elapsed Time," *Daily Jefferson* (Cambridge, Ohio), Apr. 13, 1929.

8. "Derby Runners Ride in Cars, Deputies Say," *Bellaire Daily Leader* (Ohio), Apr. 13, 1929; "Pyle Brands Derby Charges as Deliberate Falsehoods," *Zanesville Signal* (Ohio), Apr. 14, 1929.

9. "Guernsey Co. Deputies Claim Derby Runners Caught Riding Autos," *Zanesville Signal* (Ohio), Apr. 13 1929.

10. Tulloh, *Four Million Footsteps*, 20

11. Pollock, *Our State, Ohio*, 13.

12. Newton, *Running in Three Continents*, 71.

13. Appendix C, "Pace by Stage Finishers," Stage 14.

14. "Salo Picks Up Speed," *Daily Herald* (Passaic, N.J.), Apr. 15, 1929; Ed A. Fetting, "Salo's Seriousness and Grit," *Daily Herald* (Passaic, N.J.), Apr. 29, 1929.

15. Alan J. Gonder, "The Sports Wheel," *Zanesville Signal* (Ohio), Apr. 14, 1929.

16. Pollock, *Our State, Ohio*, 13; Kastner, *Bunion Derby*, 4.

17. Newton, *Running in Three Continents*, 71.

18. "Pyle Derby Runners," *Columbus Evening Dispatch* (Ohio), Apr. 15, 1929.

19. Appendix C, "Pace by Stage Finishers," Stage 15.

20. "Pyle Derby Runners," *Columbus Evening Dispatch* (Ohio), Apr. 15, 1929.

21. "C. C. Pyle's Autos Attached by Sheriff for Debt," *Daily Jefferson* (Cambridge, Ohio), Apr. 15, 1929; "Salo Picks Up Speed in Pyle Race," *Daily Herald* (Passaic, N.J.), Apr. 15, 1929; "Pyle Leaves Runners," *Columbus Evening Dispatch* (Ohio), Apr. 15, 1929.

22. "Coast to Coast Runners in Springfield," *Dayton Journal* (Ohio), Apr. 16, 1929.

23. Michael J. Rodden, "On the Highway of Sport," *Globe and Mail* (Toronto), Apr. 16, 1929.

24. *World 1931 Almanac*, 186; Pollock, *Our State, Ohio*, 66.

25. "Pyle Runners Due at 3:30 O'Clock Today," *Richmond Item* (Ind.), Apr. 16, 1929.

26. "Salo Again Held Back by Illness," *Daily Herald* (Passaic, N.J.), Apr. 16, 1929; Appendix D, "Cumulative Pace by Stage Finishers," *Stage 16*.

27. Berry, *L. A. to New York*, 94; Kastner, *Bunion Derby*, 144, 166.

28. Berry, *L. A. to New York*, 94

29. Ibid.

30. "Granville Sixth in Elapsed Time," *Globe and Mail* (Toronto), Apr. 17, 1929.

31. "Salo Leading as Pyle's Derbyists Reach Richmond," *Seattle Post Intelligencer*, Apr. 17, 1929.

32. Appendix C, "Pace by Stage Finishers," Stage 17.

33. Arthur G. McMahon, "Salo Beats Gavuzzi by One Hour," *Daily News* (Passaic, N.J.), Apr. 17, 1929.

34. Ibid.

35. "Salo's Wife Cheered Him to Victory," *Daily Herald* (Passaic, N.J.), Apr. 17, 1929.

36. "John Salo Takes Lead as Runners Leave Richmond," *Richmond Palladium* (Ind.), Apr. 17, 1929.

37. Ibid.

38. "Marathoners Speed on Today to Knightstown," *Richmond Item* (Ind.), Apr. 17, 1929.

39. Newton, *Running in Three Continents*, 71.

40. Walter McMullen, "Sports Trail," *Hamilton Spectator* (Ontario, Canada), Apr. 16, 1929.

41. Ibid.

42. "Granville's Trainer Tires of Heavy Work," *Hamilton Spectator* (Ontario, Canada), Apr. 16, 1929.

43. Newton, *Running in Three Continents*, 71.

44. "Johnny Takes Lead," *Richmond Palladium* (Ind.), Apr. 19, 1929; Appendix C, "Pace by Stage Finishers," Stage 18; Appendix F, "Marathon Pace by Mile."

45. "Salo Wins 34 Mile Run," *New York Times*, Apr. 18, 1929.

46. "The Bunion Derbyists Visit Knightstown," *Knightstown Banner* (Ind.), Apr. 19, 1929; Arthur G. McMahon, "Salo Wins Again in Indiana," *Daily News* (Passaic, N.J.), Apr. 18, 1929.

47. McMahon, "Salo Wins Again," *Daily News* (Passaic, N.J.), Apr. 18, 1929.

48. Arthur G. McMahon, "Salo Wins Third Time in Indiana," *Daily News* (Passaic, N.J.), Apr. 19, 1929.

49. Appendix C, "Pace by Stage Finishers." Stage 18.

50. McMahon, "Salo Wins Third Time," *Daily News* (Passaic, N.J.), Apr. 19, 1929; "Thirty-One Runners Head for Brazil after Overnight Rest," *Indianapolis News*, Apr. 19, 1929.

51. Tulloh, *Four Million Footsteps*, 20.

52. Kastner, *Bunion Derby*, 23, 28, 84–85.

53. Gibson, "Granville, Gardner," *Afro-American* (Baltimore, Md.), Apr. 13, 1929.

54. Ibid.

55. Appendix D, "Cumulative Pace by Stage Finishers," Stage 19.

56. Walter McMullen, "Sports Trail," *Hamilton Spectator* (Ontario, Canada), Apr. 18, 1929.

57. "Famous Trainer May Handle Phil Granville," *Hamilton Herald* (Ontario, Canada), Apr. 17, 1929.

58. "Thirty-One Runners," *Indianapolis News*, Apr. 19, 1929.

59. Ibid.

60. Newton, *Running in Three Continents*, 71.

61. Appendix C, "Pace by Stage Finishers," Stage 20; "Derby Runners at Brazil, Ind.," *Terre Haute Star* (Ind.), Apr. 20, 1929.

62. Arthur G. McMahon, "Salo Runs 57 Miles in Fast Time," *Daily News* (Passaic, N.J.), April 20, 1929.

63. "Derby Runners," *Terre Haute Star* (Ind.), Apr. 20, 1929.

64. "Thirty-One Runners," *Indianapolis News*, Apr. 19, 1929.

65. "Pyle Bunion Derby Reported in Serious Financial Difficulties," *Terre Haute Tribune* (Ind.), Apr. 21, 1929.

66. Ibid.

67. Ibid.

68. Ibid.

69. Ibid.

70. Newton, *Running in Three Continents*, 71.

71. "Throngs Greet Pyle Runners," *Terre Haute Star* (Ind.), Apr. 21, 1929.

72. *World 1931 Almanac*, 179; "Throngs Greet Pyle Runners," *Terre Haute Star* (Ind.), Apr. 21, 1929.

73. "Throngs Greet Pyle Runners," *Terre Haute Star* (Ind.), Apr. 21, 1929.

74. Ibid.

75. Ibid.; Appendix C, "Pace by Stage Finishers," Stage, 21.

76. "Simpson Wins Lap," *New York Times*, Apr. 21, 1929.

77. *WPA Guide to Illinois*, 604; "Newton, Bunion Runner, Is Hit by Auto," *St. Louis Post Dispatch*, Apr. 21, 1929.

78. "Throngs Greet Pyle Runners," *Terre Haute Star* (Ind.), Apr. 21, 1929.

79. "Salo Leads Down Grade Past Boulder at 2:30 and Umek 7 Minutes Behind," *Calexico Chronicle* (Calif.), June 12, 1929.

80. Newton, *Running in Three Continents*, 72.

81. Ibid.

82. *WPA Guide to Illinois*, xxvi.

83. "Pyle Bunion Derby," *Terre Haute Tribune* (Ind.), Apr. 21, 1929.

84. Newton, *Running in Three Continents*, 72.

85. *World 1931 Almanac*, 178; *WPA Guide to Illinois*, 427.

86. Newton, *Running in Three Continents*, 72.

87. "Salo Wins Second Place in Illinois," *Daily Herald* (Passaic, N.J.), Apr. 22, 1929; Appendix C, "Pace by Stage Finishers," Stage 22; Appendix E, "Marathon Pace by Mile."

88. "Salo Wins Second," *Daily Herald* (Passaic, N.J.), Apr. 22, 1929.

89. "Salo Wins and Passes Gardner," *Daily News* (Passaic, N.J.), Apr. 22, 1929.

90. "Salo Draws Nearer to Leader in Derby," *Globe and Mail* (Toronto), April 22, 1929; Appendix D, "Cumulative Pace by Stage Finishers," Stage 22.

91. "Eddie Sheik Gardner Tells His Own Story of Why He Quit Pyle's Race," *Black Dispatch* (African American, Baltimore), May 23, 1929; *WPA Guide to Illinois*, 427.

92. "Eddie Sheik Gardner," *Black Dispatch* (African American, Baltimore), May 23, 1929.

93. Ibid.

94. "Geo. Curtis, Trainer of Ed Gardner, Writes Letter to the Enterprise about Ed's Race," *Enterprise* (African American, Seattle), Apr. 25, 1929.

95. Ibid.

96. "Send a Letter or Telegram to Gardner and His Manager," *Enterprise* (African American, Seattle), Apr. 25, 1929.

97. Newton, *Running in Three Continents*, 72.

98. Raitz, *National Road*, 307.

99. "Gavuzzi Wins Lap," *Los Angeles Times*, Apr. 23, 1929.

100. "C. C. Pyle and Thirty Six of His Runners Spend Afternoon and Night Here," *Vandalia Union* (Ill.), Apr. 25, 1929; Appendix C, "Pace by Stage Finishers," Stage 23.

101. "C. C. Pyle and Thirty Six," *Vandalia Union* (Ill.), Apr. 25, 1929.

102. Ibid.

103. Ibid.

104. "Noted Runners Here," *Effingham Daily Record* (Ill.), Apr. 22, 1929.

105. "Vandalia Has a Bunion Derby Runner Now," *Vandalia Union* (Ill.), Apr. 25, 1929.

106. "Marathon to Be Staged Here at Vandalia," *Vandalia Union* (Ill.), May 2, 1929.

107. "Vandalia Has a Bunion" *Vandalia Union* (Ill.), Apr. 25, 1929.

108. "Marathon to Be Staged," *Vandalia Union* (Ill.), May 2, 1929

109. Charles Kastner, "Bunion Derby Fever: How the First Footrace across America Pulled the Average Working Joe into Ultramarathoning," *Marathon and Beyond*, March–April 2008, 69–71.

110. Ibid., 70.

111. Kastner, *Bunion Derby*, 25–30.

112. "Race Success," *Baltimore Sun*, Apr. 6, 1929.

113. Safford, "Pyle and Racers," *St. Louis Post Dispatch*, Apr. 23, 1929.

114. Ibid.; Newton, *Running in Three Continents*, 72.

115. Safford, "Pyle and Racers," *St. Louis Post Dispatch*, Apr. 23, 1929.

116. Ibid.

117. Raitz, *Guide to the National Road*, 310.

118. "Salo Makes Headway on First Place," *Daily Herald* (Passaic, N.J.), Apr. 24, 1929; Appendix C, "Pace by Stage Finishers," Stage 24.

119. "Salo, Chased By Dog, Wins Day's Pyle Derby Lap," *St. Louis Post Dispatch*, Apr. 24, 1929.

120. "Salo Makes Headway," *Daily Herald* (Passaic, N.J.), Apr. 24, 1929; Appendix D, "Cumulative Pace by Stage Finishers," Stage 24.

5. On Familiar Ground

1. *World 1931 Almanac*, 181; Arthur G. McMahon, "Grind On for Today," *Daily News* (Passaic, N.J.), Apr. 25, 1929.

2. Newton, *Running in Three Continents*, 72.

3. Appendix C, "Pace by Stage Finishers," Stage 25; Appendix E, "Marathon Pace Chart."

4. "First into St. Louis in Cross Country Race," *St. Louis Post Dispatch*, Apr. 24, 1929.

5. "Pyle's Runners Go through City on the Way West," *St. Louis Post Dispatch*, Apr. 24, 1929.

6. Alwyn Barr, *Black Texans: A History of African Americans in Texas, 1528–1995*, 2nd ed. (Norman: Univ. of Oklahoma Press, 1996), 158–59; Lorenzo J. Greene, Gary R. Kremer, and Antonio F. Holland, *Missouri's Black Heritage*, rev. ed. (Columbia: Univ. of Missouri Press, 1993), 148–49; Kyvig, *Daily Life*, 19; William E. Leuchtenburg, *Perils of Prosperity, 1914–1932*, 2nd ed. (Chicago: Univ. of Chicago Press, 1993), 37; Greene, *Missouri's Black Heritage*, 148.

7. "Granville, Gardner Taboo," *Pittsburgh Courier* (African American), May 5, 1928; Bernd Heinrich, *Why We Run: A Natural History* (New York: Harper Collins, 2002), 191; Tom McNabb, *Flanagan's Run* (London: Hodder and Stoughton, 1982), 58.

8. Louis R. Harlan, *Booker T. Washington: The Wizard of Tuskegee, 1901–1915* (New York: Oxford Univ. Press, 1983), 161, 170, 266, 267.

9. McMahon, "Grind On for Today," *Daily News* (Passaic, N.J.), Apr. 25, 1929.

10. Ed A. Fetting, "Salo's Seriousness and Grit," *Daily Herald* (Passaic, N.J.), Apr. 29, 1929.

11. "Picher's Entry in Pyle's Bunion Derby," *Joplin Globe* (Mo.), May 1, 1929.

12. Fetting, "Salo's Seriousnes and Grit," *Daily Herald* (Passaic, N.J.), Apr. 29, 1929; "Salo Loses 20 Minutes to Gavuzzi," *Daily Herald* (Passaic, N.J.), Apr. 30, 1929.

13. "Pyle's Runners Go," *St. Louis Post Dispatch*, Apr. 24, 1929.

14. Ibid.

15. Ibid.

16. "Britisher Leads into Springfield," *Joplin Globe* (Mo.), Apr. 29, 1929; "Dalzell Gets Warm Sendoff," *Springfield Leader* (Mo.), Apr. 30, 1929.

17. Bill Crawford, *All American: The Rise and Fall of Jim Thorpe* (Hoboken, N.J.: Wiley, 2005), 145, 195, 173, 201.

18. Ibid., 227; "Britisher Leads," *Joplin Globe* (Mo.), Apr. 29, 1929; "Dalzell Gets Warm Sendoff," *Springfield Leader* (Mo.), Apr. 30, 1929.

19. "Britisher Leads," *Joplin Globe* (Mo.), Apr. 29, 1929; "Dalzell Gets Warm Sendoff," *Springfield Leader* (Mo.), Apr. 30, 1929.

20. Phyllis Rossiter, *A Living History of the Ozarks* (Gretna, La.: Pelican, 2001), 17, 21; *Missouri: The WPA Guide to the "Show Me" State Compiled by Workers of the Writers' Program of the Works Progress Administration in the State of Missouri with a New Introduction by Walter A. Schroeder and Howard W. Marshall* (1941; repr., St. Louis: Missouri Historical Society Press, 1998), 407–8.

21. Kastner, *Bunion Derby*, 112.

22. "Ed Gardner 48 Minutes Behind Salo," *Seattle Times*, Apr. 25, 1929; *Missouri: The WPA Guide*, 408–9.

23. "Salo Cuts Gavuzzi's Lead by Almost an Hour," *St. Louis Star*, Apr. 27, 1929.

24. "Eddie Sheik Gardner," *Black Dispatch* (African American, Okla.), May 23, 1929.

25. Appendix C, "Pace by Stage Finishers," Stage 26; Appendix D, "Cumulative Pace by Stage Finishers," Stage 26.

26. "Sullivan Gives Bunioneers Great Reception," *Sullivan News* (Mo.), May 2, 1929.

27. Kastner, *Bunion Derby*, 71, 115.

28. "Pyle's Troupers Come Here Today: Gavuzzi Leading," *Springfield Daily News* (Mo.), Apr. 29, 1929.

29. "Ed Gardner Forced Out of Marathon," *Enterprise* (African American, Seattle), May 29, 1929.

30. "Quits Pyle's Coast Derby," *Chicago Defender* (African American), May 11, 1929.

31. Newton, *Running in Three Continents*, 73.

32. Kastner, *Bunion Derby*, 136.

33. Arthur G. McMahon, "Simpson Wins First Place in 45 Mile Grind," *Daily News* (Passaic, N.J.), Apr. 27, 1929.

34. Newton, *Running in Three Continents*, 71.

35. *Missouri: The WPA Guide*, 412; Jack D. Rittenhouse, *A Guide Book to Highway 66* (1946; facsimile, Albuquerque: Univ. of New Mexico Press, 2000), 25.

36. *Missouri: The WPA Guide*, 412, 421.

37. "Paul Simpson Wins Lap in Pyle's Bunion Derby," *Globe and Mail* (Toronto), Apr. 27, 1929; Appendix C, "Pace by Stage Finishers," Stage 27.

38. Rittenhouse, *A Guide Book*, 24–25.

39. McMahon, "Simpson Wins First," *Daily News* (Passaic, N.J.), Apr. 27, 1929.

40. "Salo Runs Dead Heat into Rolla, Mo., with Leaders," *Daily Herald* (Passaic, N.J.), Apr. 27, 1929; Appendix C, "Pace by Stage Finishers," Stage 27; Appendix D, "Cumulative Pace by Stage Finishers," Stage 27.

41. *Missouri: The WPA Guide*, 417.

42. "Gavuzzi Victor to Waynesville in Pyle's Derby," *Seattle Post Intelligencer*, Apr. 28, 1929; Appendix C, "Pace by Stage Finishers," Stage 28.

43. "Pyle's Troopers Here Today; Gavuzzi Leading," *Springfield Daily News* (Mo.), Apr. 29, 1929; Appendix D, "Cumulative Pace by Stage Finishers," Stage 29.

44. Newton, *Running in Three Continents*, 73; Rittenhouse, *A Guide Book*, 28–29.

45. Newton, *Running in Three Continents*, 72.

46. Ibid., 73.

47. Ibid.

48. *Missouri: The WPA Guide*, 330, 414, 420; Rittenhouse, *A Guide Book*, 30–31; *World 1931 Almanac*, 181.

49. Arthur G. McMahon, "Gavuzzi Wins the 30th Lap," *Daily News* (Passaic, N.J.), Apr. 30, 1929; Appendix C, "Pace by Stage Finishers," Stage 30; Appendix E, "Marathon Pace by Mile," Stage 30.

50. "Britisher Leads," *Joplin Globe* (Mo.), Apr. 29, 1929; Appendix C, "Pace by Stage Finishers," Stage 30.

51. McMahon, "Gavuzzi Wins," *Daily News* (Passaic, N.J.), April 30, 1929.

52. "Sporting Editor," *Springfield Leader* (Mo.), May 1, 1929.

53. "Britisher Leads," *Joplin Globe* (Mo.), Apr. 29, 1929.

54. "Marathoners in Springfield by Quick Time," *Springfield Leader* (Mo.), Apr. 29, 1929.

55. Kastner, *Bunion Derby*, 19–30.

56. Berry, *L. A. to New York*, 97; "Marathoners in Springfield," *Springfield Leader* (Mo.), Apr. 29, 1929.

57. "Marathoners in Springfield," *Springfield Leader* (Mo.), Apr. 29, 1929.

58. Ibid.; "Blister Brigade Comes into City about 4 O'Clock," *Muskogee Daily Phoenix* (Okla.), May 4, 1929.

59. "Dalzell Hurt," *Springfield Daily News* (Mo.), May 1, 1929; "Dalzell Gets Warm Send Off," *Springfield Leader* (Mo.), Apr. 30, 1929.

60. "Dalzell Hurt," *Springfield Daily News* (Mo.), May 1, 1929

61. "Sporting Editor," *Springfield Leader* (Mo.), May 1, 1929.

62. Ibid.

63. Ibid.

64. Appendix D, "Cumulative Pace by Stage Finishers," Stage 31.

65. "Salo Is Nearly Four Hours Back of Pack Leader," *Daily Herald* (Passaic, N.J.), May 1, 1929.

66. Ibid.

67. "Dalzell Hurt," *Springfield Daily News* (Mo.), May 1, 1929.

68. Newton, *Running in Three Continents*, 72.

69. "Bunion Derbyists Leave Here at 7 A.M. for Miami," *Joplin Globe* (Mo.), May 2, 1929; "Salo Heads Race," *Seattle Post Intelligencer*, May 2, 1929.

70. "Salo Heads Race," *Seattle Post Intelligencer*, May 2, 1929; *Missouri: The WPA Guide*, 505.

71. Appendix C, *Pace by Stage Finishers*, Stage 32; Arthur G. McMahon, "Salo Flies Home First with Wind," *Daily News* (Passaic, N.J.), May 2, 1929.

72. "Bunion Derbyists," *Joplin Globe* (Mo.), May 2, 1929.

73. "Shin Splint Holds Back Ed Gardner," *Seattle Times*, May 1, 1929.

74. "Arrangements Completed for Arrival of Bunionists," *Joplin Globe* (Mo.), Apr. 27, 1929.

75. *Missouri: The WPA Guide*, 234.

76. Rossiter, *Living History*, 93; *Missouri: The WPA Guide*, 233–34, 237.

77. "2,200 Witness Pyle's Show," *Miami News Record* (Okla.), May 3, 1929; "Arrangements Completed," *Joplin Globe* (Mo.), Apr. 27, 1929.

78. "2,200 Witness Pyle's Show," *Miami News Record* (Okla.), May 3, 1929.

79. "Jesse Dalzell Crippled, Walks Entire Joplin Lap," *Springfield Leader* (Mo.), May 2, 1929.

80. Newton, *Running in Three Continents*, 74; "Salo Trims Margin of Pete Gavuzzi," *Joplin Globe* (Mo.), May 3, 1929; *The WPA Guide to 1930s Oklahoma Compiled by the Writers' Program of the Works Progress Administration in the State of Oklahoma with a Restored Essay by Angie Debo and a New Introduction by Anne Hodges Morgan* (1941; repr., Lawrence: Univ. Press of Kansas, 1986), 220.

81. Appendix D, *Cumulative Pace by Stage Finishers*, Stage 33.

82. "Picher's Entry in Pyle's Bunion Derby," *Joplin Globe* (Mo.), May 1, 1929.

83. "Galena Sees Runners," *Galena Times* (Kans.), May 3, 1929; "Shields Is Given Ovation Here by Admiring Friends," *Baxter Springs Citizen and Herald* (Kans.), May 2, 1929.

84. "He Showed Them Now," *Baxter Springs Citizen and Herald* (Kans.), May 2, 1929.

85. "Shields Is Given Ovation," *Baxter Springs Citizen and Herald* (Kans.), May 2, 1929.

86. "Picher's Entry," *Joplin Globe* (Mo.), May 1, 1929.

87. "Chelsea Perked for Pacing Pack of Pyle Plodders," *Muskogee Daily Phoenix* (Okla.), May 3, 1929; Newton, *Running in Three Continents*, 74.

88. "70-Mile Drag for Pyle Runners Today," *Joplin Globe* (Mo.), May 4, 1929.

89. Appendix D, "Cumulative Pace by Stage Finishers," Stage 34.

90. "Derby Leaders," *Miami News Record* (Okla.), May 3, 1929.

91. "Salo Loses to Paterson Marathoner," *Daily News* (Passaic, N.J.), May 4, 1929.

92. "Thousands Crowd Highway to See Bunioneers Pass," *Muskogee Daily Phoenix* (Okla.), May 4, 1929.

93. Kastner, *Bunion Derby*, 88.

94. Ibid.

95. "Dribbles of the Derby," *Muskogee Daily Phoenix* (Okla.), May 3, 1929.

96. Ibid.

97. "Bunioneers Who Came Here Today," *Muskogee Daily Phoenix* (Okla.), May 4, 1929; "Dribbles of the Derby," *Muskogee Daily Phoenix* (Okla.), May 3, 1929.

98. "Salo Leads Runners into Holdenville," *Holdenville Daily News* (Okla.), May 6, 1929.

6. Heading to the Promised Land

1. "Pyle's Bunion Derby," *Wilmington Evening Journal* (Del.), Apr. 4, 1929; Safford, "Pyle and Racers," *St. Louis Post Dispatch*, Apr. 23, 1929.

2. "Bunion Derby Runners," *Frederick Post* (Md.), Apr. 6, 1929.

3. Newton, *Running in Three Continents*, 74.

4. "Blister Brigade," *Muskogee Daily Phoenix* (Okla.), May 4, 1929.

5. "Runners Getting 44 Mile Workout after Tough Run," *Sunday Times Democrat* (Okmulgee, Okla.), May 5, 1929; Appendix C, *Pace by Stage Finishers*, Stage 35, ; Appendix E, "Marathon Pace by Mile."

6. "Runners Getting 44 Mile Workout," *Sunday Times Democrat* (Okmulgee, Okla.), May 5, 1929.

7. "Umek Wins Run to Muskogee," *Miami News Record* (Okla.), May 5, 1929; Berry, *L.A. to New York*, 98; Appendix D, "Pace by Stage Finishers," Stage 35.

8. Newton, *Running in Three Continents*, 74.

9. "Eddie "Sheik" Gardner, *Black Dispatch* (African American, Okla.), May 23, 1929; A. D. Williams, "Injured Leg Forces Runner to Quit Race," *Kansas City Call* (African American, Mo.), May 10, 1929.

10. Bill Gibson, "Passing Review," *Afro-American* (Baltimore, Md.), May 11, 1929.

11. "Eddie 'Sheik' Gardner," *Black Dispatch* (African American, Okla.), May 23, 1929.

12. *WPA Guide to 1930s Oklahoma*, 181.

13. "Bunioneer Field Reduced to 24," *Miami News Record* (Okla.), May 6, 1929; Appendix C, "Pace by Stage Finishers," Stage 36; Newton, *Running in Three Continents*, 74.

14. "Elmer Cowley of Clifton in Best Run," *Daily Herald* (Passaic, N.J.), May 6, 1929; Appendix D, "Cumulative Pace by Stage Finishers," Stage 36.

15. "Bunioneer Field," *Miami News Record* (Okla.), May 6, 1929.

16. Kastner, *Bunion Derby*, 16, 166.

17. Arthur G. McMahon, "Guisto Umek Is Really a Cliftonite," *Daily News* (Passaic, N.J.), June 3, 1929.

18. "Trimble in First," *Philadelphia Inquirer*, Apr. 3, 1929; "Peter Gavuzzi Holds Lead in Pyle Derby; Runners Here Today," *Calexico Chronicle* (Calif.), June 11, 1929.

19. "Sports Section," *Hamilton Herald* (Ontario, Canada), Apr. 6, 1929.

20. Kastner, *Bunion Derby*, 152.

21. Staley A. Cook, "Blistered Toe May End Race for Simpson," *Burlington Daily Times* (N.C.), Apr. 5, 1929.

22. Ibid.

23. Ibid.; Appendix D, "Cumulative Pace by Stage Finishers," Stage 36.

24. "They're At It Once Again," *Seattle Times*, Apr. 1, 1929; "Bunioneers Leave Today for Coalgate," *Holdenville Daily News* (Okla.), May 7, 1929; Kastner, *Bunion Derby*, 54.

25. Kastner, *Bunion Derby*, 79.

26. Ibid.

27. Ibid., 64, 138–39.

28. Appendix D, "Cumulative Pace by Stage Finishers," Stage 36.

29. "Bunioneer Field," *Miami News Record* (Okla.), May 6, 1929.

30. "Shields Would Enter Long Run," *Baxter Springs Citizen and Herald* (Kans.), Mar. 18, 1929; Kastner, "Bunion Derby Fever," *Marathon and Beyond*, March–April 2008, 64.

31. "Sketches of the Runners," in *Official Program: C. C. Pyle's Second Annual International-Trans-Continental Foot Race, 1929*.

32. "Salo Gives Hard Brush to Gavuzzi," *Daily Herald* (Passaic, N.J.), May 7, 1929.

33. Ibid.

34. Appendix D, "Cumulative Pace by Stage Finishers," Stage 37; "Salo Leads Field," *Holdenville Daily News* (Okla.), May 6, 1929.

35. "Salo Gives Hard Brush," *Daily Herald* (Passaic, N.J.), May 7, 1929.

36. Newton, *Running in Three Continents*, 75.

37. *WPA Guide to 1930s Oklahoma*, 349.

38. Newton, *Running in Three Continents*, 75.

39. "Gavuzzi Gains on Salo," *Daily News* (Passaic, N.J.), May 8, 1928; Appendix C, "Pace by Stage Finishers," Stage 38.

40. Appendix D, "Cumulative Pace by Stage Finishers," Stage 38.

41. "Tuesday Was a Big Day Here," *Coalgate Courier* (Okla.), May 9, 1929; "Pyle's Bunioneers Here Tuesday Night," *Coalgate Record Register* (Okla.), May 9, 1929.

42. "Pyle's Bunioneers Here," *Coalgate Record Register* (Okla.), May 9, 1929.

43. Newton, *Running in Three Continents*, 75; *WPA Guide to 1930s Oklahoma*, 320.

44. "Salo Gains 43 Minutes on Gavuzzi," *Daily Herald* (Passaic, N.J.), May 9, 1929.

45. Ibid.

46. Newton, *Running in Three Continents*, 74.

47. "Salo Wins 50-Mile Race," *New York Times*, May 9, 1929; Appendix C, "Pace by Stage Finishers," Stage 39.

48. "Salo Wins 50-Mile Race," *New York Times*, May 9, 1929.

49. "Salo Gains," *Daily Herald* (Passaic, N.J.), May 9, 1929.

50. Newton, *Running in Three Continents*, 75; *The WPA Guide to Texas with a New Introduction by Don Graham: The Federal Writers' Project Guide to Texas* (1949; repr., Austin: Texas Monthly Press, 1986), 414.

51. *WPA Guide to Texas*, 413; Leon C. Metz, *Roadside History of Texas* (Missoula, Mont.: Mountain Press, 1994), 327.

52. "Simpson Ahead in Run," *New York Times*, May 10, 1929; Appendix C, "Pace by Stage Finishers," Stage 40.

53. "Salo Loses in 33-Mile Texas Run," *Daily Herald* (Passaic, N.J.), May 10, 1929.

54. Alan J. Gould, "C. C. Pyle Will Profit On Bunion Derby, He Declares," *Daily News* (Passaic, N.J.), May 10, 1929.

55. Synopsis of *Breckenridge American* articles related to the Bunion Derby for May 13–15, 1929, by Jean Hayworth, ed., *Breckenridge American* (Tex.).

56. Newton, *Running in Three Continents*, 75.

57. "Salo First to Dallas," *Los Angeles Times*, May 11, 1929; "Thousands Look On When Pyle' Runners Reach City," *Dallas Journal*, May 11, 1929; Newton, *Running in Three Continents*, 75.

58. Newton, *Running in Three Continents*, 75.

59. Ibid.

60. "Salo Gains 52 Minutes On Rival," *Daily News* (Passaic, N.J.), May 11, 1929; Appendix D, "Cumulative Pace by Stage Finishers," Stage 41.

61. "Salo Gains," *Daily News* (Passaic, N.J.), May 11, 1929.

62. Ibid.

63. Ibid.

64. "Thousands Look On," *Dallas Journal*, May 11, 1929.

65. *WPA Guide to Texas*, 225; Metz, *Roadside History of Texas*, 353.

66. "Bunioneers on Way to Albany," *Sweetwater Reporter* (Tex.), May 13, 1929.

67. Ibid.

68. Appendix D, "Cumulative Pace by Stage Finishers," Stage 41.

7. Under Western Skies

1. Ray Allen Billington, *Western Expansion: A History of the American Frontier*, 4th ed. (New York: Macmillan, 1974), 548, 550; *The WPA Guide to 1930s New Mexico Compiled by the Workers of the Writers' Program of the Work Projects Administration in the State of New Mexico* (1940; Tucson: Univ. of Arizona Press, 1989), 374; *Arizona: A State Guide Compiled by the Workers of the Writers' Program of the Work Projects Administration in the State of Arizona* (New York: Hastings House, 1940), 47, 340.

2. *WPA Guide to Texas*, 7, 68, 245, 250.

3. Ibid., 20.

4. Newton, *Running in Three Continents*, 75.

5. Ibid., 75; *WPA Guide to Texas*, 259, 553.

6. *WPA Guide to Texas*, 259.

7. Ibid., 231, 232, 262.

8. "Salo and Gavuzzi Run Even," *Daily News* (Passaic, N.J.), May 13, 1929.

9. Ibid.

10. "Guisto Umek Cops Lead in Pyle Bunion Derby," *Los Angeles Times*, May 13, 1929.

11. "Granville Keeps Place," *Montreal Gazette*, May 13, 1929; Walter McMullen, "Sports Drift," *Hamilton Spectator* (Ontario, Canada), May 22, 1929.

12. *WPA Guide to Texas*, 454–55; Metz, *Roadside History of Texas*, 374.

13. "Pyle Again Dealt Blow with Derby," *Dallas Journal*, May 13, 1929.

14. Newton, *Running in Three Continents*, 76.

15. Ibid.; "Richman and Hedeman Lead Pyle Runners," *Los Angeles Times*, May 14, 1929.

16. "Richman and Hedeman," *Los Angeles Times*, May 14, 1929.

17. Kastner, *Bunion Derby*, 30, 174–75.

18. Appendix D, "Cumulative Pace by Stage Finishers," Stage 44.

19. Ibid.

20. Ibid.; "Richman and Hedeman," *Los Angeles Times*, May 14, 1929.

21. Metz, *Roadside History of Texas*, 375.

22. Synopsis, *Breckenridge American* (Tex.), May 13–16, 1929.

23. Ibid.

24. Ibid.; "Race Gets Big Crowd," *Pecos Enterprise and Gusher* (Tex.), May 24, 1929.

25. "Pyle Again Dealt Blow," *Dallas Journal*, May 13, 1929.

26. Mike Corona, "Hit or Miss," *El Paso Times* (Tex.), May 25, 1929.

27. "Pyle Expects Great Finish," *Los Angeles Times*, June 10, 1929.

28. Ibid.

29. Synopsis, *Breckenridge American*, May 13–16, 1929.

30. Ibid.; Newton, *Running in Three Continents*, 76.

31. Newton, *Running in Three Continents*, 76.

32. Synopsis, *Breckenridge American*, May 13–16, 1929; Newton, *Running in Three Continents*, 76.

33. Ibid.; Appendix D, "Cumulative Pace by Stage Finishers," Stage 45.

34. Appendix C, "Pace by Stage Finishers," Stage 45.

35. *WPA Guide to Texas*, 470.

36. "Salo Cuts Gavuzzi's Lead," *Los Angeles Times*, May 16, 1929; Appendix D, "Cumulative Pace by Stage Finishers," Stage 46.

37. "Salo Fast on Way to Lead Pack," *Daily Herald* (Passaic, N.J.), May 16, 1929.

38. Newton, *Running in Three Continents*, 77.

39. "Salo Nears Gavuzzi," *Daily Herald* (Passaic, N.J.), May 17, 1929; *WPA Guide to Texas*, 557.

40. "Salo Nears Gavuzzi," *Daily Herald* (Passaic, N.J.), May 17, 1929.

41. Ibid.

42. "John Salo Cuts Gavuzzi's Lead," *Los Angeles Times*, May 17, 1929; Appendix D, "Cumulative Pace by Stage Finishers," Stage 47.

43. "Thursday Event to Be Headlined by Pyle Runners," *El Paso Times* (Tex.), May 16, 1929.

44. Newton, *Running in Three Continents*, 77; "Richman First in Derby Lap," *Los Angeles Times*, May 18, 1929.

45. "Salo Only 33 Minutes from Lead," *Daily Herald* (Passaic, N.J.), May 18, 1929.

46. Newton, *Running in Three Continents*, 77.

47. "Salo Only 33 Minutes from Lead," *Daily Herald* (Passaic, N.J.), May 18, 1929.

48. "$500 Voted to Salo by Turner League," *Daily Herald* (Passaic, N.J.), May 18, 1929.

49. "Salo Nears Gavuzzi," *Daily Herald* (Passaic, N.J.), May 17, 1929.

50. Walter McMullen, "Sports Trail," *Hamilton Spectator* (Ontario, Canada), May 22, 1929.

51. Newton, *Running in Three Continents*, 77; "Salo Annexes Lead in Derby," *Los Angeles Times*, May 19, 1929.

52. Newton, *Running in Three Continents*, 77; Appendix C, "Pace by Stage Finishers," Stage 49.

53. "Granville Badly Hurt," *Montreal Gazette*, May 23, 1929; McMullen, "Sports Trail," *Hamilton Spectator* (Ontario, Canada), May 22, 1929; "Granville Fourth in Monday's Heat Despite Handicap," *Hamilton Herald* (Ontario, Canada), May 14, 1929; Newton, *Running in Three Continents*, 77.

54. "Richman Wins Lap in Derby," *Los Angeles Times*, May 24, 1929.

55. *WPA Guide to Texas*, 558.

56. "Derby Runners and Road Show in Odessa," *Reporter-Telegram* (Midland, Tex.), May 20, 1929.

57. June Naylor Rodriguez, *Texas: Off the Beaten Path*, 3rd ed. (Guilford, Conn.: Globe Pequot Press, 1999), 253.

58. *WPA Guide to Texas*, 559.

59. "Richman and Salo in Dead Heat," *Los Angeles Times*, May 20, 1929; Appendix C, "Pace by Stage Finishers," Stage 50.

60. Arthur G. McMahon, "Cowley Continues to Gain," *Daily News* (Passaic, N.J.), May 20, 1929.

61. Rodriguez, *Texas: Off the Beaten Path*, 253; *WPA Guide to Texas*, 559.

62. "Derby Runners and Road Show in Odessa," *Reporter-Telegram* (Midland, Tex.), May 20, 1929.

63. Newton, *Running in Three Continents*, 77.

64. Appendix C, "Pace by Stage 51 Finishers," Stage 51; Appendix E, "Marathon Pace by Mile."

65. "Salo Holds Spotlight in Tie Run," *Daily Herald* (Passaic, N.J.), May 21, 1929.

66. "Richman Cops Lap in Derby," *Los Angeles Times*, May 21, 1929.

67. Newton, *Running in Three Continents*, 78.

68. *WPA Guide to Texas*, 560.

69. "Richman and Umek Tie in Lap of Derby," *Los Angeles Times*, May 22, 1929; Appendix C, "Pace by Stage Finishers," Stage 52.

70. Arthur G. McMahon, "Salo and Gavuzzi Run Even," *Daily News* (Passaic, N.J.), May 22, 1929.

71. Rodriguez, *Off the Beaten Path*, 256.

72. Mike Corona, "Cruces Will Be Host of Caravan Next Day," *El Paso Times* (Tex.), May 22, 1929.

73. "Richman Cops Another Pyle Marathon," *Los Angeles Times*, May 23, 1929; Appendix D, "Cumulative Pace by Stage Finishers," Stage 53.

74. "Salo and Gavuzzi in Fourth Tie," *Daily Herald* (Passaic, N.J.), May 23, 1929; Appendix C, "Pace by Stage Finishers," Stage 53.

75. "Race Gets Big Crowd from Area," *Pecos Enterprise and Gusher* (Tex.), May 24, 1929.

8. West of the Pecos

1. "Salo, Gavuzzi Fifth Tie Over 54 [sic] Miles," *Daily Herald* (Passaic, N.J), May 24, 1929; "Richman Wins," *Los Angeles Times*, May 24, 1929.

2. "Race Gets Big Crowd," *Pecos Enterprise and Gusher* (Tex.), May 24, 1929.

3. Metz, *Roadside History of Texas*, 29–30.

4. "Another Lap Is Annexed by Richman," *El Paso Times* (Tex.), May 24, 1929; Newton, *Running in Three Continents*, 78.

5. "Richman Wins Lap in Derby," *Los Angeles Times*, May 24, 1929.

6. Ibid.; Appendix C, "Pace by Stage Finishers," Stage 54; Appendix E, "Marathon Pace by Mile."

7. Appendix C, "Pace by Stage Finishers," Stage 54; Appendix E, "Marathon Pace by Mile."

8. Appendix D, "Cumulative Pace by Stage Finishers," Stage 54

9. Kastner, *Bunion Derby*, 164–65.

10. "Richman Wins," *Los Angeles Times*, May 24, 1929.

11. "Salo, Gavuzzi Fifth Tie," *Daily Herald* (Passaic, N.J.), May 24, 1929.

12. Ibid.

13. Newton, *Running in Three Continents*, 78.

14. *WPA Guide to Texas*, 562; Newton, *Running in Three Continents*, 78.

15. "Cowley in 14th Place, Salo in Tie," *Daily Herald* (Passaic, N.J.), May 25, 1929.

16. Ibid.

17. Newton, *Running in Three Continents*, 79; *WPA Guide to Texas*, 562.

18. Kastner, *Bunion Derby*, 158–59.

19. Newton, *Running in Three Continents*, 79; *WPA Guide to Texas*, 562.

20. "Salo, Gavuzzi," *Daily Herald* (Passaic, N.J.), May 24, 1929; "Granville and Umek in Tie for Lead in Derby," *Los Angeles Times*, May 26, 1929; Appendix D, "Cumulative Pace by Stage Finishers," Stage 56.

21. Mike Corona, "Hit or Miss," *El Paso Times* (Tex.), May 25, 1929.

22. Ibid.

23. Ibid.

24. Synopsis, *Breckenridge American* (Tex.), May 13–16 ,1929.

25. *WPA Guide to Texas*, 562.

26. Newton, *Running in Three Continents*, 79; Appendix C, "Pace by Stage Finishers," Stage 57.

27. "Salo Gains, Runners in Old Mexico," *Daily Herald* (Passaic, N.J.), May 27, 1929.

28. "Salo Swells Lead in Derby," *Los Angeles Times*, May 27, 1929; Appendix D, "Cumulative Pace by Stage Finishers," Stage 57.

29. "Salo Gains," *Daily Herald* (Passaic, N.J.), May 27, 1929.

30. "Introducing Elmer Cowley," *Daily Herald* (Passaic, N.J.), May 27, 1929.

31. Ibid.

32. "Fabens Will Be Host to Bunioneers Today," *El Paso Times* (Tex.), May 26, 1929.

33. *WPA Guide to Texas*, 243.

34. Ibid.

35. Newton, *Running in Three Continents*, 79.

36. Ibid.

37. "Gavuzzi Wins Lap in Derby," *Los Angeles Times*, May 28, 1929; Appendix C, "Pace by Stage Finishers," Stage 58; Appendix E, "Marathon Pace by Mile."

38. "Salo Lead Is Sheared by Gavuzzi," *Daily Herald* (Passaic, N.J.), May 28, 1929.

39. Newton, *Running in Three Continents*, 79; Berry, *L.A. to New York*, 103.

40. Newton, *Running in Three Continents*, 79.

41. Anderson, "C. C. Pyle and Vanguard of Bunion Derby," *El Paso Times* (Tex.), May 23, 1929.

42. Ibid.

9. Across a Rough and Unforgiving Land

1. "Bunionists Leave Today," *El Paso Times* (Tex.), May 28, 1929.

2. Appendix D, "Cumulative Pace by Stage Finishers," Stage 58.

3. Ibid.

4. "Bunioneers May Run over Desert without Trainers," *El Paso Times* (Tex.), May 28, 1929.

5. *WPA Guide to 1930s New Mexico*, 259.

6. "Salo Retains Lead," *Montreal Gazette*, May 29, 1929; Appendix C, "Pace by Stage Finishers," Stage 59.

7. "Salo Loses to Gavuzzi in New Mexico," *Daily Herald* (Passaic, N.J.), May 31, 1929.

8. "Gavuzzi Again Tops Runners," *Los Angeles Times*, May 30, 1929; Appendix C, "Pace by Stage Finishers," Stage 60; Appendix D, "Cumulative Pace by Stage Finishers," Stage 60.

9. "Have We Been Honored," *Deming Headlight* (N.Mex.), May 31, 1929; "Derbyists Here Wednesday," *Deming Headlight* (N.Mex.), May 31, 1929.

10. Kastner, *Bunion Derby*, 56–57.

11. *WPA Guide to 1930s New Mexico*, 375.

12. Newton, *Running in Three Continents*, 80.

13. Kastner, *Bunion Derby*, 56–57.

14. "Returns Home," *Daily Herald* (Passaic, N.J.), Aug. 7, 1929; Arthur G. McMahon, "John Salo Is Trailing Gavuzzi," *Daily News* (Passaic, N.J.), May 31, 1929.

15. "Returns Home," *Daily Herald* (Passaic, N.J.), Aug. 7, 1929.

16. "Hedeman Sets Derby Record," *Los Angeles Times*, May 31, 1929.

17. Appendix D, "Cumulative Pace by Stage Finishers," Stage 61.

18. Newton, *Running in Three Continents*, 80.

19. *Arizona: A State Guide*, 340–41.

20. "Salo Runs Tie Race in Desert Sands," *Daily Herald* (Passaic, N.J.), June 1, 1929; Newton, *Running in Three Continents*, 80; *Arizona. A State Guide*, 340.

21. "Salo Runs Tie," *Daily Herald* (Passaic, N.J.), June 1, 1929.

22. "Salo Takes Lead," *Daily Herald* (Passaic, N.J.), June 3, 1929.

23. "Salo Takes Lead," *Daily Herald* (Passaic, N.J.), June 3, 1929; Appendix C, "Pace by Stage Finishers," Stage 63.

24. Appendix C, "Pace by Stage 63 Finishers," Stage 63.

25. "Pyle Harriers Smash Records," *Los Angeles Times*, June 2, 1929.

26. Appendix D, "Cumulative Pace by Stage Finishers," Stage 63; Kastner, *Bunion Derby*, 164–65.

27. "First of Bunion Racers Arrive Noon Saturday," *Guardian-Farmer* (Safford, Ariz.), June 7, 1929; Appendix D, "Cumulative Pace by Stage Finishers," Stage 63.

28. "Salo in Lead," *Calexico Chronicle* (Calif.), June 12, 1929.

29. Ibid.

30. "First of Bunion Racers," *Guardian-Farmer* (Safford, Ariz.), June 7, 1929.

31. "Pyle Harriers," *Los Angeles Times*, June 2, 1929.

32. Gould, "C. C. Pyle," *Daily News* (Passaic, N.J.), May 10, 1929.

33. "Pyle Harriers," *Los Angeles Times*, June 2, 1929.

34. *Arizona: The State Guide*, 344; "Two First in Lap of Derby," *Los Angeles Times*, June 3, 1929.

35. Appendix C, "Pace by Stage Finishers," Stage 63; Appendix E, "Marathon Pace by Mile"; Newton, *Running in Three Continents*, 80.

36. "Two First," *Los Angeles Times*, June 3, 1929.

37. Newton, *Running in Three Continents*, 80.

38. Ibid.

39. Arizona: A State Guide, 344; Newton, *Running in Three Continents*, 80.

40. Newton, *Running in Three Continents*, 81; "Gavuzzi Leads Runners Again," *San Diego Union*, June 4, 1929.

41. *Arizona: A State Guide*, 202.

42. Ibid., 205.

43. "Salo Leads in Hot Grind over Arizona Roads," *Daily Herald* (Passaic, N.J.), June 5, 1929; "First Bunion Racers," *Guardian-Farmer* (Safford, Ariz.), June 7, 1929.

44. *Arizona: A State Guide*, 348.

45. Ibid., 349.

46. "Pyle Here Today," *Los Angeles Times*, June 5, 1929.

47. Ibid.

48. *Arizona: A State Guide*, 349.

49. Ibid., 350.

50. "Thousands See Bunion Derby Leader Sprint," *Arizona Republican* (Phoenix), June 6, 1929.

51. "Another Big Gain by Salo," *Daily Herald* (Passaic, N.J.), June 6, 1929; Appendix C, "Pace by Stage Finishers," Stage 67.

52. "Weary Runners of Pyle Derby Approach Goal," *Mesa Journal-Tribune* (Ariz.), June 6, 1929.

53. "Another Big Gain," *Daily Herald* (Passaic, N.J.), June 6, 1929.

54. Ibid.

55. "Thousands See Bunion," *Arizona Republican* (Phoenix), June 6, 1929.

56. Appendix C, "Pace by Stage Finishers," Stage 67.

57. "Weary Runners," *Mesa Journal-Tribune* (Ariz.), June 6, 1929.

58. "Thousands See Bunion," *Arizona Republican* (Phoenix), June 6, 1929.

59. Ibid.

60. Ibid.

61. "Guarantors of Pyle Bunion Derby Will Pay Over Small Sum," *Mesa Journal-Tribune*, June 6, 1929.

62. "Thousands See Bunion," *Arizona Republican* (Phoenix), June 6, 1929.

63. Ibid.

64. "Derby to Cut Path around Phoenix," *Phoenix Evening Gazette*, June 4, 1929.

65. *Arizona: A State Guide*, 462.

66. "Salo Adds to Lead in Bunion Marathon," *Los Angeles Times*, June 7, 1929; Appendix C, "Pace by Stage Finishers," Stage 68.

67. Appendix C, "Pace by Stage Finishers," Stage 68.

68. Arthur G. McMahon, "Salo Is Enjoying Big Lead," *Daily News* (Passaic, N.J.), June 7, 1929.

69. Ibid.

70. "Derbyists Await L.A. Welcome!," *Phoenix Evening Gazette*, June 6, 1929.

71. Kastner, *Bunion Derby*, 32–33, 118.

72. Gordon and Baker, "Observations."

73. *Arizona: A State Guide*, 387.

74. Newton, *Running in Three Continents*, 82.

75. "Gavuzzi and Salo Run Tie," *Daily Herald* (Passaic, N.J.), June 8, 1929.

76. *Arizona: A State Guide*, 463–64.

77. Ibid., 463.

78. Ibid.

79. Ibid., 389.

80. Ibid., 389–90.

81. "Gavuzzi Gains in Pyle Run," *Los Angeles Times*, June 9, 1929.

82. Ibid.; *Arizona: A State Guide*, 389.

83. Arthur G. McMahon, "Salo and Gavuzzi in Tie Again," *Daily News* (Passaic, N.J.), June 8, 1929.

84. "Pyle Expects Great Finish," *Los Angeles Times*, June 10, 1929.

85. "Salo Loses 29 Minutes to Gavuzzi," *Daily Herald* (Passaic, N.J.), June 10, 1929.

86. *Arizona: A State Guide*, 389.

87. Barry Lewis, *Running the Trans-America Footrace: Trials and Triumphs of Life on the Road* (Mechanicsburg, Pa.: Stackpole Books, 1994), 21.

88. Arthur G. McMahon, "Gavuzzi Gains on Johnny," *Daily News* (Passaic, N.J.), June 10, 1929.

89. Ibid.

90. *Arizona: A State Guide*, 389.

91. "Bunion Derby About to Run in Sand Hills," *Calexico Chronicle* (Calif.), June 6, 1929.

92. "Pyle Grind Ends Sunday," *Los Angeles Times*, June 9, 1929.

93. Ibid.

94. Ibid.

95. Ibid

96. "Pyle Expects Great Finish," *Los Angeles Times*, June 10, 1929.

97. Ibid.

98. Ibid.

99. Ibid.

100. "Gavuzzi Takes Lead on Wellton Andrade Lap," *Yuma Morning Sun* (Ariz.), June 12, 1929.

101. Ibid.

102. Berry, *L.A. to New York*, 107.

103. "Gavuzzi Takes Lead," *Yuma Morning Sun*, June 12, 1929; Appendix C, "Pace by Stage Finishers," Stage 72.

104. Arthur G. McMahon, "Gavuzzi Leading in Race," *Daily News* (Passaic, N.J.), June 11, 1929.

10. "Overcoming the Killing Distances"—The Last Five Days to Los Angeles

1. Newton, *Running in Three Continents*, 84.

2. Appendix D, "Cumulative Pace by Stage Finishers," Stage 73.

3. *The WPA Guide to California: The Federal Writers' Project Guide to 1930s California with a New Introduction by Gwendolyn Wright* (1939; repr., New York: Pantheon Books, 1984), 464.

4. "10 Years Ago," *Calexico Chronicle* (Calif.), June 12, 1929.

*5. Appendix C, "Pace by Stage Finishers," Stage 73; "Peter Gavuzzi Holds Lead," *Calexico Chronicle* (Calif.), June 11, 1929.

6. "Salo Runs Triple Tie in Desert," *Daily Herald* (Passaic, N.J.), June 12, 1929.

7. "Peter Gavuzzi Holds Lead," *Calexico Chronicle* (Calif.), June 11, 1929.

8. Ibid.

9. Ibid.

10. Ibid.

11. Arthur G. McMahon, "Gavuzzi and Salo Run Even," *Daily News* (Passaic, N.J.), June 12, 1929.

12. Ibid.

13. "Peter Gavuzzi Holds Lead," *Calexico Chronicle* (Calif.), June 11, 1929.

14. *WPA Guide to California*, 634–41.

15. Ibid., 641–42.

16. Arthur G. McMahon, "Salo Only 20 Minutes in Rear," *Daily News* (Passaic, N.J.), June 12, 1929.

17. Ibid.

18. "Salo in Lead Down Grade Past Boulder at 2:30 and Umek 7 Minutes Behind," *Calexico Chronicle* (Calif.), June 12, 1929.

19. Ibid.; Edward K. Anderson, "Bunion Blisters," *El Paso Times* (Tex.), May 28, 1929.

20. "Salo in Lead," *Calexico Chronicle* (Calif.), June 12, 1929.

21. "Salo Gains on Bunion Rival," *Los Angeles Times*, June 13, 1929; Appendix D, "Cumulative Pace by Stage Finishers," Stage 74.

22. "Turner League to Officially Welcome Salo," *Daily News* (Passaic, N.J.), June 12, 1929.

23. Newton, *Running in Three Continents*, 84; *WPA Guide to California*, 642.

24. Newton, *Running in Three Continents*, 84.

25. Braven Dyer, "Gavuzzi Holds Lead in Derby," *Los Angeles Times*, June 14, 1929.

26. Ibid.; *WPA Guide to California*, 643–44.

27. Dyer, "Gavuzzi Holds Lead," *Los Angeles Times*, June 14, 1929.

28. Arthur G. McMahon, "Gavuzzi Holds On to Lead," *Daily News* (Passaic, N.J.), June 14, 1929.

29. *WPA Guide to California*, 259; *World 1931 Almanac*, 177.

30. Front page, *San Diego Union*, June 13, 1929.

31. Dyer, "Gavuzzi Holds Lead," *Los Angeles Times*, June 14, 1929; Frank Boydstum, "Gavuzzi and Salo Finish Lap Together," *San Diego Union*, June 13, 1929; Newton, *Running in Three Continents*, 84.

32. Boydstum, "Gavuzzi and Salo," *San Diego Union*, June 13, 1929.

33. Ibid.

34. Arthur G. McMahon, "Gavuzzi Holds On to Lead," *Daily News*, June 14, 1929.

35. Dyer, "Gavuzzi Holds Lead," *Los Angeles Times*, June 14, 1929.

36. McMahon, "Gavuzzi Hold On to Lead," *Daily News* (Passaic, N.J.), June 14, 1929.

37. Dyer, "Gavuzzi Holds Lead," *Los Angeles Times*, June 14, 1929.

38. *WPA Guide to California*, 404.

39. Arthur G. McMahon, "Gavuzzi Staggers in Rear," *Daily News* (Passaic, N.J.), June 16, 1929.

40. *WPA Guide to California*, 404–7.

41. McMahon, "Gavuzzi Staggers," *Daily News*, June 16, 1929.

42. Berry, *L.A. to New York*, 108; Braven Dyer, "Derby Lap Won by Abramowitz," *Los Angeles Times*, June 15, 1929; McMahon, "Gavuzzi Staggers," *Daily News*, June 16, 1929.

43. Newton, *Running in Three Continents*, 85; Berry, *L.A. to New York*, 108.

44. McMahon, "Gavuzzi Staggers," *Daily News* (Passaic, N J), June 16, 1929; Appendix C, "Pace by Stage Finishers," Stage 76.

45. McMahon, "Gavuzzi Staggers," *Daily News* (Passaic, N.J.), June 16, 1929.

46. Dyer, "Derby Lap Won," *Los Angeles Times*, June 15, 1929; McMahon, "Gavuzzi Staggers," *Daily News* (Passaic, N.J.), June 16, 1929.

47 Dyer, "Derby Lap Won," *Los Angeles Times*, June 15, 1929; McMahon, "Gavuzzi Staggers," *Daily News* (Passaic, N.J.), June 16, 1929; Appendix C, "Pace by Stage Finishers," Stage 77; Appendix D, "Cumulative Pace by Stage Finishers," Stage 99.

48. McMahon, "Gavuzzi Staggers," *Daily News* (Passaic, N.J.), June 16, 1929; Appendix C, "Pace by Stage Finishers," Stage 77; Appendix D, "Cumulative Pace by Stage Finishers," Stage 77.

49. "Guisto Umek Captures Another Bunion Derby; Salo, "Gavuzzi Second," *San Diego Union*, June 16, 1929; Appendix D, "Cumulative Pace by Stage Finishers," Stage 77.

50. "In Home Stretch of the Bunion Derby," *San Francisco Chronicle*, June 16, 1929.

51. "Guisto Umek," *San Diego Union*, June 16, 1929.

52. Maxwell Stiles, "Peter Gavuzzi Retains Lead in Pyle Derby," *San Francisco Examiner*, June 16, 1929.

53. *World 1931 Almanac*, 177; Kevin Starr, *Material Dreams: Southern California through the 1920s* (New York: Oxford Univ. Press, 1990), 69; *WPA Guide to California*, 208–9, 211, 213.

11. The End of the Rainbow

1. Braven Dyer, "'Cash and Carry' Pyle's Transcontinental Race Ends Tonight," *Los Angeles Times*, June 16, 1929.

2. Appendix D, "Cumulative Pace by Stage Finishers," Stage 78.

3. Dyer, "'Cash and Carry,'" *Los Angeles Times*, June 16, 1929.

4. Berry, *L.A. to New York*, 110; Newton, *Running in Three Continents*, 86.

5. Newton, *Running in Three Continents*, 86.

6. Dyer, "'Cash and Carry,'" *Los Angeles Times*, June 16, 1929.

7. Berry, *L.A. to New York*, 110.

8. Newton, *Running in Three Continents*, 86.

9. Berry, *L.A. to New York*, 110.

10. Tulloh, *Four Million Footsteps*, 21.

11. Ibid.

12. Berry, *L.A. to New York*, 110.

13. Ibid., 114; Newton, *Running in Three Continents*, 86.

14. Berry, *L.A. to New York*, 111.

15. Ibid., 111–12.

16. "Pyle Intends to Hold Bunion Derby in 1930," *San Diego Union*, June 18, 1929; "Bunion Derby Ends in Fast 26-Mile Run," *San Francisco Chronicle*, June 17, 1929; "Salo Leads in Derby," *Los Angeles Times*, June 17, 1929.

17. Berry, *L.A. to New York*, 111.

18. Ibid.

19. "Johnny Salo Wins," *San Diego Union*, June 17, 1929.

20. Berry, *L.A. to New York*, 112; Newton, *Running in Three Continents*, 86.

21. Arthur G. McMahon, "Salo Wins the Bunion Derby with a Great Burst of Speed; Flying Cop Gets $25,000 Prize," *Daily News*, June 17, 1929.

22. "Pyle to Try Marathon Again," *Los Angeles Times*, June 18, 1929.

23. Appendix C, "Pace by Stage Finishers," Stage 78; "Johnny Salo Wins," *San Diego Union*, June 17, 1929; Berry, *L.A. to New York*, 114.

24. Berry, *L.A. to New York*, 114.

25. "Policeman's Terrific Pace in Last Leg of Long Race Brings Home $25,000 Prize," *Daily Herald* (Passaic, N.J.), June 17, 1929; "Pyle May Use Salo in 26-Hour Run at Convention of Elks," *Daily Herald* (Passaic, N.J.), June 18, 1929; McMahon, "Salo Wins," *Daily News* (Passaic, N.J.), June 17, 1929.

26. "Policeman's Terrific Pace," *Daily Herald* (Passaic, N.J.), June 17, 1929.

27. "Returns Home," *Daily Herald* (Passaic, N.J.), Aug. 7, 1929.

28. "Pyle May Use Salo," *Daily Herald* (Passaic, N.J.), June 18, 1929.

29. "Policeman's Terrific Pace," *Daily Herald* (Passaic, N.J.), June 17, 1929.

30. "Police Director Turner Happiest Man in Passaic," *Daily News* (Passaic, N.J.), June 17, 1929.

31. Berry, *L.A. to New York*, 110-11.

32. Ibid., 112.

33. Ibid.

34. Arthur F. H. Newton, "Gavuzzi Has a Fine Record," *Hamilton Herald* (Ontario, Canada), Apr. 2, 1931.

35. McMahon, "Salo Wins," *Daily News* (Passaic, N.J.), June 17, 1929; Dyer, "Pyle to Pay," *Los Angeles Times*, June 23, 1929.

36. "Arthur G. McMahon Home after Long Trip," *Daily News* (Passaic, N.J.), July 24, 1929; "Returns Home," *Daily Herald* (Passaic, N.J.), Aug. 7, 1929; "Paul Simpson Comes Home; Pockets Empty," *Burlington Daily Times* (N.C.), July 8, 1929; "Harbine Returns after Completing Pyle Derby Run," *Santa Rosa Free Democrat Press* (Calif.), June 19, 1929; "Cowley Speaks at Capital Benefit," *Daily Herald* (Passaic, N.J.), June 19, 1929.

37. Berry, *L.A. to New York*, 144.

38. "Salo, Payne, and Gavuzzi to Run Race in Passaic," *Daily News* (Passaic, N.J.), Aug. 16, 1929; "Salo and Andy Payne to Race at Stadium," *Daily News* (Passaic, N.J.), Sept. 7, 1929.

39. "Policeman's Terrific Pace," *Daily Herald* (Passaic, N.J.), June 17, 1929.

40. "'Cash and Carry,'" *Los Angeles Times*, June 16, 1929.

41. Tulloh, *Four Million Footsteps*, 20.

42. Ibid., 20–21.

43. "Harbine Returns," *Santa Rosa Free Democrat* (Calif.), June 19, 1929.

44. Appendix A, "List of Starters"; Appendix D, "Cumulative Pace by Stage Finishers," Stage 78.

12. Searching for the Pot of Gold

1. "Pyle Intends," *San Diego Union*, June 18, 1929.

2. Ibid.; "Harbine 12th, Wins $900 in Pyle Marathon," *Santa Rosa Free Democrat Press* (Calif.), June 18, 1929.

3. Berry, *L.A. to New York*, 115.

4. "Pyle May Use Salo," *Daily Herald* (Passaic, N.J.), June 18, 1929.

5. "Arthur G. McMahon Is Home after Long Trip," *Daily News* (Passaic, N.J.), July 24, 1929.

6. Braven Dyer, "Salo to Be Honored," *Los Angeles Times*, June 23, 1929; Braven Dyer, "Pyle to Pay Off Tuesday," *Los Angeles Times*, June 23, 1929.

7. Dyer, "Pyle to Pay," *Los Angeles Times*, June 23, 1929.

8. Ibid.

9. Berry, *L.A. to New York*, 115.

10. "Promoter Pyle in Trouble Again," *Montreal Gazette*, June 19, 1929; "Bunion Derby Man," *Hamilton Spectator* (Ontario, Canada), June 18, 1929; "Pyle's Troubles Piling Up in California," *Daily News* (Passaic, N.J.), June 18, 1929.

11. "Promoter Pyle," *Montreal Gazette*, June 19, 1929.

12. "Johnny Salo Returns Home, Minus $21,000," *Daily News* (Passaic, N.J.), Sept. 5, 1929; Arthur G. McMahon, "Salo Has No Plans to Come Home," *Daily News* (Passaic, N.J.), July 13, 1929.

13. Derderian, *Boston Marathon*, 156.

14. "Paul Simpson Comes Home, Pockets Empty," *Burlington Daily Times* (N.C.), July 8, 1929.

15. "Harbine Return," *Santa Rosa Free Democrat Press* (Calif.), June 19, 1929.

16. "Pyle, Behind in Paying Runners, May Face Court" *Daily Herald* (Passaic, N.J.), July 29, 1929.

17. "Pyle Broke, To Stand Trial in a Coast Court," *Daily News* (Passaic, N.J.), Aug. 30, 1929.

18. Reisler, *Cash and Carry*, 192.

19. McMahon, "Salo To Get His Money," *Daily News* (Passaic, N.J.), July 2, 1929.

20. Ibid.

21. "Arthur G. McMahon Home," *Daily News* (Passaic, N.J.), July 24, 1929.

22. "Returns Home," *Daily Herald* (Passaic, N.J.), Aug. 7, 1929; Derderian, *Boston Marathon*, 156.

23. "Johnny Salo Returns," *Daily News* (Passaic, N.J.), Sept. 5, 1929.

24. "Salo and Andy Payne," *Daily News* (Passaic, N.J.), Sept. 7, 1929.

25. "Winners of Two Pyle Derbies Sign Contract for Events," *Daily News* (Passaic, N.J.), Aug. 16, 1929.

26. Arthur G. McMahon, "South African Runner Beats Gavuzzi, Second Man, By a Half Mile," *Daily News* (Passaic, N.J.), Sept. 23, 1929.

27. Sears, *Running through the Ages*, 139–51.

28. "Salo, Ray Win Grind," *Daily News* (Passaic, N.J.), Sept. 30, 1929; Berry, *L.A. to New York*, 117.

29. "Salo Is Officially Welcomed," *Daily News* (Passaic, N.J.), Oct. 3, 1929.

30. "Salo Returns to Work; Assigned to Patrol Duty by Acting Chief De Groot," *Daily News* (Passaic, N.J.), Oct. 13, 1929.

31. Rearson, "Patrolman Dies," *Daily Herald* (Passaic, N.J.), Oct. 5, 1931.

32. Ibid.

33. Ibid.

34. Ibid.

35. J. Newman Wright, "Passaic Pays Tribute to Iron-Hearted Johnny Salo," *Daily Herald*, Oct. 7, 1931; "C. C. Pyle Sends Regrets," *Daily Herald* (Passaic, N.J.), Oct. 7, 1931; Manro

Magarill, "A Local Hero, He Won a Transcontinental Foot Race on 2nd Try, Met Untimely Death," *Herald News* (Passaic, N.J.), June 7, 2002.

36. Vivian Eney Cross, *Carved on These Walls . . .* , http://www.nleomf.org/memorial.

37. Berry, *L.A. to New York*, 118.

38. "Long Race Unpopular," *Hamilton Spectator* (Ontario, Canada), Apr. 4, 1931; Sears, *Running through the Ages*, 231.

39. Hadgraft, *Tea with Mr. Newton*, 195, 198, 219.

40. Ibid., 194.

41. Derderian, *Boston Marathon*, 156–57.

42. Hadgraft, *Tea with Mr. Newton*, 198.

43. Ibid.

44. Ibid., 199; Kastner, *Bunion Derby*, 187.

45. Reisler, *Cash and Carry*, 196; Braven Dyer, "Death Ends Colorful Career of C. C. Pyle," *Los Angeles Times*, Feb. 4. 1939.

46. Reisler, *Cash and Carry*, 196.

47. Dyer, "Death Ends," *Los Angeles Times*, Feb. 4, 1939.

48. Kastner, *Bunion Derby*, 188.

49. James H. Thomas, *The Bunion Derby: Andy Payne and the Transcontinental Footrace* (Oklahoma City: Southwestern Heritage Books, 1980), 133.

50. Crawford, *Jim Thorpe*, 227.

51. Peterson, *Pigskin*, 120.

52. Charles Kastner, "Hart, Frank 'Black Dan.'" *BlackPast.org*, http://www.blackpast .org/?q=aah/hart-frank-black-dan-1859; Marshall, *King of the Peds*, 332, 359; Sears, *Running through the Ages*, 146; Kastner, *Bunion Derby*, 172.

53. "Coast to Coast Walker Spends Hour in Auburn," *Post Standard* (Syracuse, N.Y.), Apr. 9, 1915; "Long Distance Walker Hikes to California," *New York Age* (African American), May 4, 1929.

54. "Youthful Cyclist Has Driven across Continent," *Halifax Evening Mail* (Nova Scotia, Canada), June 15, 1927.

55. "Around the World Hikers," *Enterprise* (African American, Seattle), June 20, 1929; "Youth, 20, Ends 5,000-Mile Hike For $1,000 Prize," *Enterprise* (African American, Seattle), Mar. 30, 1928.

56. Heinrich, *Why We Run*, 191.

57. McNabb, *Flanagan's Run*, 58; Thomas, *Bunion Derby*, 36, 84, 105–6, 123–24.

58. Hadgraft, *Tea with Mr. Newton*, 197.

59. Charles Kastner, "The 1928 Bunion Derby, America's Brush with Integrated Sports," *Perspective on African American History, BlackPast.org*, "An Online Reference Guide to African American History," http://www.blackpast.org/?q=perspectives/1928-bunion -derby-america-s-brush-integrated-sports.

60. Sears, *Running through the Ages*, 152–56.

61. "Boy Leads in Catalina Swim," *Seattle Times*, Jan. 16, 1927.

62. Charles Kastner, "Awakening the Spirit of the Lake Hike," *Northwest Runner Magazine*, March 2001, 28–32.

Glossary

Ballyhoo: sensational promotion and advertising

Bunion Derby: C. C. Pyle's first (1928) or second (1929) Annual International Trans-Continental Foot Races across America

Bunioneers: men who competed in the 1928 and/or 1929 Bunion Derby

C. C. Pyle's Cross Country Follies: Pyle's traveling vaudeville show, which accompanied the 1929 Bunion Derby

Control point: finish line

Dancing debutantes: a New York dance troupe that was part of Pyle's follies

Director general: race director

Dogs: common nickname for feet in the 1920s

Flying cop from Passaic: nickname for Johnny Salo

Pedestrians: long-distance racers who competed for cash prizes in the 1800s

Race patrol: a six-man force that monitored men during the race to ensure they did not accept rides

Rubber: massage therapist

Sheik of Seattle: nickname for Eddie Gardner

Shin splints: a common injury among the bunioneers; extreme pain in the leg between the knee and ankle brought on by overuse.

Stage race: daily race

Bibliography

Films

Bunion Derby. Tape Master 5404, Catalog 56943. Orland Park, Ill.: WPA Film Library.

Newspapers

Afro-American (Baltimore, Md.)
Amsterdam News (African American, N.Y.)
Arizona Republican (Phoenix)
Baltimore Sun
Baxter Springs Citizen and Herald (Kans.)
Bellaire Daily Leader (Ohio)
Black Dispatch (African American, Okla.)
Breckenridge American (Tex.)
Burlington Daily Times (N.C.)
Calexico Chronicle (Calif.)
Chicago Defender (African American)
Cleveland Plain Dealer
Coalgate Courier (Okla.)
Coalgate Record Register (Okla.)
Columbus Evening Dispatch (Ohio)
Cumberland Daily News (Md.)
Daily Herald (Passaic, N.J.)
Daily Jefferson (Cambridge, Ohio)
Daily News (Passaic, N.J.)
Daily News Standard (Uniontown, Pa.)
Dallas Journal (Tex.)

Dayton Journal (Ohio)

Deming Headlight (N.Mex.)

Democrat Messenger (Waynesburg, Pa.)

Effingham Daily Record (Ill.)

Elizabeth Daily Journal (N.J.)

El Paso Times (Tex.)

Enterprise (African American, Seattle)

Frederick Daily News (Md.)

Frederick Post (Md.)

Galena Times (Kans.)

Globe and Mail (Toronto, Ontario, Canada)

Guardian-Farmer (Safford, Ariz.)

Halifax Evening Mail (Nova Scotia, Canada)

Hamilton Herald (Ontario, Canada)

Hamilton Spectator (Ontario, Canada)

Herald News (Passaic, N.J.)

Holdenville Daily News (Okla.)

Indianapolis News

Joplin Globe (Mo.)

Kansas City Call (African American, Mo.)

Knightstown Banner (Ind.)

Los Angeles Times

Mesa Journal-Tribune (Ariz.)

Miami News Record (Okla.)

Montreal Gazette (Quebec, Canada)

Muskogee Daily Phoenix (Okla.)

New York Age (African American)

New York Post

New York Times

Pecos Enterprise and Gusher (Tex.)

Philadelphia Inquirer

Phoenix Evening Gazette

Pittsburgh Courier (African American)

Post Standard (Syracuse, N.Y.)

Reporter-Telegram (Midland, Tex.)

Richmond Item (Ind.)

Richmond Palladium (Ind.)

St. Louis Post Dispatch

St. Louis Star

San Diego Union

San Francisco Chronicle

San Francisco Examiner

Santa Rosa Free Democrat Press (Calif.)

Seattle Post Intelligencer

Seattle Times

Springfield Daily News (Mo.)

Springfield Leader (Mo.)

Standard News Daily (Uniontown, Pa.)

Sullivan News (Mo.)

Sunday Times Democrat (Okmulgee, Okla.)

Sweetwater Reporter (Tex.)

Terre Haute Star (Ind.)

Terre Haute Tribune (Ind.)

Vandalia Union (Ill.)

Wheeling Daily News (W.Va.)

Wheeling Register (W.Va.)

Wilmington Evening Journal (Del.)

Yuma Morning Sun (Ariz.)

Zanesville Signal (Ohio)

Other Sources

Arnett, Earl, Robert J. Brugger, and Edward C. Papenfuse. *Maryland: A New Guide to the Old Line State.* 2nd ed. Baltimore: The Johns Hopkins Univ. Press, 1999.

Barr, Alwyn. *Black Texans: A History of African Americans in Texas, 1528–1995.* 2nd ed. Norman, Okla.: Univ. of Oklahoma Press, 1996.

Berry, Harry. *From L.A. to New York, from New York to L.A.* Self-published, 1990.

Billington, Ray Allen. *Westward Expansion: A History of the American Frontier.* 4th ed. New York: Macmillan, 1974.

Crawford, Bill. *All American: The Rise and Fall of Jim Thorpe.* Hoboken, N.J.: Wiley, 2005.

Cross, Vivian Eney. *Carved on These Walls* . http://www.nlcomf.org/memorial.

Derderian, Tom. *Boston Marathon: The First Century of the World's Premier Running Event.* Champaign, Ill.: Human Kinetics, 1994.

Gordon, Burgess, and John C. Baker. "Observations on the Apparent Adaptability of the Body to Infections, Unusual Hardships, Changing Environment and Prolonged Strenuous Exertion." In *From L.A. to New York, from New York to L.A.*, by Harry Berry. 158–63.

Greene, Lorenzo J., Gary R. Kremer, and Antonio F. Holland. *Missouri's Black Heritage*. Rev. ed. Columbia: Univ. of Missouri Press, 1993.

Hadgraft, Rob. *Tea with Mr. Newton: 100,000 Miles: The Longest Protest March in History*. Essex, UK: Desert Island Books, 2009.

Harlan, Louis R. *Booker T. Washington: The Wizard of Tuskegee, 1901–1915*. New York: Oxford Univ. Press, 1983.

Heinrich, Bernd. *Why We Run: A Natural History*. New York: HarperCollins, 2002.

Hudson, John C. *Across This Land: A Regional Geography of the United States and Canada*. Baltimore: The Johns Hopkins Univ. Press, 2002.

Ierley, Merritt. *Traveling the National Road: Across the Centuries on America's First Highway*. Woodstock, N.Y.: Overlook Press, 1990.

Kastner, Charles. "Awakening the Spirit of the Lake Hike." *Northwest Runner Magazine*, March 2001.

———. *Bunion Derby: The 1928 Footrace across America*. Albuquerque: Univ. of New Mexico Press, 2007.

———. "Bunion Derby Fever: How the First Footrace across America Pulled the Average Working Joe into Ultramarathoning." *Marathon and Beyond*, March–April 2008.

———. "Hart, Frank 'Black Dan'" (1858–1908). Encyclopedia entry, *BlackPast.org, An Online Reference Guide to African American History*. http://www.blackpast.org/?q=aah/hart-frank-black-dan-1859.

Klein, Maury. *Rainbow's End: The Crash of 1929*. New York: Oxford Univ. Press, 2001.

Klingaman, William K. *1929: The Year of the Great Crash*. New York: Harper and Row, 1990.

Kyvig, David E. *Daily Life in the United States, 1920–1940*. Chicago: Ivan R. Dee, 2004.

Leuchtenburg, William E. *Perils of Prosperity, 1914–1932*. 2nd ed. Chicago: Univ. of Chicago Press, 1993.

Lewis, Barry. *Running the Trans-America Footrace: Trials and Triumphs of Life on the Road*. Mechanicsburg, Pa.: Stackpole Books, 1994.

Marshall, P. S. *King of the Peds*. Bloomington, Ind.: AuthorHouse, 2008.

McNab, Tom. *Flanagan's Run*. London: Hodder and Stoughton, 1982.

Metz, Leon C. *Roadside History of Texas*. Missoula, Mont.: Mountain Press, 1994.

Milroy, Andy. "Herbert Hedemann—Tough Versatile Veteran," http://www
.ultralegends.com/herbert-hedemann-tough-versatile-veteran.

———. "Mike McNamara," http://www.aura.asn.au/MikeMcNamara.html.

Noakes, Tim. *Lore of Running*. 4th ed. Champaign, Ill · Human Kinetics, 2001.

Newton, Arthur F. H. *Running in Three Continents*. London: H. F. and G. Witherby,
1940.

*Official Program: C. C. Pyle's Second Annual International-Trans-Continental Foot
Race*. New York: Longacre Press, ca. 1929.

Parrish, Michael E. *Anxious Decades: America in Prosperity and Depression, 1920–
1941*. New York: W. W. Norton, 1992.

Peterson, Robert W. *Pigskin: The Early Years of Professional Football*. New York:
Oxford Univ. Press, 1997.

Pollock, Mabel V. *Our State, Ohio, 1803–2003: A Bicentennial History*. Newcomer-
stown, Ohio: 1st Book Library, 2001.

Raitz, Karl B., ed. *A Guide to the National Road*. Baltimore: The Johns Hopkins Univ.
Press, 1996.

Reisler, Jim. *Cash and Carry: The Spectacular Rise and Fall of C. C. Pyle, America's First
Sports Agent*. Jefferson, N.C.: McFarland, 2009.

Rittenhouse, Jack D. *A Guide Book to Highway 66*. 1946; facsimile, Albuquerque:
Univ. of New Mexico Press, 2000.

Rodriguez, June Naylor. *Texas: Off the Beaten Path*. 3rd ed. Guilford, Conn.: Globe
Pequot Press, 1999.

Rossiter, Phyllis. *A Living History of the Ozarks*. Gretna, La: Pelican, 2001.

Sears, Edward. *Running through the Ages*. Jefferson, N.C.: McFarland, 2001.

Starr, Kevin. *Material Dreams: Southern California through the 1920s*. New York:
Oxford Univ. Press, 1990.

Stone, John, Jr. *The Hells of the Bunion Derby: Written to Be Understood*. Self-
published, ca. 1928.

Thomas, James H. *The Bunion Derby: Andy Payne and the Great Transcontinental
Footrace*. Oklahoma City: Southwestern Heritage Books, 1980.

Tulloh, Bruce. *Four Million Footsteps: Los Angeles to New York—The Famous Runner's
Account of His Record Breaking Marathon*. London: Mayflower, 1970.

Williams, John Alexander. *West Virginia: A Bicentennial History*. New York: W. W.
Norton, 1976.

The World 1931 Almanac and Book of Facts. New York: The World, 1932.

WPA State and City Guides (alphabetically by state or city)

Arizona: A State Guide Compiled by the Workers of the Writers' Program of the Work Projects Administration in the State of Arizona. New York: Hastings House, 1940.

The WPA Guide to California: The Federal Writers' Project Guide to 1930s California with a New Introduction by Gwendolyn Wright. 1939. Reprinted with an introduction. New York: Pantheon Books, 1984.

Delaware: A Guide to the First State Compiled and Written by the Federal Writers' Project of the Works Progress Administration for the State of Delaware. New York: Viking Press, 1938.

The WPA Guide to Illinois: The Federal Writers' Project Guide to 1930s Illinois with a New Introduction by Neil Harris and Michael Conzen. 1939. Reprint, New York: Pantheon Books, 1983.

Missouri: The WPA Guide to the "Show Me" State Compiled by Workers of the Writers' Program of the Works Progress Administration in the State of Missouri with a New Introduction by Walter A. Schroeder and Howard W. Marshall. 1941. Reprinted with a new introduction. St. Louis: Missouri Historical Society Press, 1998.

New Jersey: A Guide to Its Present and Past Compiled and Written by the Federal Writers' Project of the Works Progress Administration for the State of New Jersey. 1939. Reprint, New York: Hastings House, 1959.

The WPA Guide to 1930s New Mexico Compiled by the Workers of the Writers' Program of the Work Projects Administration in the State of New Mexico. 1940. Reprint, Tucson: Univ. of Arizona Press, 1989.

The WPA Guide to New York City: The Federal Writers Project Guide to 1930s New York with an Introduction by William H. Whyte. 1939. Reprint, New York: New Press, 1992.

The WPA Guide to 1930s Oklahoma Compiled by the Writers' Program of the Works Progress Administration of the State of Oklahoma with a Restored Essay by Angie Debo and a New Introduction by Anne Hodges Morgan. 1941. Reprinted with a new introduction. Lawrence: Univ. Press of Kansas, 1986.

Pennsylvania: A Guide to the Keystone State Compiled and Written by Workers of the Writers' Program of the Works Progress Administration in the State of Pennsylvania. 1940. Reprint, New York: Oxford Univ. Press, 1963.

The WPA Guide to Texas with a New Introduction by Don Graham: The Federal Writers' Project Guide to Texas. 1940. Reprinted with a new introduction. Austin: Texas Monthly Press, 1986.

Index

Page numbers in italics refer to photographs or illustrative material.

Abramowitz, Harry, 4, 132, 172, 178
accidents. *See* cars and motorcycles
advertising and promotion, 18–19, 105, 113, 126, 143
African Americans, 68, 77–78, 98, 184–86
Albany, Tex., *108*, 113–14
Albuquerque, N.Mex., 133–34
Algodones, Mexico, 149, *151*
Allegheny Mountains, 40, 46–51
amenities and facilities: lack of, 47, 64, 67, 80–81, 123–24; racism and, 45–46, 68–69, 83. *See also specific location*
American Football League (AFL), 29
Anson, Tex., *108*, 114–15
Apache Indians, 137–38
Apelquist, Karl (Swedish), 67, 50
Appalachian Mountains, 12, 32, 36–52
Appleby, Delmar, 70
Arizona, *131*, 135–49, *151*
Arnold, Ben "Red," 48, 60
Australian participants, 22, 33, 132, 171–72
Aztec, Ariz., *131*, 145–46

Balcolm, Cleo, 90
ballyhoo, defined, 126, 289

Baltimore, Md., *13*, 32, 34–35, 37–39, *38*, *39*, 40, 98
bankruptcy, 28, 29, 35, 67, 71, 148, 175, 183
Barren, George (trainer), 12, 16, 17, 42, 51, 62, 78, 85, 169
baseball, 81
Baxter Springs, Kans., 80, 91–92
Belgian participants, 4, 19, 24. *See also* Cools brothers (Belgium)
Bell, Brian, 29
Berry, Harry, 16, 157, 162, 176
Big Spring, Tex., *108*, 117–18
Boston Marathon, 147, 178, 182
Brazil, Ind., 54, 63–64
Breckenridge, Tex., *108*, 110–19, *112*, *113*
Buckeye, Ariz., *131*, 143–44
Bunion Derby (1928), 5–8, *6*, *7*, 14–23; business and financial aspects, 29, 67, 71; daily pace, 136; dropouts, 6, 14, 20, 22; Gardner and, 19–20, 44, 62, *92*; Gavuzzi and, 14, 19–20, 100, 170; Gonzales and, 59; Granville and, 48; Hart and, 6; Joyce and, 58; Newton and, 6, 14, 18; Payne and, 4, 5, 8, 14, 22–23, 87, 88, 93–94, 123; route, 73–74, 134; Salo and, 5, 19–20, 60, 125, 170; Umek and, 47; writings about, 16, 23, 36, 37, 161–62, 181

Bunion Derby (1929): critics of, 26–28, 71, 144; cultural setting for, 1–2, 128, 179, 183, 184–87; cumulative pace by stage finishers, 223–52; daily and cumulative mileage, 195–97; finishers, 170–74; first day, 1–11; last day, 161–70; legacy of, 144, 169, 183–87; logistics of, 8–11, 18–19, 28, 53, 80–81, 88, 114–15, 162; memorabilia, *3, 21*; pace by mile, 253; pace by stage finishers, 199–222; rules, 8–11, 18–19, 56, 167; starters, 191–93; writings about, 16, 161–62, 181. *See also* prize money; route maps; *specific location or participant*
Burlington, N.C., 165, 176–77
business and financial aspects: advertising and promotion, 18–19, 105, 113, 126, 143; bankruptcy fears, 28, 29, 35, 67, 71, 148, 175, 183; cash-flow issues, 34, 67, 71–72, 80–81, 103–4, 137, 175–77; of choosing cities, 18–19, 35, 53, 92, 95, 102, 126, 128, 133, 143; fans as contributors and sponsors, 48, 63, 80, 90, 100–101, 111–12, 116–17, 148, 171; 1928 race, 29, 67, 71; participant costs and fees, 23–24, 29, 67, 80, 111. *See also* Cross Country Follies; legal aspects; prize money
Bylas, Ariz., *131,* 137–38

Calexico, Calif., *151,* 152–53, 154
California, 150–70, *151,* 176. *See also specific location*
Cambridge, Ohio, *54,* 55–56
Canadian participants, 41. *See also* Granville, Philip (Canada)
cars and motorcycles: accidents and injuries, 6, 8, 22, 51, 66, 84, 87–88, 93, 110, 112–13, 126, 128; breakdowns, 127, 130, 134, 166; race support vehicles, 34,

57–58, 127, 130, 134, 166; traffic issues, 2, 4, 5–6, 57, 152, 162, 165
Carthage, Mo., 89
"C. C. Pyle's Cross Country Follies." *See* Cross Country Follies
"C. C. Pyle's Second Annual International-Trans-Continental Foot Race." *See* Bunion Derby (1929)
cheating, accusations of, 47, 56, 124, 166–68, 170
Chelsea, Okla., *79,* 93–94, *96*
Chicago Bears football, 28–29
Chubb, D. S. "Dye," 91–92
class, social, 26–27, 71, 101, 169, 185
Cleveland, Ohio, 29, 58, 172
Cleveland National Forest (Calif.), 155
climate. *See* weather and climate conditions
Coalgate, Okla., *96,* 101–2
codes and permits, 7–8, 21–22, 30, 167
Collinsville, Ill., *38, 54,* 72–74, *79*
Colorado City, Tex., *108,* 115–16
Columbus, Ohio, *38, 54,* 55, 57–58
Comrades Marathon (South Africa), 14
"control point"/finish line, defined, 9, 289
Conway, Mo., 85
Cools, Juuls (Belgium), 19, 23
Cools, Karl (Belgium), 19, 23
Cools brothers (Belgium), 4, 19–20, 23–24, 41
Corona, Mike, 126
costs and fees, participant, 23–24, 29, 67, 80, 111. *See also* sponsorship
Cotton, Toby Joseph, Jr., 186
Cowley, Elmer, 23, 80, 116, 156, 165, 180
Creek Nation, 98–99
Crompton, Tom, 48, 60
Cross, Vivian Eney, 180
Cross Country Follies: in Arizona, 137, 138, 139, 143, 147; cash-flow issues, 8, 29–30, 34, 48–49, 67, 71–72, 80–81,

95–97, 105; cast members, 21–22, 25, 28, 60, 90, 94, 123–24, 125; codes and permits, 7–8, 21–22; in Delaware, 32–33; in Illinois, 70, 71–72; lawsuits, 21–22, 24, 57–58; in Maryland, 33–34, 35, 42, 50; memorabilia, 25; in Mexico, 128–29, 149; in Missouri, 80–81, 90; in New Jersey, 7–8; in New Mexico, 133; in Ohio, 58; in Oklahoma, 94; in Pennsylvania, 48–49, 50; reviews of, 48, 50, 60, 70, 80, 90, 118, 120, 143; in Texas, 105, 109, 110, 111, 115, 118, 119, 120, 123–24, 127; theme of, 24–28; Thorpe as master of ceremonies, 81–82, 90, 182–83; in Virginia, 60

Cumberland, Md., 38, 39, 43–44, 46, 50

Curtis, George (trainer), 45–46, 62, 64, 68–69, 83, 86, 88, 97

daily races/stage race, defined, 9, 289

Dallas, Tex., 96, 104–6, 108

Dalzell, Jesse, 23, 46, 85–88, 90–91; accidents and injuries, 87, 93, 110, 115, 118, 121

Dalzell, O. B., 90

Davis, William T., 185

Deal Barber Shop (Vandalia, Ill.), 70

Delaware, 13, 31–33, 38

DeMar, Clarence, 147

Deming, N.Mex., 127, 131, 133, 134

desert running, 62, 121, 126, 130–32, 134, 135, 141–49, 152–55

detours, 49, 50, 104, 133–34, 144

discrimination. See racism; sexism

disqualifications, 11, 47, 56, 124. See also cheating, accusations of

Downing, Bill, 50

Downing, W. M. A., 102

dropouts: Arizona, 136; Cools brothers, 41; Dalzell, 121; Delaware, 33, 34;

desert, 130, 132; early, 8, 11, 20; Gardner, 91, 93, 97–98; Gonzales, 59; Granville, 110; Indiana, 64, 66; Maryland, 41; Missouri, 83–84; Newton, 66; 1928 race, 6, 14, 20, 22; Ohio, 59; Oklahoma, 97–98; Pandolfi, 136; Pennsylvania, 23, 47, 49, 50; role of daily lengths and, 64; Texas, 110, 121; Trimble, 47; West Virginia, 52

Duncan, Ariz., 131

Durant, Okla., 96, 102–3

Duval, Madame, 60, 90

Dyer, Braven, 157, 161, 165, 176

Effingham, Ill., 54, 67–68

El Centro, Calif., 153–54

Elizabeth, N.J., 4, 5–8, 13

Ellis, Tom, 41

Ellis, Tom (Canada), 41

El Paso, Tex., 120, 121, 122, 126, 127–29, 130

Empire Games, 182

English participants, 100, 161, 170, 186. See also Gavuzzi, Pete (England); Hart, Charley (England); Newton, Arthur (England/South Africa)

entry fees. See courts and fees, participant

exhaustion, 36–37, 97, 102, 148, 150; Cools brothers, 23; Gardner, 43; Gavuzzi, 109, 127; Hart, 6, 14, 100; heat, 40, 41; Kester, 100; rookies and, 20, 23, 34, 40; Salo, 43, 103, 109, 158; Trimble, 47; Umek, 99, 105–6, 114, 115

extended distances: to Breckenridge, Tex., 110; to Collinsville, Ill., 72; to Dallas, Tex., 104; to Effingham, Ill., 67–68; to Fabens, Tex., 133; to Holdenville, Okla., 101; to Muskogee, Okla., 97–98; Newton on, 64–65, 67, 73, 97–98, 101, 104, 110; to San Juan Capistrano, Calif., 157

Fabens, Tex., *122*, 127

facilities. *See* amenities and facilities

fans, 7, 26–28, 51, 95, 132, 142–43; of
Dalzell, 87; economic importance
of, 19, 28; as financial sponsors and
contributors, 48, 63, 80, 90, 100–101,
111–12, 116–17, 148, 171; of Flowers, 113;
of Gardner, 44, 68–69, 77, 89, 184–85;
"go as you please" racing and, 26, 178,
184–85, 186; of Owen, 142; of Payne,
93–94, 142; of Salo, 4, 8, 105, 116, 125,
155, 163, 175, 179; of Shields, 91–92

fees. *See* costs and fees, participant

Fetting, E. A., 78–80

finances. *See* business and financial
aspects

finishers, list of, 170–74

finish line/"control point," defined, 9

Finnish participants, 20, 83–84, 178

First Annual Transcontinental Foot Race.
See Bunion Derby (1928)

Fleetwood (horse), 179

Flowers, Tiger, 113–14

follies. *See* Cross Country Follies

football, 28–29, 63, 67, 81, 183

Fort Worth, Tex., *108*, 109

*Four Million Footsteps: Los Angeles to New
York* (Tulloh), 162

Frederick, Md., *38*, *39*, 40–42, 50

*From L. A. to New York, From New York to
L. A.* (Berry), 16, 162

Gardner, Eddie "the Sheik," *45*, 75–78,
76, *92*; Arnold on, 60; background, 44;
death of, 182; death threats against, 4,
43–46, 62, 77–78, 82, 83; drops out of
race, 91, 97–98, 182; education, 44, 77,
98; exhaustion, 43; fans of, 44, 68–69,
77, 89, 184–85; legacy of, 184–86; leg

injuries, 63–64, 65, 68, 82, 83, 85, 86, 88,
89, 91, 93, 97–98, 168; news coverage
of, 68–69, 98; nickname, 44, 289; 1928
race, 19–20, 44, 62, *92*; post-race life,
182; racism and, 4, 8, 43–46, 62, 68–69,
74, 77–78, 82, 83, 98, 168, 184–86; style
and technique, 44, 135, 168; support
vehicle breakdown, 134. *See also* Curtis, George (trainer)

Gavuzzi, Pete (England), 12–20, *15*, *17*;
background, 12–14; back injury, 84;
exhaustion, 109, 127; finish line, 161–
70; fluid loss, 149; goes on offensive,
86; C. Hart and, 14, 100; infected tooth,
14, 100, 170; interviews with Tulloh,
162, 164; news coverage of, 60, 155,
156–58, 159; nickname, 58; 1928 race,
14, 19–20, 100, 170; post-race life, 176,
178–79, 180–82; prize money received,
170, 176; Prohibition and, 128; on race
cheaters, 56; ruptures Achilles tendon,
157–58, 161, 168; slows pace, 110, 125,
134, 159; style and technique, 12–13,
90–91, 154, 169; support vehicle breakdown, 134, 166. *See also* Barren, George
(trainer); Newton, Arthur (England/
South Africa)

Gibson, Bill, 98

Gila Bend, Ariz., *131*, 145

"go as you please" racing, 26, 178, 184–85,
186

Gonder, Alan J., 57

Gonzales, Seth, 59

Grand Ladies' International Tournament
for the Championship of the World,
186–87

Grange, Harold "Red," 28–29

Granville, Philip (Canada): accidents
and injuries, 110, 116, 117–18, 154;
background, 47–48, 171; 1928 race, 48;

post-race life, 180–81; prize money received, 171; sponsors, 48, 63, 117, 171; training team, 60, 63, 64

Hancock, Md., *39*
Harbine, Edwin, 165, 177
Harrison, Pat, 83
Hart, Charley (England), 33, 46; drops out, 14, 50; exhaustion, 6, 14, 100; as Gavuzzi's trainer, 14, 100; knee injury, 6, 11; 1928 race, 6; as Simpson's trainer, 100, 114, 132, 171
Hart, Frank "Black Dan," 26, 27, 184–85, 186
Havre de Grace, Md., *13*, 33–34
Hazelgreen, Mo., 85
health and safety, 18, 47, 49, 60, 144. *See also* exhaustion; injuries
Hedeman, Herbert (Australia), 22, 33, 34, 89, 132, 135, 172
Hells of the Bunion Derby, The (Stone), 23, 36, *37*
Holdenville, Okla., 101
Howard, Amy, 186–87

Illinois, *38*, 54, 65, 74, 79. *See also specific location*
Imperial Valley, Calif., 154, 155
Indiana, *38*, 54, 59–66
Indianapolis, Ind., *38*, *54*, 61–63
Indian Territory, 98–99
injuries: Achilles tendon, 157–58, 161, 168; ankle, 8, 87; arm, 66, 78, 112–14; back, 84; foot, 110, 115, 116, 117–18, 121, 154, 171; knee, 6, 11, 29, 156. *See also* leg injuries
Italian participants, 4, 22, 98–101, 136, 170–71

Jacumba, Calif., *151*, 154–55, 167
Jinks, Harold, 59
Joplin, Mo., *79*, 89–90
Joyce, Mike, 58–59, 172
Joyce, Mrs. Mike, 58–59
Juarez, Mexico, 128–29
Jusnick, George (Poland), 4, 137

Kansas, 91–92
Kent, Tex., 121–24, *122*
Kester, Herman, 100
Klein, Herbert, 179
Knightstown, Ind., 61
Kolehmainen, Willie (Finland), 20

La Belle Rene, Miss, 21–22
Las Cruces, N.Mex., 127, *131*, 133
legal aspects: codes and permits, 7–8, 21–22, 30, 167; lawsuits, 21–22, 24, 47, 57–58, 59, 176–77; writs of attachment, 21–22, 64
Leggett, Joe, 64
leg injuries: Dalzell, 87; Ellis, 41; Gardner, 63–64, 65, 68, 82, 83, 85, 86, 88, 89, 91, 93, 97, 99, 104; Newton, 14, 66; Salo, 80; shin splints, 8, 43, 50, 289; Umek, 51
Lenglen, Suzanne, 29
Lewis, Leonard, 20, 21
Lindbergh, Charles, 24, 26–28
long-distance running. *See* transcontinental running
Lordsburg, N.Mex., *131*, 134, 135
Los Angeles, Calif., *151*, 158–70, 177; news coverage from, 136, 137, 144, 147–48, 155, 156–57, 161, 163, 165, 176

Maplewood, Mo., *79*

marathons: Boston Marathon, 147; Comrades Marathon (South Africa), 14; "go as you please" racing and, 26, 178, 184–85, 186; women and, 186–87

Marini, Pietro, 4

Marshall, Ill., *54*, 65–66

Maryland, *13*, 31, 32, 33–35, 37–42, *38*, *39*

McMahon, Arthur G., 61–62, 78, 84, 89, 105, 144, 147, 149, 153, 154; on fan turnout, 118; on final leg, 156–58; at finish line, 163, 165; on return of Amelia Salo, 59–60; on Salo's homecoming, 177–78; on Salo's recovery, 52

McNamara, Mike (Australia), 33, 135, 171–72, 181

memorabilia, *3*, *21*, *25*

Mesa, Ariz., *131*, 141–42, 143

Mexico, 128–29, 149, *151*

Miami, Ariz., *131*, 138–39

Miami, Okla., *79*, 90, 91–92, 99

Midland, Tex., *108*, 118

Miller, Mo., *79*

Mineral Wells, Tex., *108*, 109–10

Missouri, *38*, 76–90, *79*

Mojave Desert, 23, 83, 99, 146–47

Monahans, Tex., *108*, 119

Morristown, Pa., 22

motorcycles. *See* cars and motorcycles

mountain running, 12, 32, 36–52, 81, 127, 133, 138–39, 153–56

Mulcahy, Michael J., 7–8

Mullen, Ken, 23

Muskogee, Okla., 94, *96*, 97–98

National Football League (NFL), 28–29

National Law Enforcement Memorial (D.C.), 180

National Road (U.S. Route 40), 37–40, *38*, *39*, 49

Native Americans, 98–99, 137–38

Newark, N.J., 6

New Jersey, 4–8, *13*, 17, 21–22, *38*, 52. *See also specific location*

New Mexico, *131*, 132–35

Newton, Arthur (England/South Africa), 14–18, *16*, *17*, *181*; on African American runners, 186; background, 14; Breckenridge, Tex., match, 113–14; drops out of race, 66; on extended distances, 64–65, 67, 73, 97–98, 101, 104, 110; finish line, 161–70; on Gavuzzi, 127–28, 145, 157, 161; on Granville, 118; Hart and, 100; hit by car, 66, 78, 85; legacy of, 186; on local amenities, 88; 1928 race, 6, 14, 18; physical description of, 14; post-race life, 178–79, 180–82; returns to race, 78, 85; rookies and, 19, 34, 40, 41; *Running in Three Continents* (autobiography), 161–62, 181; on Salo, 102, 128, 133, 145; on short laps, 57; on Spangler, 154; stomach issues, 60; as technical advisor, 114–15, 116, 119, 150; on Umek's wins, 99. *See also* Barren, George (trainer); Gavuzzi, Pete (England)

New York City, 1–4, 8, 17, 186–87

New York Yankees (football), 29, 63

Nielson, Neils, 47

nonviolent resistance, running as form of, 77–78

Northwest Territory, 53–55, *54*. *See also specific location*

Oakes, Robert, 87–88

Odessa, Tex., *108*, 119

Ohio, *38*, *54*, 55–59. *See also specific location*

Oke, Teddy, 63, 117, 171

Oklahoma, *79*, 90–94, *96*, 97–103

Okmulgee, Okla., *96*, 98–99, 101

Olympic Games, 147, 178

Owen, Steve, 4, 63, 97, 124, 142, 167, 183

Ozark Highlands, 81–94

pace by stage finishers, 199–222

Pandolfi, Colombo (Italy), 136

participants: costs and fees for, 23–24, 29, 67, 80, 111; social class and, 26–27, 71, 101, 169, 185; sponsorship of, 48, 63, 80, 90, 100–101, 111–12, 116–17, 148, 171

Passaic, N.J., 5, *6*, *7*, 125, 177–78. *See also* McMahon, Arthur G.; Salo, Johnny

Payne, Andy, *9*; death of, 182; fans of, 93–94, 142; Gavuzzi and, 14; 1928 race, 4, 5, 8, 14, 22–23, 87, 88, 93–94, 123; post-race life, 178, 182; style of, 4, 94, 123

Pecos, Tex., *108*, 120, 121, *122*

pedestrians, defined, 26, 178

Pegler, Westbrook, 2, 8, 17, 21–22

Pegram, William, 184

Pennsylvania, *13*, 18, 22–23, 24, 31, *38*, *39*, 46–49, 50 *See also specific location*

permits and codes, 7–8, 21–22, 30, 167

Perrella, Louis, 8

Philadelphia, Pa., *13*, 18, 22–23, 24, 31, 178–79

Phoenix, Ariz., 144

Pinal Mountains, 138

Polish participants, 4, 137

prize money: actual, 175–77; promised, 9–11, 71–73, 95, 135, 137, 162, 170–72

Prohibition, 1, 4, 48, 128

promotion. *See* advertising and promotion

Pyle, Charley C., *30*, *31*, *183*; arm injury, 112–13, 126, 128; business ventures, 24–31, 182; death of, 182; Lindbergh and, 26–28; managerial style, 7–8, 67, 71–72, 167; marriages of, 182; offers ranch to Salo, 176; physical description of, 30–31, 126; suffers stroke, 177, 182

racism, 8, 44–46, 74, 168, 184–86; amenities and facilities and, 45–46, 68–69, 83; death threats, 4, 44, 62, 77, 82, 83; running as form of nonviolent resistance, 77–78, 98

Radio Transcription Company of America, 182

Ray, Joie, 178

Redwing (horse), 179

Richman, Arthur, 110–12

Richman, Ben, 110–11

Richman, Morris, 110–12, 137, 156, 171

Richman, Sammy, 4, 8, 118, 136–37; background, 110–12, 171; finish line, 161–70; post-race life, 176; prize money received, 171; stomach issues, 135; style and technique, 111, 142; Umek and, 119, 120, 123, 124–25

Richman, Sid, 171

Richmond, Ind., 34, 59–60

Robinson, Sammy, 186

Rogers, Will, 2

Rolla, Mo., *79*

rookies, 12, 18, 19–23, 34, 37, 40, 47, 168

Route 40, U.S. (National Road), 37–40, *38*, *39*, 49

Route 66, 73–74, 82, 84, 134

route maps, *10*, *38–39*; Arizona, *131*; California, *151*; detours, 49, 50, 104, 133–34, 144; Eastern Seaboard, *13*; Midwest and Plains, *79*, *96*, *108*; New Mexico, *131*; 1928 race, 73–74, 134; Northwest Territory, *54*; Southwest, *131*; Texas, *108*, *122*

Running in Three Continents (Newton), 161–62, 181

safety. *See* health and safety
Safford, Ariz., *131*, 136–37
Safford, Robert W., 72
Salo, Amelia, 8, 43, 60, 62, 101, 103; death of Johnny, 180; at finish line, 164; leaves derby, 32, 52; post-race life, 178; rejoins derby, 32, 55; as trainer, 32, 64, 78–80, 146, 147, 152, 169, 170, 176
Salo, Helen, 32, 55, 180
Salo, Johnny, 4–7, 31–33, *140, 141*; Arnold on, 60; background, 4–5; birthday celebration for, 125; blisters, 78–80; car accidents, 22, 93; death and memorials, 179–80; employment, 5–*6*, 7, 125, 179; exhaustion, 43, 103, 109, 158; fans, 4, 8, 105, 116, 125, 155, 163, 175, 179; finish line, 161–70; funding for, 116–17; homecoming, 155, 164, 177–78, 179; leg injury, 80; news coverage of, 52, 59, 61, 68, 84, 89, 101, 105, 118, 119, 142, 144, 147, 153, 154, 155, 156–57, 159, 163; nickname, 5, 63, 289; 1928 race, 5, 19–20, 60, 125, 170; post-race life, 175–80; prize money received, 170, 176; Pyle offers ranch to, 176; resurgence of, 62, 73; slows pace, 110, 125, 134, 159; stomach issues, 32, 42, 43, 49, 52, 55, 56, 58, 69, 127, 133; style and technique, 90–91, 142, 154, 169. *See also* Wicklund, Bill (trainer)
Salo, Leo, 32, 55, 180
San Carlos Apache Indian Reservation, 137–38
San Diego, Calif., *151*, 155–57, 159, 163
San Francisco, Calif., 159
San Juan Capistrano, Calif., *151*, 157–58, 167–68

Second Annual Transcontinental Foot Race. *See* Bunion Derby (1929); *specific location*
Seeley, Calif., 153
Sentinel Peak, 145
sexism, 186–87
"shadow runners," 20
Shanley, Francis Patrick, 156
Shelton, Henry "The Cuban Wonder," 185
Sherman, Tex., *96*, 103–4
Shields, Guy, 80, 91–92
shin splints, 8, 43, 50, 289
Sierra Blanca, Tex., *122*, 125–26
Simpson, Paul "Hard Rock": background, 19, 99–100, 171; finish line, 176–77; C. Hart and, 100, 114, 132, 171; news coverage of, 165; nickname, 99; post-race life, 181
social class, 26–27, 71, 101, 169, 185
Sonora Desert, 135, 139, 145–46
Souminen, Arnie, 41
South African participants, 14
Spangler, Joe, 116, 154
sponsorship, participant, 48, 63, 80, 90, 100–101, 111–12, 116–17, 148, 171
Springfield, Mo., *79*, 86–88
Springfield, Ohio, *54*, 58
stage races/daily races, defined, 9, 289
starters, list of, 191–93
"stepping along," 4, 94, 123
St. Louis, Mo., *38*, 75–81, *76, 79*
Stone, Claire, 60, 90
Stone, John, Jr., 23, 36, *37*
style and technique: Gardner, 44, 135, 168; Gavuzzi, 12–13, 90–91, 154, 169; Payne, 4, 94, 123; rookies, 44; Salo, 90–91, 142, 154, 169; "stepping along," 4, 94, 123; Umek, 47, 99, 142
Sullivan, Frank "Sully," 63
Sullivan, Mo., *79*, 83

Superior, Ariz., *131*, 139
Superstition Mountain, 154
Swedish participants, 47, 50
Sweetwater, Tex., *108*, 115

Tacna, Ariz., 146
techniques. *See* style and technique
tennis, 29
Terre Haute, Ind., *38*, 65, 66
Texas, 95–97, *96*, 103–30, *108, 112, 113, 117,
    122. See also specific location*
Thomas Deming Furniture Company
    (New York), 21, 24
Thorpe, Jim, 81–82, 90, 128, 182–83
training/trainers, women as, 32, 169
Trans-American Footrace (1992), 146–47
transcontinental running: effects of
    1929 race on, 168, 184–87; origins
    and growth of, 26–27, 70–71, 168, 178,
    184–87; women and, 186–87
Trapp, Merle A., 8
Trenton, N.J., *13*, 17, 21–22
Trimble, Troy, 22, 47
Tulloh, Bruce, 162, 164, 168
Turner, John, 116, 164, 178, 180
Tuskegee Institute (Alabama), 44, 77, 98

ultramarathoning. *See* transcontinental
    running
Umek, Guisto (Italy), 22, 102, 156, 162;
    background, 46–47, 170–71; exhaus-
    tion, 99, 105–6, 114, 115; leg injury, 51;
    news coverage of, 99, 152–53; 1928 race,
    47; post-race life, 176; prize money
    received, 170; Richman and, 119, 120,
    123, 124–25; slows pace, 109; style and
    technique, 47, 99, 142; support vehicle
    breakdown, 127, 166

Uniontown, Pa., *39*, 46–49, 50
U.S. Route 40 (National Road), 37–40, *38,
    39, 49*
U.S. Route 66, 73–74, 82, 84, 134

Vandalia, Ill., *38*, 69–72
Van Horn, Tex., *122*, 124–25

Wanttinen, Olli (Finland), 83–84, 178
Waynesburg, Pa., *39*, 49, 50
Waynesville, Mo., 79, 84–85
weather and climate conditions: in Cali-
    fornia, 154; in Illinois, 67–68, 69–70; in
    Maryland, 34, 40; in Missouri, 84, 85,
    87, 89; in Ohio, 58; in Oklahoma, 91,
    102; in Texas, 104, 115–16, *117*–18, 119,
    120, 121–23, 127. *See also* desert run-
    ning; mountain running
Wellton, Ariz., *131*, 146–47
West Virginia, *38, 39*, 50–51, *54*
Wheeling, W.Va., *38, 39*, 50–51, *52, 54*
Wicklund, Bill (trainer), 8, 43, 55, 62, 130,
    146, 149, 170; background, 32; at finish
    line, 164; as mechanic, 134, 169; post-
    race life, 177–78, *179*
Williams, Nebraska, 185
Williams, Wesley, 100
Wilmington, Del., *13*, 31–33
Wimbledon championship, 29
women: as athletes, 29, 32, 186–87; as
    trainers, 32, 169
Woodward, Bertha, 187

Yuma, Ariz., *131*, 148–49, *151*

Zanesville, Ohio, *54*, 56–57

OTHER TITLES IN SPORTS AND ENTERTAINMENT

Abel Kiviat, National Champion: Twentieth-Century
Track & Field and the Melting Pot
　　Alan S. Katchen

Beyond Home Plate: Jackie Robinson on Life after Baseball
　　Michael G. Long, ed.

Blacks at the Net: Black Achievement
in the History of Tennis, Two Volumes
　　Sundiata Djata

Fair Dealing and Clean Playing: The Hilldale Club
and the Development of Black Professional Baseball, 1910–1932
　　Neil Lanctot

My Los Angeles in Black and (Almost) White
　　Andrew Furman

The New Cathedrals: Politics and Media in the History of Stadium Construction
　　Robert C. Trumpbour

The Sport of Kings and the Kings of Crime: Horse Racing,
Politics, and Organized Crime in New York, 1865–1913
　　Steven A. Riess

Tarnished Rings: The International Olympic
Committee and the Salt Lake City Bid Scandal
　　Stephen Wenn, Robert Barney, and Scott Martyn

The Rise of American High School Sports and the Search for Control, 1880–1930
　　Robert Pruter

Sport and the Shaping of Italian American Identity
　　Gerald R. Gems